William Humphrey

The Living God

William Humphrey

The Living God

ISBN/EAN: 9783744653169

Printed in Europe, USA, Canada, Australia, Japan

Cover: Foto ©Lupo / pixelio.de

More available books at **www.hansebooks.com**

"HIS DIVINE MAJESTY"

OR

THE LIVING GOD.

BY

WILLIAM HUMPHREY, S.J.

LONDON.
THOMAS BAKER, SOHO SQUARE.
1897.

"HIS DIVINE MAJESTY."

1. —MAN'S KNOWLEDGE OF GOD'S EXISTENCE.
2. —MAN'S KNOWLEDGE OF WHAT GOD IS.
3. —THE ESSENCE AND THE ATTRIBUTES OF GOD.
4. —THE ABSOLUTE PROPERTIES OF THE DIVINE ESSENCE.
5. —THE NEGATIVE PROPERTIES OF THE DIVINE ESSENCE.
6. —GOD'S KNOWLEDGE.
7. —GOD'S SINCERE WILL OF MAN'S SALVATION.
8. —GOD, THE ONE CREATOR.
9. —GOD, AS THE AUTHOR OF NATURE.
10. —GOD, AS THE AUTHOR OF THE SUPERNATURAL.
11. —THE PARADISE OF GOD'S CREATION.
12. —THE INNER LIFE OF GOD.

PREFACE.

THE subject of this volume will be of interest not only to Catholics, but to Protestants—and not only to members of the Established Church of England, and to English Nonconformists, but also to members of the Established Church of Scotland, and of the two Presbyterian bodies which are separated from it—and again, not to those only who make profession of the Christian religion, but to Jews, Mahometans, Buddhists, and other Unitarians of all denominations—and even to those to whom God is as yet unknown, as a personal God, but who are "seeking God, if haply they may feel after or find Him."

I have borrowed the bulk of my material for this work from the lectures of two of my old professors in the Gregorian University of Rome, Father (afterwards Cardinal) Franzelin, and Father Palmieri, both of them of the Society of Jesus. These were the two Professors of Dogmatic Theology in my day, some seven-and-twenty years ago.

While I was sitting on the benches of the Collegio Romano, listening to the lectures of those theologians of world-wide renown, in company with fellow students, of many nations, English and Scotch, French and Germans, Spaniards and Italians, Poles and Lombards, Belgians and South Americans, and many more; the Bishops of the world were assembled in Council, with the Vicar of Christ, in the transept of St. Peter's in the Vatican.

There were men in those days who went wild over the second Dogmatic Constitution of the Council, which defined the infallibility of the Roman Pontiff. The same men had given but little heed to the Dogmatic Constitution which preceded it, and by which they might have well been startled.

The Catholic Church does not define for the pleasure of defining, but defines then only when necessity arises, and when that necessity is pressing. Doctrinal errors may abound, and, nevertheless, many years may pass away before she lays the errors under her anathema, and defines the truths which those errors contradict.

Not till the fourth century did the Church define the personal divinity of Jesus Christ. Not till the eleventh century did she define His real presence in the Blessed Sacrament. The existence of God is contained, as an article of faith, in the Catholic Creeds, but it was reserved to this nineteenth century for the Church to say—If any one shall deny the one true God, the Creator and Lord of the visible and the invisible, Let him be anathema.

These words are a startling revelation of a state of affairs which made them necessary. It is true that the Vatican decree on this point is in great part a reproduction of a decree of the Fourth Lateran Council, held in 1215, but that Decree was directed mainly against a Manichean error of the Albigenses, some at least of whom held that God produced Lucifer and his angels, and that Lucifer after his revolt produced the visible world.

In the first Dogmatic Constitution of the Vatican Council, which is known as the *Dei Filius*, from the words with which the prologue to it opens, there are two Chapters, and eight Canons, which bear directly on our subject. The first chapter is headed—Concerning God, the Creator of all things; and is as follows—The Holy Catholic Apostolic Roman Church believes and confesses, that there is one true and living God, the Creator and Lord of heaven and earth, almighty, eternal, immense, incomprehensible, infinite in intellect and will, and in every perfection, Who, since He is one, singular, wholly simple and unchangeable spiritual substance, is to be proclaimed as distinct in reality and essence from the world, and to be in Himself and of Himself most blessed, and ineffably exalted above all things which are and can be conceived besides Him.

He the only true God, by His goodness and almighty power, not to increase or to acquire His own beatitude, but to manifest His perfection through the goods which He imparts to creatures, in His most free counsel made at once in the beginning of time both creations, the spiritual and the corporeal, that is, the angelic and the earthly, and then the human, as if common and constituted both of spirit and of body.

All things which He has made God guards and governs by His providence, which reaches from end to end mightily, and orders all things sweetly. For all things are naked and open to His eyes, and those things also which shall be in the future, through free action of creatures.

To this Chapter are appended five Canons, under the same heading—Concerning God, the Creator of all things.

1.—If any one shall deny the one true God, the Creator and Lord of the visible and of the invisible, Let him be anathema.

2.—If any one shall dare to affirm that there is nothing besides matter, Let him be anathema.

3.—If any one shall say that the substance or essence of God, and of all things, is one and the same, Let him be anathema.

4.—If any one shall say that finite things, both corporeal and spiritual, or that spiritual things at least, are emanations from the Divine substance—or that the Divine essence, by the manifestation or evolution of itself, becomes all things—or that God is universal or indefinite being which, by determining itself, constitutes the universe of things, and the distinction of it into genera, species, and individual things, Let him be anathema.

5.—If any one shall not confess that the world, and all things which are contained therein, both spiritual and material, have, in the whole of their substance, been produced by God from nothing—or shall say that God created, not by a will which is free from all necessity, but as necessarily as He necessarily loves Himself—or shall deny that the world was made for the glory of God, Let him be anathema.

The second Chapter, which is headed—Concerning Revelation, is as follows—The same holy mother the Church holds and teaches that God, the principle and end of all things, can with certainty be known by the natural light of human reason, from created things, for the invisible things of Him, from the creation of the world, are clearly seen, being understood by the things that are made; but it has pleased His wisdom and goodness, by another, and that a supernatural, way to reveal Himself, and the eternal decrees of His will, to the human race; as the Apostle says—God, Who at sundry times and in divers manners spoke in times past to the fathers by the prophets, last of all in these days hath spoken to us by His Son.

To this Divine revelation, it is indeed to be attributed that those matters which in Divine things are not in themselves impervious to the human reason, may also, in the present condition of the human race, be known by all with expedition, with firm certainty, and without any admixture of error. Revelation is not, however, for this reason, to be said to be absolutely necessary; but because God, of His infinite goodness, has ordained man to a supernatural end, that is, to a participation of Divine goods which utterly surpass the understanding of the human mind, for eye hath not seen, nor ear heard, neither hath it entered into the heart of man, what things God hath prepared for them that love Him.

To this Chapter are appended three Canons, under the same heading, Concerning Revelation.

1.—If any one shall say that the one and true God, our Creator and Lord, cannot be known with certainty by the natural light of human reason, through the things that are made, Let him be anathema.

2.—If any one shall say that it cannot be, or that it is not expedient, that man should be taught through Divine revelation concerning God, and the worship to be given to Him, Let him be anathema.

3.—If any one shall say that man cannot be Divinely raised to a knowledge and perfection which surpasses that which is natural; but that of himself he can, and ought, by a perpetual progress, to at last arrive at possession of all the true, and all the good, Let him be anathema.

In the Chapters, the Council declares the true doctrine; while in the Canons, it stigmatizes the heresies which contradict that doctrine. Chapters and Canons mutually complete each other, and form one definition in two parts—positive in the Chapters—negative in the Canons—and infallible in both. Chapters are infallible in all that they propound as being the doctrine of the Church; but the proofs and arguments which they may contain do not enter into the infallible object of the definition. Canons are of great service in determining what is of Catholic faith in the Chapters.

Every detail of any truth which directly concerns His Divine Majesty, the one only true and living God, must necessarily be of supreme interest to every thinking man. Many of these details must, necessarily, of the very nature of them, remain abstruse, however popularly they may be treated. Hence, not a few of those who would otherwise be eager to study God, at least as minutely as they are wont to study other objects of knowledge, are repelled by what seems to them to be the abstruseness of the argument. They shrink at any rate from uninterrupted reading of the whole of a treatise on the subject. To such persons I would suggest that they should use this volume as a book of reference, to which they may turn for information on particular points. There are many words and phrases in common use, with which they are familiar, but of the precise meaning of which they have not as yet a clear, or at least an adequate idea. They might be glad to know exactly, neither more nor less, what is meant by such words as essence—attributes—substance—being—nature — person — eternal — immense — incomprehensible—natural—supernatural—preternatural—pure, in the sense of a pure spirit, a pure act, pure nature, and the like, which meet them so often in their reading. I have had the benefit of such readers specially in view, along with the convenience of the general reader, in providing a very copious Table of Contents.

The title of this volume has been suggested by the Spiritual Exercises of St. Ignatius. *His Divine Majesty* is a phrase which in that short work the Saint uses no fewer than twenty-four times. The honour and glory of His Divine Majesty—the praise and service of His Divine Majesty—our offering and giving to His Divine Majesty—our being created to the image and likeness of His Divine Majesty—our love and fear of His Divine Majesty—the homage due to His Divine Majesty—the Throne of His Divine Majesty—the pleasing of His Divine Majesty—the offence of His Divine Majesty—giving thanks to His Divine Majesty—merit in sight of His Divine Majesty—disposal by His Divine Majesty, in accordance with His most holy will, of all that we are and have—are examples of the connection and way in which St. Ignatius uses this, his favourite phrase, in speaking of our Creator and Lord.

Every thing which is contained within the Spiritual Exercises, has been approved, and with a singular approbation, by the Apostolic See. It is impossible, therefore, for any loyal

Catholic to take objection to the title *His Divine Majesty*. It is to all who have been trained in the Spiritual Exercises, "familiar in their ears as household words." No other words could so well express the precise purpose of this Volume. It will not have been written altogether in vain if it serves to render familiar, in the ears of those who read it, a title which crystallises in three words the idea of the infinite sovereignty, and sovereign prerogatives, of that absolute Monarch Who is man's Master, because He is man's Maker.

WILLIAM HUMPHREY, S.J.

CONTENTS.

CHAPTER I.

MAN'S KNOWLEDGE OF GOD'S EXISTENCE.

	PAGE
Theology—in its wider sense—in its more restricted sense	1
God as the *principal object* of theology	2
Philosophy—its place and office	3
Direct arguments from reason for God's existence	3
Reflex arguments	4
Philosophical arguments for God's existence	5
God knowable to man, through creatures	16
God's manifestation of Himself	16
Manifestation in the *physical* order	17
Manifestation in the *historical* order	18
First knowledge of God. More finished knowledge	19
Ignorance of God "inexcusable"	21
Natural knowledge of the moral law	22
Connection between knowledge of God, and knowledge of the moral law	22
Rational nature, and the moral order	26
Implanted knowledge. "Innate ideas"	27
Manifestation of God, through the *supernatural* order	28
Transformation of society wrought through Christianity	30
The cause of it	31
Office of Judaism	33
Reason and Faith. Objective certainty. Evidence	36
Knowledge of God's existence. Belief in it	37
The Vatican decree on man's knowledge of God's existence	40

CHAPTER II.

MAN'S KNOWLEDGE OF WHAT GOD IS.

	PAGE
Man's *mediate* knowledge of God	42
Affirmation in God of every perfection of the creature	43
Negation in God of all imperfections	44
Supereminence of God's perfection	44
Man's conceptions limited, and inadequate	45
Need of manifold notions of the one God	46
Intuitive vision of God	46
Four orders of vision	47
The *light of glory*	48
What the Blessed see in God	49
Comprehension. The Incomprehensible	54

CHAPTER III.

THE ESSENCE AND THE ATTRIBUTES OF GOD.

Various meanings of the word *Essence*	57
The *physical* essence of a thing	58
The *metaphysical* essence of a thing	58
Self-existent being. Participated being	61
Plenitude of being. Absolute being	67
Divine *attributes*—absolute and negative	68
God's name *I am*	69
Analogous being	70
Universal being	72
Abstract being. Divine being	73

CHAPTER IV.

THE ABSOLUTE PROPERTIES OF THE DIVINE ESSENCE.

Absolute perfection. Abstract perfection	74
Impossibility of two infinites	74
The composite, and the simple	75

	PAGE
Various kinds of composition	76
Metaphysical composition	58, 161, 77
Absolute *simplicity* of God	78
Changelessness of the Divine will	86
The notion of the *true*	89
Truth—formally—fundamentally—morally	89
Veracity. Moral truth	89
God infinitely *intelligible*, and infinitely *intelligent*	90
Substantial Truth	91
Participation of truth in creatures	93
The notion of the *good*	95
Goodness in the moral order	98
Substantial Goodness	100
God, as His own end	101
God, as cause of created goodness	102
Objective manifestations of Divine goodness	103
Beatitude	106
External glory of God	109
Communication of goodness	110
The notion of the *beautiful*	113
Beauty of the senses. Spiritual beauty	114
The Beauty of God	115

CHAPTER V.

THE NEGATIVE PROPERTIES OF THE DIVINE ESSENCE.

The notion of *eternity*	119
The Divine Eternity	120
"The Beginning"	121
Co-existence of the temporal with the eternal	122
The notion of *immensity*, or unmeasuredness	124
The manner of a spirit's presence	125
The Divine Immensity	126
Omnipresence	126

A

	PAGE
Place. Space	127
God in all things by essence—by presence—by power	128
Imaginary space. Imaginary time	129

CHAPTER VI.

GOD'S KNOWLEDGE.

Simplicity in a spirit	131
Intellectuality of a spirit	132
God, as He is a Spirit	134
Understanding in God	135
The *true* as the terminus of God's knowledge	164, 137
Principal, and formal object of God's knowledge	166, 143
Secondary, and material objects	173, 144
God's knowledge *of vision*	179, 146
God's knowledge *of simple understanding*	179, 146
God's *mediate* knowledge	179, 147
Practical knowledge	149
Divine knowledge *of approbation*	150
Divine knowledge *of disapprobation*	150
Divine predefinition. Divine permission	151
God's foreknowledge. Man's freedom	155
God's knowledge, an act	159
The possible, extrinsically, and intrinsically	168
The future, as knowable	173
God's volition	180
Prescribing will—efficient will	181
Adequate will—efficacious, and inefficacious will	182

CHAPTER VII.

GOD'S SINCERE WILL OF MAN'S SALVATION.

God's *antecedent* will. God's *consequent* will	181, 184
God's *absolute* will. God's *conditionated* will	180, 188

CONTENTS. xix

	PAGE
God's will of the salvation of infants	189
God's will, in view of second causes	193
Free causes, in the *moral* order	194
Necessary causes, in the *physical* order	195
God's common providence. Special providences	196
Predestination	196
Gratuitousness of grace. Prevision of merits	198
Order of predestination. Order of execution	199
Reprobation, the fault of man	203

CHAPTER VIII.

GOD THE ONE CREATOR.

Notion of creation. Various definitions	205
Formal object of creation	207
God's dominion of ownership	208
Infinite, self existent, necessary Being	210
Finite, participated, contingent being	210
Atheism, Dualism, Pantheism, Creation	211
The creative act *formally* immanent—*virtually* transient	212
Directive knowledge. Efficacious will	182, 215
God's freedom of will, in creating	218
Divine goodness, as diffusive of itself	219
Principal causes. Instrumental causes	220
Creation, as exclusively proper to God	222
The Creator of *some* things, Creator of *all* things	223
Impossibility of *instrumental* causes in creation	223
Three Persons create. One Creator	224
Appropriation of Creation	225
Representation of causes by *trace*—by *image*	227
Representation of the Trinity in creatures	229
God, as *exemplary* cause of all creatures	232
An *idea* in the mind of an artificer	233
No *final* cause of creation in God	236

	PAGE
Difference between a *reason* and a *cause*	239
Divine goodness, the *reason* of creation	240
Objective extrinsic glory	241
Formal extrinsic glory	241
Formal reason of God's love of creatures	246
The best of worlds	247
The world's *material* perfection. Its *formal* perfection	249
Manifestation of the Divine goodness	250
Creation *in* time, and *with* time	255
Eternity of the world impossible	257

CHAPTER IX.

GOD, AS THE AUTHOR OF NATURE.

Mode, and *order*, of the world's formation	258
God's works a commentary on God's word	259
Advantage of natural sciences	259
Subordination of them to Divine Revelation	260
Distinction of operations in God	262
Formation of material *substance* into corporeal *natures*	262
Why six epochs are called six *days*	263
Existence of angels, or *pure* spirits	264
Relation of angels to place, and to space	265
Superiority of the angelic intellect	266
The angels' knowledge. How far they *reason*	267
Knowledge of *free acts*, and of *future events*	268
Knowledge of "cogitations of the heart"	269
God alone the Searcher of hearts	269
Hearing, and *speech*, among the angels	272
Nobility of man	272
Man, made *immediately* in human species	273
Man's transformation from the brute impossible	272

Two elements only in human nature	275
Man, one *subject*, and one *substance*	275
Man's soul, as the *form* of man's body	276
Specific oneness. Oneness of *origin*	277
Human souls, distinct creations	278
Immortality of the soul, a *law* of its nature	279

CHAPTER X.

GOD, AS THE AUTHOR OF THE SUPERNATURAL.

What is *nature?*	283
The natural order. The supernatural order	284
Nature. The *natural*	285
Activity of a nature. Capacity of a nature	291
What is *exacted by*, and *due to* nature?	293
What is *gratuitous*, and *not due* to nature?	294
The *supernatural*. The *preternatural*	296
Sonship. Slavery. Strangers	297
Divine *adoptive* sonship	299
Deification of the creature	303
Supernatural knowledge, *not due* to human nature	304
Innate appetites. Elicited appetites	306
Obediential power in the creature	311
Concupiscence	315
Struggle of natural inclinations	319
Immunity from concupiscence	320
Physical evils. Moral advantages	334, 322
Infused knowledge, *not due* to human nature	329
Human immortality	332
Mortality, *natural* to man	333
The *simply* evil. The *absolutely* evil	335
Pure, or mere, nature	336

xxii CONTENTS.

CHAPTER XI.

THE PARADISE OF GOD'S CREATION.

	PAGE
Integrity of nature	338
Adam's knowledge	340
Conditional immortality	344
Immunity from suffering and sorrow	344
Connection of *preternatural* gifts with *supernatural* grace	345

CHAPTER XII.

THE INNER LIFE OF GOD.

Man's conception of God's perfections	347
Formal objective ideas	348
Distinction *in idea*, with foundation *in reality*	349
Formal ideas of the *absolute*, and the *relative*	349
Relation in creatures. Relation in God	350
Substantial relations	351
A word, or mental conception	352
Divine understanding. Divine loving	353
Divine persons	357
Persons. Hypostases	358
Substance. Accidents	359
No accidents in God	360
The whole. The part	362
No parts in God	367
Specific oneness. Numerical oneness	368
Dignities of the *personal*	369
Will follows the *nature*, and not the *person*	369
Real distinctness of the Divine Persons	370
Identity of Divine *relations* with the Divine *essence*	371
No priority among Divine relations	374
Analogical conception of the Divine Persons	375

	PAGE
Subsistence. Subsistence in God	376
Opposition of relations	379
The unbegottenness of God the Father	385, 380
Procession of the Holy Ghost	380
The Father and the Son, one principle of procession	381
Notion of two Divine processions only	388
Difference between Divine processions	392
Generation. God the Son. The Eternal Word	393
Generation in pure spirits—in corporeal beings—in God	397
Essence of generation. Three notes	399
Procession of the Holy Ghost, not *generation*	404
Absolute attributes. Oneness with the Divine essence	405
External operations, common to the Divine Persons	406
Appropriation of works, and attributes, to one Person	408
Scope of appropriation. Foundation of appropriation	409
Inexistence of the Divine Persons, one in another	411
The Trinity, a mystery	414
Two constituents of a mystery	415
The "hidden wisdom"	419
Existence of the Trinity, incapable of demonstration	422
Place of analogical conceptions of super-rational truths	424
Understanding, and faith	430
Mysteries above reason, not contrary to reason	434
Right use of philosophy in theology	435

CHAPTER I.

MAN'S KNOWLEDGE OF GOD'S EXISTENCE.

THEOLOGY is the study of God. In a wide sense of the word, theology extends to the study of many other beings besides God. The study of these, as included under theology, is however the study of them not merely as they are in themselves, but as they are in their relation to God. God thus remains in theology the principal object of it, although in this case not the only object of it. It is in reality God Himself who is being studied in those beings that are not God.

In a less wide sense of the word, theology is restricted to the study of God Himself—the nature of God—the attributes of God—and the internal processions in God.

Under its wider aspect, theology embraces the study of all the works of God, whether in the order of creation and nature—or in the order of sanctification and grace—along with all the results of these works of God, and all that takes place in God's doing of them.

Knowledge and explanation of the works of God is *theological* only in so far as these works are being considered in their relation to God, as

God is the supreme principle, or first beginning, from which they have both their being, and their own proper nature and character—and as God is also the last end to which they have been, one and all of them, of the very nature of their existence as His creatures, ordained.

In every science, the *principal object* of it is that to which all other matters which are treated in that science are subordinated, and under the idea of which they are being considered.

In the science of theology, the *principal object* is God, as He has revealed Himself by means of supernatural manifestations to man's reason, which He has Himself enlightened with the light of faith.

God's enlightening of man's reason with the light of faith does not create or give existence to that reason, or to the natural force and light of reason. His enlightening presupposes these, and it raises them to a higher order than that of nature.

In like manner the *supernatural* manifestations by means of which God reveals Himself to the reason which He has raised above its natural level, presuppose *natural* manifestations by means of which God exhibits Himself to the natural light of reason in order that He may be known.

The demonstration and the explanation of the existence and of the attributes of God, as understood by man's reason from God's *natural* manifestations of Himself, belong to the domain of Philosophy.

In Theology this natural knowledge of God provided by Philosophy prepares the way for a clearer and more complete understanding of those truths which God has revealed through His supernatural manifestations of Himself. Theology makes use of the natural knowledge of God which Philosophy supplies, not as if it were a proper principle of its own teaching, but as it is a subsidiary aid.

In this sense Philosophy has been called a pedagogue and propædeutic, a prelude and preamble to Theology. Theology is the Queen of Sciences, and Philosophy is the most noble of her handmaids.

The arguments by which the existence of God is demonstrated in Philosophy may be regarded both directly and reflexly. Regarded *directly*, they are drawn from the existence of *contingent* beings, that is to say, of beings the existence of which is not of their own nature necessary—from the perfections of those beings, along with their essential imperfections—from the existence of a rational nature, an existence which is immediately apprehended by the natural reason itself—from the essential dependence of the whole universe, and the order and disposition of it towards an end—and from the absolute force of the moral law to bind. From all of these it is that man's reason recognizes that it cannot be that there should not exist a *necessary* Being as the creative cause of all effects—the most wise and the most perfect of all beings—a just and holy foreseer and lawgiver—the principle or first beginning, and the end of all things that are.

The whole of this train of argument rests on the intrinsic bond which is perceived by man's intelligence as existing between those truths which are known by the light of reason. The argument belongs therefore to Philosophy.

The arguments for the existence of God which are supplied by reason may at the same time be regarded *reflexly;* as when it is asked—What is the force and value of these arguments? Are there in human reason implanted forces in order that it should arrive at certainty that God exists? Is human reason, moreover, in virtue of its own natural light, able to ascend from its knowledge of creatures to knowledge of the existence of their Creator as a true and personal God Who is utterly distinct and separate from the whole universe of His creatures?

This *reflex* consideration has its proper place both in Philosophy and in Theology, but in different ways; and these correspond with the differences which are characteristic of the two sciences. In Philosophy the reflex question itself is solved through the direct demonstration, since the human reason which has evident knowledge of the object, understands at the same time by reflection that this knowledge is true knowledge. The reflex knowledge of its trueness can, however, be made still more perfect and distinct through analysis of the arguments.

From the point of view of Philosophy we understand by the name of God a Supreme Being, from whom other beings are necessarily dependent. This conception, although imperfect and confused, is nevertheless in reality a conception of God. In God alone is this conception verified. It moreover implicitly contains other notes which belong to God.

As matter of historical fact, the existence of such a Being has been admitted by the human race with a constant consent which is morally universal. It is testified to by the sacred books not only of the Hebrews, but of the Chinese and the Indians. It is witnessed, among Greek authors, by Hesiod and Homer, Plato and Aristotle, Herodotus and Xenophon. Among Latin authors, Tacitus and Cæsar, Cicero and Seneca bear witness to it. In countries which have been discovered since their time there is also found evidence of recognition of a divinity. Languages express the common ideas and sense of peoples, and in all languages are found words to designate a Supreme Being. Sacrifices, festivals, altars, oracles, and oaths are proofs of belief in a deity. Knowledge of a God is simultaneous with all the known primeval records of every nation. The Hebrew Scriptures, which are at least genuine records, trace this knowledge to the origin of the human race.

Mankind as a whole has admitted the existence of a divine nature. Even when men have multiplied that nature they have recognized some one divine being as greater than other divine beings, and as a Supreme Being from whom other beings are dependent. Belief in a plurality of gods proves that the believers in it had not a *distinct* conception of divinity, or a recognition of all the attributes of divinity which are capable of being known; but it does not prove the absence of a conception of the difference of one Being from other beings, or of the conception of one Supreme Being. Even Polytheists have revered a Supreme Being as a prince among other gods.

Pantheism which denies, or at least does not admit distinction between God and other beings, excludes indeed the true conception of God as He is in Himself; but even in pantheism there still remains the conception of a Supreme Being from whom flows forth whatsoever is, and from whom in some way all and every thing that is depends.

If the Greeks called certain nations atheistic, it was because those nations did not worship the Greek gods; and in this sense Socrates and, in after times, the Christians were called atheists.

It is not one and the same thing to have a knowledge of God, and to adore God with an external and public worship; and absence of this worship does not negative the existence of that knowledge.

This constant and morally universal consent of men in holding the existence of a God cannot have had its rise in prejudices of education. Although the persuasion may have been and was fostered and propagated through education, yet the first origin of what afterwards became common, cannot have been education. It must either have existed from the beginning of the human race, or it must have been from the author of human nature, or from human nature itself. Prejudices from education are, moreover, not the same in all nations, and they are liable on reflection to be laid aside, and especially if they run counter to natural inclination. We find that in this case the prejudice in favour of the existence of a God, even if prejudice it was, came to be confirmed and completed by reflection upon it.

The evidence wherewith the truth of the existence of some supreme being is known to all men, is not immediate, but mediate; and so this truth requires demonstration.

A proposition which is *known of itself* is one which is knowable without the intervention of demonstration. This it can be in two ways, either because by aid of experience, or because by aid of analysis, the predicate is seen in the subject. The predicate may be seen in the subject either as regards itself only, or also as regards us. As regards itself, a proposition is *known of itself* when that which is enunciated in it has in itself the reason why it is *immediately* knowable. Of this kind are all propositions the predicate of which is of the *essence* of the subject. When the subject is completely known, the predicate can be thereby known. It would therefore be better said that the proposition is *knowable* of itself. An intellect is, of course, supposed which is capable of knowing that truth *immediately*. Knowableness has its relation to him who knows.

A proposition is *known of itself*, on the other hand, *as regards us*, when it is such that we also can *immediately* know it. This is the case when the terms, that is, the subject and the predicate being understood, the bond between the two is at once apparent to us; or, when the truth of the proposition is made manifest to us solely through analysis of its terms, the subject and the predicate, without the aid of any other means. These are called *immediately evident* propositions, such as first principles.

In the proposition *God is*—the predicate is of the *essence* of the subject. Existence is essential to God. Hence this proposition, so far as concerns itself, is *known of itself.* It is not however known of itself *to us.* It is not *immediately* evident.

We are here speaking not of some obscure and confused knowledge of God in which God is not seen as distinct from other beings, but of a knowledge which, although imperfect, is nevertheless in so far clear and distinct as to contain some notes of God, and He is perceived as distinct from all other beings which are not God. That He is so, we know when we know that *God is.* It is known of itself *to us.* The knowledge is certain, that is to say, we affirm with certainty that which is contained in, and brought forth from the proposition. It is a matter of judgment, and not solely of apprehension. That which is predicated in the proposition *God exists*—is real existence, and so it is the reality of the subject. The reality of a subject cannot be *immediately* seen and affirmed, unless the subject is seen through *intuition* of it. The reason is because so long as we have only an *idea* of the subject, there always remains the question whether there is a real object which corresponds to this idea. Apart from intuition, this can be known by *demonstration* alone. That which falls to be known by the aid of demonstration is not *immediately* evident. Some knowledge of God must precede every demonstration of the existence of God. This is not a certain judgment with regard to that existence. It is a simple apprehension, which is equivalent to a nominal definition. This is the case when the truth of the existence of God is sought and found by demonstration. When the same truth, without being sought, is found through demonstration, then a notion which exhibits God—such as, for instance, the notion of a supreme being from which all beings depend, the notion of a first cause, and the like—is obtained in the process of demonstration itself, and there is required only the notion which is virtually or implicitly contained in the principles which are assumed. For example, if a thing begins to exist, the cause of it exists, and there cannot be an infinite procession of causes, and therefore there must exist a first cause. To this first cause we give the name of God.

In this process of reasoning the notion of a first cause is explicitly acquired. Before it, the notion was held only implicitly.

Demonstration *a priori* proceeds from this that

in the ontological order, or order of real being, there is first a reason or cause of that which is demonstrated. There is nothing, however, in the ontological order which can be a cause of God, or in which God can have a reason for His being. There cannot therefore be *a priori* demonstration of God's existence. It must be demonstrated *a posteriori*. It has to be shewn that the physical order of the universe is the work of an intelligent Being. To do this we consider the first elements of this physical order, or the first conditions of its origin. If these require a disposing mind, they make manifest that the physical order which evidently exists has proceeded from an intelligence.

The primitive elements of physical order in matter are movement—certain and differing directions of this movement—and a well-adapted placing in space of that which is set in order. All physical phenomena depend on *movement*, and so that is first postulated.

From different movements, and from different directions of that which is moved, and from the difference of the subjects on which various agents can act, and do act, different phenomena are produced, and different natures are constituted. Hence, that the order which is visible to us should exist, there must have been a certain direction of movement, and a certain placing in space.

Given that in matter itself there is not to be found any reason of those three, and that they must therefore have their origin from an extrinsic agent, we go on to prove that this agent is intelligent, and as intelligent was the reason or cause of them. If the cause of them is not intelligent, either it is subordinate as an instrument to one who is intelligent, and in him we have God; or it acts by its own force, and it is impossible that from this force there should spring the physical order which we observe. The cause of this order must be a *free* agent.

There must be a cause or reason why the existing order in matter should have been established, rather than another possible order. Determination of the existence of the present order in place of other schemes of order cannot have sprung from a cause which was itself necessitated. If the cause could institute the present physical order, it could certainly have effected other systems of order, which are similar to it, or are less wonderful. In a cause which can of itself produce several effects, there is not a sufficient reason why it should be determinated to produce one particular effect, rather than other effects, unless it either determinates itself, or is determinated by another. If it determinates itself it is not a necessitated cause. It is a free cause, with power to choose. If it is determinated by another, then the reason of the effect produced is in him who determinates it, and who is therefore free, and the true cause of the order which he establishes; and so again we come back to God.

Whatever exists is either produced, or is not produced. That which is produced indicates another by which it is produced. That other is either produced, or is not produced. If it is not produced, then there exists a being which is not produced. If it is produced, we have a chain or series of producers and produced. In this series all the members of it cannot be produced. If all were produced, either they were produced from nothing—or there is an infinite procession of producers and produced—or there are at least two beings which are to each other a mutual efficient cause. Each of those two is the maker of the other. This last is impossible. That all beings should be produced from nothing, with no being to bring them out of nothing, is absurd. It is contrary to the principle of causality. If a successive series of existences, one after the other, is infinite, one existence at least in that series must be eternal. The series cannot have no beginning unless the first member of it is eternal. If a series is infinite, as a series of existences of the same character, there must always be in it one member prior to another member, and the series cannot be eternal. The very idea of it involves contradiction.

If there exists a contingent being, there must also exist a necessary being. A *contingent* being is a being the existence of which is possible, and the non-existence of which is also possible. A *necessary* being is a being which must necessarily be, and the nature of which absolutely demands existence. If a necessary being did not exist always, it never could exist. If it did not always exist, it was at some time nothing. If it was at any time nothing, it could not ever be, because nothing can begin from nothingness, nor can a thing begin of itself. For the beginning of a thing, another thing is required by the principle of causality. A being which must necessarily always be, cannot be contingent. Such a being is an adequate cause why other beings are, or why they may be; and there cannot be any effect without an adequate cause of it. An *adequate* cause is that from which is derived the whole of the reason why the effect should exist. One contingent being cannot be the adequate cause of another contingent being. A necessary being, which has in itself the reason of its own existence, can be the adequate cause of contingent beings. If, therefore, there are contingent beings—and the existence of them is evident, and cannot be disputed—there must be a *necessary* being who is *self-existent*. Thus again do we come back to the God in whom we live, and move, and are, or have our being.

A man who has full use of reason cannot for any length of time be ignorant of, or intellectually deny, the existence of God. The means of knowledge are common to all, and those means are first principles, and the existence of the visible creation. Reflection is indeed required, but reflection cannot be absent for a length of time. The visible objects which present themselves as effects, and the order which evidently obtains among them, excite reflection. There is also in man a natural avidity to know the causes of things. Given reflection, and comparing the principle of, for instance, causality with the fact of the existence of visible things, there must result some knowledge of the existence of a God, under the conception, at least, of a supreme being, from whom all things depend.

To Theology it most certainly belongs to give judgment with regard to the value of the demonstration from reason—and with regard also to the force of human reason which, along with the natural light of reason enables man to know with certainty through his knowledge of God's creatures, that God Himself exists.

2.

That God is knowable to man, through man's previous knowledge of God's creatures, is a truth which is contained in God's written revelation. In the Sacred Scriptures God is declared to be knowable to men in those attributes of His which exhibit Him as distinct from His works, as He is the Supreme Author and Lord of them. God is not only *knowable*, but He is *easily* knowable, and that without need of any very subtle or far reaching investigation. God is knowable by means of the same natural faculty wherewith men form their judgments with regard to the properties of visible nature. God is therefore an object of human knowledge, and there are forces in the human reason which are proportioned in order to man's attainment of this knowledge.

The Sacred Scriptures describe also the *mode* of God's manifestation of Himself, along with the *mode* of man's knowledge of God through his natural reason, which corresponds to that natural manifestation.

An object of knowledge cannot *actually* be known to human beings unless and except in so far as it manifests itself to their minds. The manifestation is in fact the knowableness of a thing, as made actual to him who is knowing it. An object of knowledge may be made manifest either through itself immediately, or mediately through another object which is already known. God manifests Himself to the human reason through His creatures in such wise as that from a knowledge of the perfections of the visible universe—which are, however, limited by their imperfection—man arrives at a knowledge of God. It is not as if in creatures God were seen in Himself and in His substance. It is from knowledge of an *effect*, and of the *perfection* of that effect, that the reason has understanding of the existence of God and, to some extent, of the perfection of God who is the Supreme Cause of every effect. The objectively knowable becomes the subjectively known, when God has rendered Himself *actually* knowable, through His manifestation of Himself.

The Sacred Scriptures of both Testaments—and notably in the Book of Wisdom, in St. Paul's Epistle to the Romans, and in St. Paul's speeches both at Lystra and at Athens, as these are recorded in the Book of the Acts of the Holy Apostles—set before us a twofold order in the universe of creatures, from consideration of which the human reason has knowledge of the existence of God. There is the *physical* order—and there is the *historical* order.

The whole of the physical order is a resplendent manifestation of God to the rational soul.

Scripture supposes, by way of foundation, the evidence of the *imperfection* of the creature—and from this there is understood the fact that the creature derives its being from some other Being distinct and separate from itself. The more fully the *perfections* also of creatures, as they are effects, are understood, the more clearly is there recognized the perfection of the Cause of all creatures.

When the question is—*Is there* a first cause of the universe? the Scriptures set forward the imperfections and limitations of creatures, to be considered by the human reason.

When, on the other hand, the question is—*What is* this first cause which does exist? the same Scriptures set forth the beauty—the order—and the magnificence of the universe of creatures. Both considerations, when taken together, constitute in its entirety the demonstration of the existence of God.

Both at Lystra and at Athens St. Paul set forth the *historical* order of providence as a testimony of God to all nations, from which they might and ought to have had knowledge of Him.

He notes the second causes in the physical order, as causes the actions and effects of which are directed by the God of providence for the preservation and benefit of men. Under this aspect the historical argument is in touch with the cosmological argument.

He notes also the history of peoples as divinely directed, among other ends, to this end that men of all nations may recognize a divine providence as well as a human element, in the history of those peoples as it is a whole.

He further notes the continual benefits and providence of God in His direction of individual men. "God is," he said to the men of Athens, "not far from every one of us, for in Him we live, and move, and are."

He declares that the relations of human nature towards God, and the dependence of human nature upon God, are both of them such as that in men who have come to use of reason there should, as it were, spontaneously and necessarily, spring up an at first obscure indeed and confused knowledge of a Supreme Being—and that later on, supposing this preconception, they should seek after God, and a more explicit knowledge of God. By means of this wider, deeper, and more clear knowledge, derived from consideration of God's benefits both to men in common and to individuals, they might be able to feel after God and to find Him.

The first spontaneous and obscure knowledge—which the Fathers, and not without reason, speak of as implanted in or engrafted on human nature—St. Paul distinguishes from a more finished knowledge.

He teaches that Divine deeds are ordained in order to this that, from the known fact of them, there should of itself result in men an impulse to seek after God. In this impulse towards enquiry about God, there is already and necessarily contained some confused and primordial knowledge of God. In this enquiry man can, and ought to cultivate his primitive conception. It remains, however, possible for man, by his own fault, to apply the same primitive idea of God to objects which are not God, and so to pervert that idea. It does not therefore necessarily follow from a man's seeking God in some or any sort of way that he will feel after and find God. St. Paul says "that they should seek God, *si fortè* if perhaps they may feel after him or find Him."

Hence we see how it is that the idea of the *existence* of some divinity is common to all nations, and is almost ineradicable. The perversion, however, of the *true notion* of God was nevertheless nearly as widely spread among the Gentiles.

The faculty of understanding through creatures the existence and the perfection of God and, if other aids are absent, the duty of exercising this faculty, are such that, if men taught by God's natural manifestation and testimony, which He has adapted to the congenital light of man's natural reason, do not worship God as the one true God, and a personal God, who is separate and distinct from all and every one of His creatures—and to whom it is due that He should be honoured by His rational creatures with supreme worship—they are, as St. Paul wrote to the Romans, "inexcusable."

3.

St. Paul distinctly teaches that the moral law, with its absolute force to bind the human conscience, is knowable—and was known to the Gentiles, through reason, and apart from positive revelation of that law.

This natural knowledge of the obligation of the moral law supposes and includes the natural knowableness, and the natural knowledge of God through reason; apart from positive revelation given by God, and received by man, with regard to God's existence.

Some sort of knowledge, however, and at least a confused knowledge of God, comes first in order before man's distinct knowledge of moral obligation.

The hinge of the question turns on this, that from the teaching of St. Paul, and so from the revealed word of God, it is demonstrated that a knowledge of moral obligation—or, in other words, of a law which has force to bind the conscience—is possible to man through his natural reason, without presupposing a positive revelation from which this knowledge is drawn, and on which it rests.

From this it further follows—or rather there is included in this the truth—that there can be some knowledge of the existence of God which is merely a result of reason, and is not founded in positive revelation.

A knowledge of moral obligation which essentially includes some sort of knowledge of God cannot have proceeded from the sources of reason, unless this knowledge of God was essentially included by way of foundation in that knowledge of moral obligation.

The question of the logical connection between knowledge of God's existence and knowledge of the binding force of the moral law is philosophical rather than theological. The question is—Is knowledge of the moral law, from which we may arrive at knowledge of God, the knowledge which is first in order? or, Is it only from the revealed fact of the force of reason to give knowledge of the moral law, that we may conclude that the same force of reason avails to knowledge of God? It is clear that there cannot be the former knowledge without the latter knowledge.

St. Paul instructs the Romans that a knowledge through reason, of moral principles can exist, and actually did exist amongst the Gentiles—apart from positive revelation of the moral law.

His scope, throughout the whole of his Epistle, is to refute the error and pride of the Jews in their glorying in the notion that it was sufficient for justice to be Jews by birth, and to belong to the Mosaic economy. God, he argues, does not look to race, and both Jews and Gentiles are judged in accordance with their works, whether good or evil. If the Jews glory in their prerogative of the Law and Mosaic economy, this will not free them from destruction. They have not in those privileges any foundation for their pride with reference to the Gentiles, to whom the Law was not revealed. Those who, without belonging to the Law, have sinned will perish—not for transgression of an unknown law, but—for the sins which they have committed against a law which they have known, not from revelation, but from another source. Those who belong to the Law are not thereby already saved, but will on the contrary be judged in accordance with that law which was revealed to them. "Not the hearers of the Law are just before God, but the doers of the law shall be justified."

The law which the Gentiles were said by St. Paul not to have, was not the ceremonial law of

Moses, for that law was not the law which was "written in their hearts." The law referred to was the moral law which forbids theft, adultery and idolatry. St. Paul is contrasting the form of the law which was manifested to the Jews by a positive revelation—and so far as that form is concerned, the Gentiles had not the law—with the real *matter* of the law which even the Gentiles did have, although through another mode of manifestation, that is to say, through their own rational nature. Through the light of reason the Gentiles had understanding of moral good and moral evil, and of the obligation to do the one, and to avoid the other.

The Apostle further explains the way in which the Gentiles "were to themselves a law." It was not as if their rational nature were itself a lawgiving principle. It was inasmuch as that rational nature manifested and, as it were, *promulgated* the moral law to them. This promulgation consisted in the knowledge which they had, through the natural light of reason, of moral obligation. The writing of the law in their hearts or intellects, of which he speaks, was not that kind of writing by which revealed law and doctrine is said to be written in human hearts through the more abundant internal grace of the New Testament. It was a writing of which the proximate principle was the rational nature of man itself, in contrast with God's writing through Moses on tables, and God's positive revelation.

He who by the light of reason has understanding of the obligation to avoid moral evil and to do good, has therein knowledge that this obligation avails for every rational creature. It is an absolute obligation which is binding always, everywhere, and under every conceivable hypothesis. There cannot be any circumstances whatever in which the obligation of the rational creature to avoid moral evil does not remain in all its vigour. He who has understanding of this obligation as absolute, has therein understanding of his own dependence on a superior to whom, for observance of due order, he is bound to submit himself and obey—and in whose pre-eminence over all creatures this obligation is founded. He has thus at least an obscure and confused knowledge of a Supreme Lord to whom an absolute homage is due.

The same light of reason which gives understanding of the obligation of a law, necessarily embraces also the existing of a God who is Supreme Lawgiver, and supreme principle of moral obligation; and without the idea of whom there could not be conceived the notion of that absolute obligation. It is clear that knowledge of absolute obligation cannot be presupposed as a foundation from which to arrive at the first knowledge of God, since this knowledge is itself the foundation of that other knowledge.

Human reason can, from other divine manifestations, ascend by way of analysis to a knowledge of the existence of God and, God's existence once known, can have distinctness in its understanding of the absolute obligation of the moral law. From this more distinct knowledge there can be, as it were, a retracing in order to a more clear and confirmed understanding of God's existence and perfection.

A clear knowledge of moral obligation does not necessarily suppose a clear and distinct knowledge of the existence of God; although it cannot consist with an utter absence of all knowledge of God's existence.

Perfect knowledge of absolute obligation is one thing, and some knowledge of the moral order in its wider aspect is another thing.

From the very consideration of rational nature, as it is ordained towards the *true* and the *good*—and from consideration of human society—man can easily arrive at understanding of the necessity and existence of a moral order—of the existence of an ultimate end in the enjoyment of the *true* and of the *good*—and of the necessity and the existence of *rights* and *duties*. These are *essential* relations of a rational nature. Without them the idea of such a nature would involve contradiction. Such a nature would be as impossible as it is inconceivable. These essential relations would be destitute of all ultimate foundation, if there did not actually exist one Supreme Being, who is a holy and just lawgiver, and supreme judge. As, therefore, from understanding of the *physical* order the human reason can come to know that God exists; so from its perception of the essential relations of the *moral* order the human reason can rise to a knowledge of God, as He is the exemplary cause or pattern, and as He is the efficient cause of that moral order. This is the objective process of human thought. Practically, however, and as matter of fact, these notions of the moral order are, as we shall see, a foundation not of first knowledge of God's existence, but of a more finished knowledge of God's perfection and attributes.

When the Fathers speak of knowledge of God as being a "seminal word" which is sown or implanted in, or engrafted on, or congenital to man's nature, they do not mean this in the sense of—to use a phrase of certain moderns—an "innate idea" of God which is created in human nature along with that nature. They mean merely that the rational soul, which is an image of God, has been so made for knowledge of God that, with the light of reason which is congenital to that soul, and by an indeliberate exercise of the reasoning faculty which belongs to it, and so by a natural movement it, as it were, spontaneously conceives—from the obvious evidence of the universe, as it is a natural manifestation of God—*some* knowledge of God. This primitive knowledge is apart both from philosophical enquiry, and from instruction through positive revelation.

The Fathers, in the use of these expressions, are contrasting this obscure or confused knowledge of God, not with *acquired* knowledge as such—for this knowledge is itself acquired—but with that more finished knowledge of God which is arrived at through more diligent and subtle consideration—and also and chiefly with that more perfect knowledge of God which is due to revelation.

It is the intellectual faculty itself, or man's reason, which they call the "seminal word." They regard the force of reason as being, as it were, a seed of wisdom which is congenital to human nature.

4.

Besides God's manifestations of Himself through His works in nature, there is another manifestation which God makes of Himself through His works in the supernatural order.

The more perfect any effects, seen to be effects, are, the more manifestly do they demonstrate the existence of the cause of them, and the perfections of that cause.

If from the works of nature the existence and attributes of the Creator of nature are so resplendent, with what exceeding clearness of splendour must they not shine forth in a manifestation of Himself which He has superadded, and which consists of works of a far higher order. By means of these works God the infinitely mighty, wise, good, and merciful, presents Himself to man's intelligence, as it were, in the midst of rays of refulgent glory. Hence the Fathers comparing the two manifestations—the natural and the supernatural—made by God of Himself, speak of the former, in the light of the latter, as being but a slender shadow seen from afar.

God's supernatural manifestation of Himself, in a series of mighty deeds and marvels, constitutes an universe apart. The existence of this universe is an historical fact which is known to us with the utmost certainty. That there is a necessary bond between the existence of this series of historical facts, and the existence of a cause of that series man's reason plainly perceives.

With no less certainty do we see by the light of reason that the cause must necessarily be none other than a Being who is entirely distinct and separate from one and all of the forces of this visible world—who is infinitely powerful, good, wise, omniscient, provident and, in one word—the God whom the doctrine which is bound up with these supernatural facts announces—and towards whom, in His manifestation of Himself in His infinite perfections to human intelligence, those facts have an intrinsic relation of order.

In order that the necessary bond between the existence of the *effects*, which constitute the manifestation, and the existence of the *cause* who manifests Himself, should be discerned by means of reason, a bare consideration of the effects, as they are historically known to us, is sufficient. Compare the state and condition of Christian society as we find it constituted in the fourth century and since, with the condition of human society as it was in the generations before the Christian era. From a comparison of the two it is clear that in the interval there has been made a mighty transformation. An universal change in religious principles and ideas, in worship, and in morals has taken place. The change is seen to pervade all institutions, both public and private, and the whole course of thought, of feeling, and of action. We see a human society regarding with hatred and contempt that which the same human society had before regarded with worship as the palladium of its common glory and wellbeing.

Learned and unlearned alike are now imbued with the most sublime of principles. Virtues, the very names of which were at one time unknown, are speculatively appreciated by all, as of the highest value, and are practised with previously unheard of fortitude by not a few. A transformation such as this demands a proportionate cause.

No cause of the change is to be found in the elements of the society which preceded it. The whole idea of heathen life and society, and the whole of this new idea of Christian life and society are so violently opposed, the one to the other, as to make it manifest that the transformation must be attributed solely to the power of Him to whom the minds and wills of men are subject, and who can superadd to nature forces which are far above it.

History, moreover, tells us that every endeavour was made by the heathen world, throughout three long centuries, with as much pertinacity as cruelty, to hinder this effect. We find no human means calculated to produce it; we find many forces in action which, apart from Divine counteraction were such as to render it impossible.

Side by side with all this, a constant and widespread series of miracles, of fulfilments of prophecy, and of supernatural enlightenings and strengthenings of souls, which were apparent in the wonderful effects of them, point towards Him as the Author of the transformation, to whom the whole universe, both corporeal and spiritual, is subject.

The Christian economy, therefore, regarded universally and as it is a whole, is seen to rest on principles, to be sustained by means, and to shine with external manifestations of internal gifts and perfections of grace, which are such that it must necessarily be the work of Him who is the infinitely good, wise and almighty Creator and Sanctifyer, whom the Christian religion professes to be the Author of that religion. The Christian economy thus presents itself as a supernatural creation of God, and by its very existence it is, and is recognized as being a supernatural manifestation of God.

In like manner as the institution and rise of the Christian society exhibits God as the creative cause of it, so is the *preservation* of that society an enduring manifestation of God, as preserving, protecting, and fostering it by supernatural power.

The history of Christianity is intimately connected with the history of the "chosen people" of God under the Old Testament; as is the perfection of a thing with the first beginning of that thing. The religious and political life of the Jewish nation, taken as a whole, was during two thousand years utterly different from the religion, the life, and the morals of all the heathen nations.

The continuity of this national characteristic, which the Jewish nation preserved amid all its vicissitudes, was bound up with supernatural facts—with prophecies uttered and fulfilled—and with appearances of God to men, not merely at intervals, but in a continuous series of them throughout many ages. The complexus of these was not an accidental adjunct. It constituted the foundation, and was an essential element of the religious and political history of the Jewish people, regarded as it forms one historical whole. Apart from these supernatural facts, that history cannot be either understood or explained. The history of the Old Testament is thus one long and continuous manifestation of God, and of His divine attributes.

All preceding manifestations of God, as forming a preparation, and all subsequent manifestations, considered as they form an effect and continuation, culminate in the one supreme manifestation of God which was made in the Incarnate God. It is true that the fact of the personal divinity of the visible God was to be learned by men through teaching, and was to be believed by men on authority. It is nevertheless equally true that Jesus Christ, regarded in His life on earth, taken as a whole, and with all its portentous wonders—and regarded at the same time in connection with the history of the Testament before His advent, which, taken as a whole, was a preparation for His coming, as for the complement of that Testament—and regarded again in connection with the subsequent history of Christianity, which taken as a whole, depends from Him as from its cause and principle—must necessarily be recognized as the crowning pinnacle of God's manifestation of Himself to man.

As therefore the visible universe is rightly called by the Fathers a herald, a proclamation, and a doctrinal utterance of God, inasmuch as it manifests God to man's intelligence; so also and much more ought the *supernatural* universe—even if it is regarded objectively only as it is a complexus of facts, and prescinding from the formal revelation of which faith is the correlative—to be called an objective doctrinal utterance by God about Himself. The Divine power, says St. Augustine, speaks by means of facts, and as novel and less common words, interspersed becomingly and with moderation in human speech, add brilliance to it, so in the significance of deeds of marvel is the Divine eloquence in a manner more resplendent.

5.

If this objective supernatural manifestation of God, as it is one whole or universe, is considered beyond the immediate scope of it, and in the light of the idea which properly belongs to it as most its own, it is clear at a glance that it is not merely metaphorically an utterance of God, as it is an objective manuduction to the knowledge of God, but that in a proper sense it constitutes an essential element of God's word and revelation.

Those supernatural facts are, as it were, a royal apparel wherewith the words are adorned as they are words of God—they are a seal of divinity wherewith the words are stamped—and whereby the teaching which is conveyed in the words is demonstrated by way of evidence, as a teaching which is credible and to be believed. The divine facts along with the divine words thus constitute *one* utterance on the part of God.

This divine utterance does not as yet exhibit a truth to the intellect in such wise as that the intellect should have understanding of that truth in itself. It exhibits it in order that the intellect should believe in that truth with supernatural faith, on the authority of God who is revealing it.

All those things, and those things only form the *material* object of faith which are enunciated either explicitly or implicitly in the doctrinal utterance of God. The doctrine of God's existence is in manifold ways enunciated in the Word of God. It is enunciated *directly*, and of the intrinsic nature of the utterance, as it is a Divine utterance, in every revelation whatsoever. It is enunciated again *reflexly*, and from the signification of the words, when God reveals Himself as, for instance, eternal, or as necessarily existing, or when it is prescribed in so many words that "he that cometh to God must believe that *He is*." Hence it is absolutely certain that the existence of God is a truth which is contained in the revealed Word of God. It is therefore a fact which is to be believed with supernatural faith.

The demonstration from evidence, and consequent knowledge of the existence of God *through the light of reason*, in no way hinders the intellect —when it is enlightened with the supernatural light of faith, and strengthened by the bidding of a will which is supernaturally moved—from assenting to the self same truth *by reason of the authority of God revealing*.

Although the material object is in this case one and the same, our knowledge of that object is nevertheless twofold. The object has a knowableness from mediate evidence, or the certainty which springs from demonstration. It has a knowableness also on Divine testimony. Through the first, that truth which presents itself to the reason is related to the reason as a truth to be *understood*. Through the second, the same truth is related to the supernatural habit of faith as a truth to be *believed*.

It follows that the same material object, under that idea or aspect of its knowableness in which it is affected by the authority of God revealing—an authority which is extrinsic to it—is objectively *certain*, but is nevertheless not *evident*. Assent to a truth under this formal idea is therefore a *free* assent.

Under the other idea of its knowableness, the same truth may be *evident*, and if so, assent to that truth by the intellect is a *necessary* assent, and independent of all free choosing by the will.

Hence we see how an object of faith is, under its own formal idea, not apparent, and how faith even in things which are evident, but evident from other sources, is a conviction or "argument of things which appear not." We see also in like manner how it is that a man who has knowledge from evidence that God exists, and so cannot deny the existence of God, is nevertheless capable of withholding *faith* in the existence of God, that is to say, he can refuse his assent to this truth *on the authority of God as speaking*. That God has spoken is objectively most *certain*, but it is not so *evident* as that assent or dissent should not depend on a free command of the will. The assent of the reason may be merely through the light of nature, while the assent of faith is elicited by supernatural forces. The two assents, therefore, as regards both the formal motive of them, and the subjective principle which elicits them, belong to distinct and different orders.

That which is the case with regard to all other of those truths which can be known both by the light of reason and revelation, is equally the case with regard to this truth of God's existence. There occurs however in the case of this primary truth a particular difficulty. The question may be asked—In what way can the existence of God be believed *by faith*, on the authority of God speaking, since the very foundation of an act of faith is knowledge, and that a supernatural knowledge, which is already possessed, of God's existing? The authority of God speaking, it may be argued, can only in so far move me towards believing as I already know that God exists, and this knowledge of mine must be a supernatural knowledge, in order that the act of faith may be supernatural. When, therefore, I say—I believe that God exists, because God, who is infinitely veracious, has said that He exists—in this very motive which is the formal motive of believing, the existence of God is already affirmed, and it cannot be to me a motive for believing, except so far as in it I embrace the existence of God as already certain.

The answer is this. In every act of faith there are comprehended, implicitly at least and virtually, certain elements. Of these elements one is a proposition which is immediately known, either evidently or obscurely, namely, that if God speaks, He is infinitely veracious and cannot either deceive or be deceived. Another is—God has revealed this particular truth. Now, looking to the character and whole mechanism, so to speak, of the motives of credibility wherewith God's utterance presents itself as being in reality a Divine utterance—or, looking to that utterance with all its component parts, or constituent elements, I understand for *certain* although not *evidently*, and so as to take from me my intellectual freedom to either assent or dissent—that this is a word of God. The assent, in the case of either proposition, as it is by way of premiss to the act of faith, does not spring from the motive of the authority of God speaking, nor is it given because God has said that He is infallible, and that He has also revealed this particular truth, but both assents when they enter the act of faith are elicited through supernatural forces. These forces are superadded through grace to the intellect and the will, so that the firmness of the adhesion should be, as it ought to be, supernatural and supreme. Then it is that, in the third place, there follows an assent to the particular truth itself which has been proposed as a revealed truth, and this assent is *on the authority of God revealing*. This is a *formal* act of faith.

In this act of faith—The infallible God has revealed that He exists, and so on His authority, and from reverence thereto, and with a pious affection of faith, I believe that God exists—there is a twofold assent to the existence of God. The two assents, however, differ both in mode and in motive. The first assent is implicit, and does not rest on authority. The second assent which is a formal act of faith, is explicit, and it rests on authority. To a truth of which already I have knowledge under one idea, I assent reflexly under another idea, namely—by reason of the infinite authority of God who speaks. To Him this supreme homage of faith and worship is due from His rational creature.

In this debt of homage is contained the answer to farther questions, such as, What is the scope, the necessity, and the use of faith and an act of faith in the existence of God, when the fact of God's existence is already known?*

The Vatican Council declared that God can with certainty be known, by the natural light of human reason, from created things; and those who dispute this truth of revelation, she laid beneath her heaviest censure—If any man shall say that the

---

* For a fuller treatment of this point see *The Sacred Scriptures*, or *The Written Word of God*, Chapter XIII, Human apprehension of Divine Revelation, p. 253, by William Humphrey, S.J. London: *Art and Book Co.*, 1894.

one and true God, our Creator and Lord, cannot be known with certainty by the natural light of human reason, through the things that are made. Let him be Anathema.

CHAPTER II.

Man's knowledge of what God is.

MORTAL men do not see God *immediately* in His own proper nature. They can have knowledge of Him only by way of conclusion, and by means of His creatures, as through a medium of which they have already knowledge.

Even in His revelation God has accommodated Himself to this mode of conception which is connatural to man.

This our *mediate* mode of knowledge of God, or knowledge through a *means* which is not God of that which God is, resolves itself, on analysis, into knowledge through *affirmation*, or ascription to God of perfections which we discern in the works of God—through *negation* of the existence in God of the imperfections which are found even in the most perfect of his creatures, and are found also even in our own objective ideas of perfections—and finally through the ideas which are conceived by conjunction of those affirmations and negations, and which result in a notion of the *supereminence* of God's perfection over every perfection which is known to us, or which can be conceived by us.

When we are directly conceiving the perfection of God *affirmatively* through ascription to Him of, for instance, wisdom or justice, our notion does not indeed objectively involve limitation and defect, as do other notions—such as the notion of the reasoning faculty. This faculty, as proceeding from truth to truth, of the very idea of it implies limitation and therefore imperfection. So does the notion of the *potential* which, of the nature of it, has to be perfected in the actual. We, nevertheless, conceive even such perfections as wisdom or justice in a limited way. We cannot conceive an idea of wisdom which shall exhibit wisdom distinctly and positively as without limit. Still less are we capable of conceiving an idea which shall exhibit at once, and in the singleness of one Being, all the perfection which, by reason of the imperfectness of our understandings, we conceive piecemeal by many notions, and call by many names. When, therefore, we speak of the wisdom of God, we presuppose that this perfection is in God not as we conceive it, but in a far higher way. The supereminence of God's wisdom we cannot possibly either conceive or express otherwise than either by negation of its being in reality no more than it is in our own apprehension of it; or by a confused conception of supereminence which we attempt to express by the use of superlatives. All our *affirmative* conceptions, therefore, of God and of His Divine attributes are accompanied by, or rather they implicitly contain, notions which are *negative* of all the imperfection of limitation, along with notions which suppose supereminence. As two negatives make an affirmative, so are our negations affirmations, as they are negations of negations. In these negations an affirmative notion is supposed by way of foundation, and they include the notion of supereminence.

There are not therefore three ways of coming to a knowledge of that which is in God, which are adequately distinct, the one from the other. In each of the three modes all the three are in a manner conjoined. One of the three is always direct, and it includes obliquely the other two.

Hence we understand in what sense the Fathers are speaking when they say that—all perfections can be affirmed of God, and all denied—God is of every name, and is of no name—our knowledge of God is then more perfect when we have come to know that God cannot be known.

2.

If we were to see and know God by immediate intuition—or without the intervention of any created medium of knowledge—and as He is in Himself, and still more, if we were to comprehend God, we should in our conception be penetrating and including the whole of His perfection. This follows from the fact that there is not in the Divine nature any real distinction. It is one most simple being. We arrive, as we have seen, at our understanding of that which God is, through our previous knowledge of the perfections which we perceive in creatures. These perfections are manifold, and every one of them shadows forth under some one aspect the perfection of its exemplary and efficient cause, that is to say, the perfection of Him who made it, and after the pattern of Whom it was made. Not any one of these perfections is, nor are all of them together, an adequate expression or representation of the Divine perfection. Hence it is that, in accordance with the multiplicity of perfections, the idea of which we abstract from creatures, we form a *mental* distinction of the Divine perfection into manifold perfections. As the Divine essence is the pattern of all the perfections which can be, or can be conceived to be in creatures; so does that essence correspond to all the ideas of perfections which our minds can possibly conceive. As, therefore, created perfections are an imperfect objective imitation and shadowing forth of the Divine perfection under various aspects; so also every one of our ideas is an inadequate and therefore an imperfect exhibition, under one or other aspect, of the one simple and infinite perfection of God.

Although it is one and the self same essence which corresponds to all and to every one of our notions of the Divine perfection, yet that perfection is more imperfectly and more confusedly exhibited by the notion of one perfection than it is by the combined notions of several perfections. Hence, by reason of the imperfection of our mode of understanding, we must necessarily multiply our notions, if we are to come to some better knowledge of God's infinite perfection.

3.

God as He is in Himself is invisible to the natural capacities and forces of the creature. The rational or intelligent creature can, nevertheless, be raised and, as matter of fact, has been raised through the grace of glory to intuitive vision of God. This is that vision in which the perfect supernatural beatitude, and the ultimate supernatural end, of the intelligent creature is constituted. This vision, inasmuch as it is an operation of a created mind, remains *finite*. The object of this vision, inasmuch as it is an infinite Being, must remain *infinitely knowable*. Hence the vision of God by the creature admits of an indefinite number of degrees in the perfection of it.

It cannot, moreover, ever adequately correspond to the whole of the infinite knowableness of its object. *Comprehension* of the infinite is proper and possible to an infinite intellect alone.

There are four kinds or orders of vision, and these are utterly different one from the other. The four are—the vision of the senses—intellectual vision—intuitive vision—and comprehensive vision.

Vision of God, who is a spirit, with the eyes of the body, which is the vision *of sense*, is impossible, and the imagination of it is absurd.

Intellectual vision which is *mediate*—and is so called because it is arrived at through the medium of creatures in which the Creator is mirrored—is the only vision of God which is possible to men in the *natural* order.

Intuitive or *immediate* vision of God is proper to the *supernatural* order, and is possible only in the ultimate perfection of that order.

Comprehensive vision of God is proper, as it is possible, to God alone.

To three perfections which are possible to the intelligent creature, the perfection of nature—the perfection of grace—and the perfection of glory, there correspond three orders of intellectual light, the natural light of reason—the light of faith through grace—and the light of glory. Of this threefold light the source is God, as He is Creator, in the order of nature—as He is Sanctifyer in the order of grace—and as He is Beatifyer in the order of glory.

As is every act of understanding, so is also the intuitive vision of God, an immanent act of the mind itself which sees. It is *produced* by the mind—remains *dependent on* the mind—and *informs* the mind.

The *light of glory* is a supernatural force, or power to understand, which stands high above every natural force, and has been superadded to the intellect of the Blessed. This light informs the mind by way of a *habit*, and raises the mind to the intuitive vision of God as He is in Himself. It is a supernatural assimilation of the created intellect to the Divine intellect, in the mode in which it has knowledge of the Divine essence.

The Blessed, in seeing God as He is, see all God's absolute perfections. Every one of these perfections is in God all perfection, and is God Himself. Hence to behold God as He is, is to behold Him as He is all and every absolute perfection.

In like manner, the Blessed, in seeing God as He is, see also the three Divine Persons. The Divine *essence*, as it is in itself, and in its own intrinsic perfection, is the Father who by His understanding produces the Word, and the Father and the Son who by their love produce the Holy Ghost. The Paternal understanding has of necessity the Filial Word as its intrinsic terminus, while the love of the Father and the Son has of equal necessity the Spirit who proceeds therefrom as its intrinsic terminus. He, therefore, who does not behold these Divine Persons does not behold the Divine essence as it is in itself.

The intellect of the Blessed is raised through that supernatural enlightenment of it, which is called the light of glory, to the perfect understanding and penetration of all facts and truths which, outside God and under God, either now are or in the future may be; so far as this knowledge befits them, and so far as the state of each of them demands.

Hence all the mysteries and all the truths which have been revealed to mortal men, the whole of the economy of revelation and of the supernatural order, which of itself belongs in this life to the object of faith, shall then be the object of intuitive vision without a veil, or of understanding without intervention of any medium. To faith, as to a beginning, shall succeed vision, as the perfection and complement of faith.

We are not speaking now of those revealed truths of faith which immediately concern God Himself, for these belong to the principal or *primary* object of beatific vision. We refer to matters of faith which lie outside God, and which are the *secondary* object of beatific vision. Among these truths of faith are the Incarnation of the Word—the way in which true God is as truly man—the exaltation of man's nature in the Word—the redemption of the human race through the Precious Blood—the mystical Body of Christ which is His Church, as founded, nourished, and fostered by Him, as is a bride by her bridegroom, and as dependent for preservation, government and assistance on the Father, the Son, and the Holy Ghost—the gifts of grace—the sacraments, and the virtue of the sacraments, which is derived to them from God the Sanctifyer, and through the merits of Jesus Christ—and the Eucharist as it is both sacrament and sacrifice. All these, and other matters which have been revealed by God for us men to believe, shall then lie open without a veil to the intelligence of the Blessed who behold God.

The Blessed who in beatific vision behold God in Himself behold Him, nevertheless, with different degrees of clearness, as He is the *exemplary* cause or eternal pattern of all beings every one of which is some shadow and participation of Him who *is*—as He is the universal, *efficient* and *preserving* cause, on whom all beings that exist are necessarily dependent, not only for production but also for continuance in being—and as He is the *final* cause to which all beings are, of the nature of them, intrinsically and necessarily ordained.

If the Blessed were to behold the Divine essence as adequately as it is knowable, that is to say, if they were to *comprehend* the Divine essence, they would also in that essence have perfect comprehension of all things that are possible, and all things that shall at any time exist. Such comprehension, however, belongs to infinite perfection, and is therefore proper to God alone.

The Blessed, nevertheless, inasmuch as they see the Divine essence as it is in itself, see also the way in which that infinite Being is the pattern and norm of all things which are capable of participated being; even if they do not see all and every one of the things themselves the existence of which is possible.

The Blessed see likewise the way in which nothing that is not God can actually exist without dependence on that infinite goodness, wisdom and power which is the God whom they behold as He is in Himself. The Blessed see also the way in which all things that exist are necessarily ordained towards that infinite good, as towards their own essential end. It does not, however, follow from this, that the Blessed see all and every one of those beings and facts which have real existence.

The light of glory avails, in accordance with

the differing degrees of its perfection, towards knowing with greater or less amplitude the possible beings, truths, and good objects, which have their pattern and foundation in the primal Being, the primal Truth, and the primal Good, who is beheld by them as He is.

In like manner the light of glory avails also to the seeing of things which actually exist; and which in their existence depend from that first cause and ultimate end of all things. It extends in all the Blessed to the beholding of the whole of the created universe, so far as that universe consists of permanent substances. It extends to perfect vision of the magnitude, the order, and the beauty of the whole universe; and of the species and essences of things, so far as is necessary to perfect beholding of the glory of God in the mirror of His created universe. The Blessed see all that is necessary in order to their seeing, shining forth in the things which are made, the essence, the power, the goodness, the wisdom and the beauty of God, who is the pattern, the creator, the preserver, and the final cause or ultimate end of all and of every one of them His creatures.

All the Blessed, both angelic and human, belong to the heavenly hierarchy which is divinely ordered in its various grades. All of them are members of one Church. This, whether triumphant in Heaven, or suffering in purgatory, or militant here on earth, is the Communion of Saints. Every individual of the Blessed, therefore, in accordance with his own state and grade in which he has been established in the Kingdom of Heaven, has his own different position in the communion of saints, and his own different relation towards the whole Church. The perfection of the Blessed demands that every one of them should see all things which belong to his own state. All the Blessed see the whole of the Heavenly Jerusalem, in which all are fellow citizens. As concerns all that is being transacted, whether in purgatory or here on earth, and especially in the supernatural order of grace, every one of the Blessed has knowledge of every thing that appertains to his own function and ministry. The Blessed, moreover, have not lost any knowledge which they had while on earth of human affairs, or of their relations with human beings. As the dead bodies of the Blessed, buried in this earth of ours, have their ordered relation towards their future life and glory in Heaven, so, and with still more reason, do the souls that are living in glory retain their special relations towards human persons and human affairs. This remains with a perfection which bears proportion to the perfection of their charity towards God, and towards men who are to be sanctified and saved by God.

4.

Although the Blessed behold God intuitively in His own essence, God nevertheless remains *incomprehensible* to every created intellect, or intelligent creature.

The word *comprehension* is used in two senses with regard to corporeal things. Comprehension may signify either the apprehension, or *laying hold of* a thing, or the *encircling embrace* of that thing; in the sense of the full inclusion of one thing in another which contains it. Following the analogy of this use of the word *comprehension* in corporeal matters, the same word is used in spiritual and intellectual matters, and in a twofold sense. Comprehension is sometimes taken, by way of metaphor derived from the runners in a race, to signify attainment of an end, as when St. Paul says "So run that you may comprehend," that is to say—reach the goal. In this sense also those who have arrived at their ultimate end are called "Blessed Comprehenders." In the same sense and way, one of the three endowments of a glorified soul is called *comprehension*. This comprehension is the correlative of *hope*, as vision is the correlative of faith, and as fruition is the correlative of charity.

In a very different sense is the word *comprehension* understood, when it is used to signify that

God cannot be comprehended by any created intellect, even in its highest state of supernatural elevation, and that God is absolutely *incomprehensible.*

The beatific vision is capable of an indefinite number of degrees, so that another and yet another more perfect degree of it remains always possible. In the minds of the Blessed this vision has different degrees of perfection, in accordance with the different degrees of their charity.

In the idea of created being, or created perfection, there is not included a supreme degree, than which there can be no higher degree, or beyond which another degree is not possible. In the idea, therefore, of created vision of God, there is not included a supreme degree of perfection. Supreme vision is *infinite* as the object of vision is infinite, and is therefore infinitely knowable. Hence supreme vision lies outside and above the whole idea of created vision. Supreme vision is proper to God alone. It is no more communicable to the creature, than is the Divine being itself communicable.

Vision which adequately corresponds to the knowableness of an object is properly, and in the strict sense of the word, *comprehensive* vision.

That *incomprehensibility* belongs to God is evident from the very notion of the infinity of

God. God cannot possibly be known in His infinite knowableness, except by an infinite intellect. In other words, *comprehension* of God is none other than knowledge of God which is adequate to the whole of God's infinite knowableness. The created Soul of Jesus Christ beholds its Creator with the very highest perfection of intuitive vision which is possible to any created intelligence. Nevertheless, that Soul, as being a created soul, is a finite soul. Hence even that Soul cannot know the infinitely knowable with other than a finite knowledge. The finite cannot contain the infinite, and the Human Soul of God cannot *comprehend* God.

CHAPTER III.

THE ESSENCE, AND THE ATTRIBUTES OF GOD.

ESSENCE is a word which is capable of three meanings, when it is used with regard to created things. The *essence* of a thing may mean all those things by which some individual thing is constituted in its particular being. Given all and every one of these constituents, the thing *is*. If any one of these constituents is absent, the thing *is not* that particular thing. In this sense, the *essence* of a thing consists of all the things which are in that individual thing, except those only which are accidental to it. These may be either present in it, or absent from it, without it ceasing to be that particular thing. This sense of the word *essence* we dismiss for the present. The use of the word in this sense might, in the subject which we are considering, lead to confusion of thought.

The *essence* of a created thing may, in another sense of the word, be understood as being the complexus of all those things which are necessarily common to every single subject of the same order. This is an essence which is abstracted indeed from individual things—and which prescinds therefore from the accidentals, and from the individuating notes of those things—but is constituted by all the essential perfections which are in individual things of the same order. This is what is called the *physical essence* of a thing.

When we make a mental distinction of those notes in a created thing, which are understood to comprehend in themselves either formally, although confusedly, or at least virtually, all other notes of that thing, we arrive at what is called the *metaphysical essence* of the thing.

This metaphysical essence contains that which is common to all subjects of the *same* order, and to these alone. Hence that which a thing is in itself, distinguishes it from all things of a *different* order; inasmuch as it at least virtually comprehends all the perfections of the *physical essence* of that thing. In the *metaphysical* essence of a thing, all the perfections of that thing have their principle. The perfections of the thing flow forth from the essence of the thing, and in it they have their being. Hence this essence is that which in a thing is first apprehended by the understanding, as the fountain and principle of all that is in that thing.

It is clear that, if we were capable of conceiving,

and were to conceive God, as God really is in Himself, there would be in our minds no distinction either of *physical essence* from personal properties, or of any *metaphysical essence* from other Divine perfections.

We, however, conceive the essence and nature of God—which is in itself absolutely simple—under a number of inadequate notions of manifold perfections. We derive our ideas of perfection from creatures; and in creatures perfections are distinct, one from the other. In creatures perfections depend one on another, and flow forth one from another, up to the *metaphysical essence* which is the principle of all of them.

When, therefore, we conceive perfections in God, we do not indeed form a judgment that one Divine perfection really *flows forth from* another Divine perfection; but it is at the same time true that the inadequate idea which we conceive of a Divine perfection *supposes* another perfection, from which it seems to us to depend, or which depends from it, as from its principle.

Although in God it is one most simple Being who is a spirit, who is wise, and who wills, yet we, in aiming at distinctness of conception, cannot conceive a *will* either in itself, or in its functions, without in our conception presupposing an *intellect*—and we cannot conceive an intellect, without in our conception presupposing a *spiritual substance*

—and a spiritual substance again we cannot conceive, without in our conception presupposing the *being* of that spiritual substance. Although, therefore, on account of the infinite simplicity of God, it is impossible for us to distinguish in God a metaphysical essence, in that way in which we distinguish a metaphysical essence in creatures, this does not, however, hinder us, in our imperfect mode of understanding, from conceiving, among the manifold ideas under which we come to know to some extent that which God is, one idea which has some similarity to *essence.*

The conception of an *essence* ought to give the notes which distinguish the thing, whose essence it is, from all other things of a different order.

These notes are also understood as constituting the thing. From them, therefore, as first in order other things which are in them may be deduced, while they themselves do not follow from any other previous things.

The *essence* of a thing, therefore, is always a perfection which is *supreme*—in the sense of there being no perfection which is previous to it—among all the perfections which constitute a thing in a certain order of beings, and which distinguish that thing from all other things.

In created things, therefore, the *essence* of them cannot be constituted by the *being* of them. Although *being* is a supreme perfection, it is not proper to one order—nor does *being* distinguish one being from other beings—nor are all the determinate perfections which are in the thing comprehended in the *being* of the thing, as in their principle. The *essence* must be *being* as contracted to a determinate perfection.

If, however, in any being the idea of *being* should be distinct and different from everything which is not being—and if it should be simply the idea of *being*, not indeed as an indeterminate conception of *being*, but of *being* as determinated by fulness of perfection—then, in this case, that idea of *being* would be a perfection which is supreme, as coming first in order. It would also distinguish this being from all other things—and it would, moreover, be a principle which contained all the perfections, not determinated in reality but determinated *in idea only*, which could be discerned in it. Such an idea of *being* would, in comparison with other perfections, be a *metaphysical essence*.

This is the idea of *being* in God, as God is absolute Being, and not a being by participation. Negation of participated being, and affirmation of absolute *being* are both of them expressed, when God is said to be *being from itself*, or selfexistent *being*.

There is the very greatest difference between *being* which is derived through participation of *being* from another, and *being* which is from itself, underived, and therefore self existent. The being of creatures is not simply *being*. It is *being* which has been determinated to a certain *grade of being*. Being is therefore found in creatures in a nobler grade, or in a less noble grade; in proportion as these creatures more nearly imitate or more remotely imitate and shadow forth the Divine being. The more restricted grade of the *rational* includes, therefore, the more universal grade of *life*. This again includes the higher grade of *being*; but not *vice versâ*. Being does not include living; and living does not include understanding. *Being* which is *from itself*, or self existent, is not restricted to any grade. When to those words *being from itself* there are not added any other words to determinate the meaning of them, they are understood as indicating *absolute perfection* throughout the whole range of *being*.

Hence, by the words *life from itself*, or selfexistent life, there is not signified a nobler grade of perfection. There is simply expressed a perfection of a determinated order, which is already comprehended in *being from itself*.

Even if the life in question were to be defined as *intellectual life*, intellectuality which is selfexistent is itself already comprehended in *selfexistent life*; and both intellectuality and selfexistent life are comprehended ultimately in *selfexistent being*.

The opposite of this is the case in *participated* being, which is the being which belongs to every creature. This *derived* being is always imperfect being. It is, therefore, higher in the scale of being when a perfection has been superadded to it.

Selfexistent Being is not, properly speaking, a *definition* of God; nor can any other definition of God be given which shall consist of, as logicians say, the proximate genus, and the ultimate differentia.

All created things are in some way compounded of that which is common to many, and of that which is proper to themselves. In God—not only as God is in Himself, but as God is conceived by us mortal men—there is not anything which is common to beings that are not God, and which is, through addition of a perfection, determinated to an idea which is *proper* to God. On the contrary, the *Being* of God, and our idea of that *being*, is in itself absolutely proper to God, and differs utterly from every other idea of *being* which can possibly be concerned. God's *Being* is itself all perfection.

Nevertheless, since the word *being* is an *analogous* term, and, while principally applied to God, may also signify *being* which belongs to others that are not God, it is possible for us to determine the word *being* to signify *the Divine Being alone*, by the addition to it of the words *from itself* or "selfexistent." This addition we may regard as an ultimate differentia, in the language of logic; as giving expression to the essential difference between *Divine Being* and *participated being*. In this way the words "selfexistent being" bear some similarity to a *definition*.

Further, definition is one thing, and description is another. Perfections which are confusedly comprehended in the conception of *selfexistent being* it is possible for us to explain more distinctly, and so to some extent to *describe* God.

We see, therefore, that although God's absolute perfections are not really distinct, one from the other, and so no one of them is prior to another, or is a foundation of other perfections—yet the distinction *of idea*, which is a necessary consequence of our imperfect mode of understanding, suffices for our making a distinction into *essence* and *properties* of essence; and for in thought placing the proper idea of the Divine essence in this that God is *selfexistent Being*.

2.

When we are treating of distinction of Divine properties and perfections from the Divine essence —and of partition and distribution of those properties into certain, as it were, categories—our distinction can have regard only to that essence and those perfections in the *mode* in which they are *known to us*. The principle of order must therefore be taken not from God's perfection, as it is in itself, for that is impossible; but from the objective intrinsic bond between perfections, as this bond exists in our mode of thought.

In the enquiry as to whether there is a God, the reason—from the limitations of the creature, by means of which the creature is known to be a *contingent* being, and a being which derives its *being* from another being—concludes that there exists a *necessary* Being, a *selfexistent* Being.

As this limitation of *contingency* and *participation* affects all perfections of the creature; so does the perfection of *selfexistent being*, and *plenitude of being* pervade all the perfections of God.

Hence both reason and faith, in their answer to the question "What is God, regarded absolutely?" do no more than render a confused conception of selfexistent being more distinct, by an unfolding of that which is contained in the idea of selfexistent being.

This is, in accordance with our mode of arriving at knowledge of God by means of creatures, done in two ways. It is done first, by declaring the perfection of *selfexistent being*, through negation of negation, or negation of the limitation by which the creature is necessarily affected. Of the very nature of such negations, the negations themselves are conceptions of *plenitude of being* under various aspects of contrast to *limited being*. By multiplication of these conceptions we come to conceive more distinctly that of which we have a confused perception in selfexistent being.

We may consider the limitations which attach to the creature by reason of its *origin*. As a *created* being, it is a being which holds its *being from another being*. Hence formally and in itself a created being is a *finite* being. It is capable, therefore, of multiplication and of change. In its relation to *time*, the endurance of a created being involves succession or, at least, the possibility of succession. In its relation to *place*, a created being is restricted in its presence, or is circumscribed by space. In its relation to *knowledge*, a created being, as it is a finite being, is comprehensible by a *finite* intellect, and is knowable *as it is in itself*.

All these limitations we understand as being so many distinct expressions of *participated being*, or of being which is derived from another being. In the inverse order, we understand in the very idea of *absolute being*, that there is comprehended in it a perfection which is above and beyond all these and similar limitations.

Since such a perfection has no analogous type corresponding to it in the creature, from which it can be apprehended, and can receive a name, while on the contrary that which corresponds to it in the creature, is the imperfection which is opposed to it, we conceive this perfection of absolute being confusedly, and express it by negations.

Hence theologians speak of *negative* attributes in God; such as His being uncreated, and His being infinite, His being one and simple, and still more, His being incorporeal, unchangeable, eternal, immense, incomprehensible, invisible and ineffable.

We can also, in the second place, come to an understanding of *selfexistent being*, and *plenitude of being*, by conceptions which directly, although confusedly, *affirm* perfections. This we do by prescinding from the limitation of the perfections which we apprehend *in* creatures, or *from* creatures. This prescinding from limitation can be made in all those perfections, and in those perfections only, of which we can form an universal conception which is not in itself restricted to limited being; but can be applied both to being which is *absolutely selfexistent*, and to being which is *participated*, or derived from another being. Among such perfections are, in the first place, those perfections which are *transcendental*, as transcending every genus, such as *being*, and the *true*—and the *good*. Among such perfections there are also substantial generic degrees, such as a *living* substance, and an *intellectual* substance, or a spirit. There are those perfections, likewise, which exclude or, at least, do not include, the imperfection of material things; such as are intellect, will, power, and all that follows from those faculties.

Through exclusion from selfexistent being of every imperfection, *duration* and *presence* are really resolved into negations of restriction to *time* and *place*, or into the negative attributes of *eternity* and *immensity*.

The Divine *attributes* are sometimes divided into *absolute* attributes, and *relative* attributes. *Absolute* attributes are Divine attributes considered in themselves, apart from any relation to creatures, as outside God. *Relative* attributes are those which have relation to creatures, as creatures are distinct from God.

When God is called by the names of Creator—Lord—the Divine Providence—the Sanctifyer, and the like, the foundation of those names is in God the necessary and eternal perfection of the Divine intellect, will, and power. That which outside God is created, subject, directed, and sanctified, does not add perfection to God. It is from it, however, that these names of God are taken.

The Divine intellect, will, and power, and the perfections which are connected with them are, as regards acts of these, conceived by us as something which concerns the Divine *essence*, and appears to us as if it were added to that essence. Hence a distribution of God's perfections into *absolute properties*, and into *attributes*, properly so called, has foundation in that mode which is the only mode in which it is possible for us men here on earth to consider the Divine perfections.

3.

The name of God, revealed by God Himself, *I am*, or *I am who am*, or *He who is*—is a name which is *proper* to God alone. This name signifies immediately the *substance* of God. The name does not admit of any analogous meaning. It is, therefore, an incommunicable name. It is as incommunicable to the creature, as is the Divine essence which the name signifies.

In other names which are given to God in the Sacred Scriptures, such as The First and The Last—The Beginning and The End—The Alpha and The Omega—He who is, and was, and is to be—there is a declaration, under the form of indefinite time, of a oneness of past, present, and future. This is a negation of succession, and so a supereminence over all relations of time. *He who is* comprehends the beginning, the middle, and the end, and all the plenitude of absolute being, and absolute perfection; to which nothing can be added, and from which nothing can be taken.

As God alone is *He who is*, the intrinsically *necessary* Being, who comprehends the whole *plenitude* of absolute being, and besides whom there cannot be any *absolute* being; so in that absolute perfection of His is found the reason why outside God there is a possibility of the existence of *analogous* imitations of God, and of beings *by participation* which derive their being from God. In the free exercise of God's will, and in His infinite power, is found the *cause* also why such beings actually are.

It belongs to the plenitude of absolute being that *outside it* there can be nothing of absolute and independent being—for otherwise God would not be that plenitude of being. It belongs also to God's plenitude of absolute being, that at His will there can be imitations of His perfection in creatures, that are in every way dependent on Him. If this were not so, God would not be perfect under all ideas of perfection, and so would not be plenitude of *being*, or plenitude of absolute perfection.

God alone *is because He is*, and no one besides God, and outside God, can *be*, or can be conceived as *being because he is*. All beings except God can *be*, only because God *is;* and they actually *are* because God wills them *to be.* They are *from Him*, as from the necessary principle of the intrinsic and extrinsic *possibility* of all things. They are *by* Him, or *through* Him, as from the *free cause* not only of the beginning of their *existence*, but also of the continuance of the existence of all created things, which are in every way dependent on Him. They are also *to* Him, as to the End of all things.

Whatsoever of perfection there is in actually existing creatures, or can be in creatures the existence of which is possible, is comprehended in God, as in the one absolute and externally imitable perfection of Him who is the *pattern* of them, and who is also their *efficient* cause.

Hence *being* and *to be* are not predicated *univocally* of the Divine Being and of beings that are outside God, and that are not God. His Being, and the *being* of them, cannot be connumerated. They differ wholly in the very idea of *being*. It is, nevertheless, not *equivocally* but *analogically* that *being* is predicated of creatures, and that because they are truly an imitation and adumbration or shadowing forth of the Divine Being. The application of the term *being*, as common to both God and His creatures, is therefore *not arbitrary*. It is founded in a likeness and relation of the lower to the higher. Hence it is that in the Sacred Scriptures creatures which, regarded simply in themselves, are said *to be*, are in comparison with the Divine Being, sometimes said *not to be*.

The most universal idea of *being* which it is possible for us to conceive, is not a being which is simple and determinate; but is an *abstraction* of actual being, or of possible being, in which, besides the opposition of it to nothingness or to *not being*, there is no determination.

The Divine *Being* is, on the other hand, *simple and determinate*, with a determination beyond which there cannot be any determination which is higher.

The *abstract* idea of *universal being*, and our idea of the Divine Being, differ in the very mode in which the two ideas are conceived. The one idea we form by way of immediate *abstraction* from that which is presented to us in creatures, the other idea we form by way of *conclusion*, so as to arrive at a conception of the pattern Being, who is the principle and fountain of all created and creatable being.

The *simplicity* of *universal* being is *negative*, on account of the abstraction of it from all determinate perfections. This is a simplicity which neither has nor can have real existence. It exists only in apprehension of the mind. The *simplicity* of the *Divine* Being is, on the contrary, *positive*, and it necessarily exists, although it is only most imperfectly and through negations that we arrive at a mental apprehension of it.

The fallacy whereby *being* which is *simple through abstraction* is substituted for Being which is *simple through absolute perfection*, is the principle of Pantheism, and is, as it were, a compendium of Pantheism in all its various forms.

This fallacy lies also at the root of the error of those who fancy that God is objectively and really, to us mortal men on earth, the object of our first intellectual idea, and of immediate intuition by us; although He is not in this life distinctly and reflexly known by us under the idea of absolute essence. God is not the first object of our knowledge, or the first object which is knowable by us. It is not through a knowledge of God which is immediate, that we have our knowledge of creatures. It is through our knowledge of creatures, that we come to knowledge of God.

CHAPTER IV.

The absolute properties of the Divine Essence.

A PERFECTION which is *absolute*—as comprehending in it the whole idea of perfection—cannot be conceived as *manifold*, or as capable of multiplication. It must be wholly *one*. Truth, goodness, wisdom, and every perfection whatsoever which can be conceived as the whole of perfection, and unlimited by any imperfection, is not a mere *abstract* conception. It is, of intrinsic necessity, a real existence. It is not, and it cannot be, only in the sphere of the ideal. In itself it is, and must be, *real being*. It is, therefore, intrinsically impossible, as involving contradiction, that absolute Divine Being should be multiplied, and that there should be a number of Gods.

To speak of two infinites, each of which is the fulness of absolute being, would be to say that one of the two is infinitely perfect, and that to it, nevertheless, is wanting the infinite perfection which is in the other—and that the other is, in like manner, the fulness of the whole of absolute being, and that, nevertheless, to it is wanting the whole fulness of absolute being, which belongs to the other infinite nature which is distinct from it. Of both infinites, the whole fulness of perfection would be at one and the same time affirmed and denied.

This is the innermost reason why multiplication of the Divine essence is impossible, as involving contradiction; and why the oneness of the Divine essence is not the same as oneness of number, but is above that oneness.

This argument is either supposed by, or it is implicitly contained in expressions used by the Fathers to demonstrate the oneness of God from the perfection of the Divine *essence*, as when they say—If there were two or more Gods, there would be no Supreme—Among several Gods there cannot be any difference—Several Gods would be superfluous, since one is sufficient.

2

The explanation of the *composite* is easier than is the explanation of the *simple*. From the idea of the composite, therefore, we can best unfold the idea of the simple. In the composite, we observe parts. Whatever has parts is in some way manifold. It is not in itself wholly undivided, and still less is it indivisible. That which has no parts, is in itself *undivided* and *indivisible*. From conjunction of parts into one whole, the *composite* formally proceeds. The immediate and direct negation of *composition* is *simplicity*.

Oneness in itself and *simplicity* do not differ in reality. They differ only in the mode of considering them. That which is *one in itself* is considered in opposition to *the many*, of which the composite consists. That which is *simple* is considered in opposition to the *composite*, which consists of many.

The composite more approaches the idea of the simple, the less the parts of the composite are really distinct, and the more intimately they coalesce into one undivided whole.

Besides corporeal substances, in which both the constituent parts and the integrating parts are *substantial*, there are spirits also in existence. Created spirits are altogether simple. In spirits there cannot be any composition, other than that of qualities, habits, and spiritual acts. These there can be, and these there are, in a substance which has no substantial parts.

There are various species of composition, such as—composition of matter and substantial form—composition of integrating parts—composition of substance and accidents—composition of essence and *esse*—composition of nature and hypostasis—and composition of genus and differentia.

By a *part* we mean a thing which is imperfect, which receives perfection through another thing communicating itself to it, and uniting itself with it. Hence *parts*, properly so called, always perfect each other through a mutual communication of themselves. The perfection of the composite whole springs from the union and mutual communication of all the parts. A part, as a part, is an incomplete being. From the intrinsic idea of parts, we see how compositions are consequences of limitation, and are among the certain signs of limitation.

Where there is *physical composition* of parts which are distinct in the thing itself, whether these parts are substantial parts, or whether one of them is an accident only, the case is clear. When each of the parts, inasmuch as it is a part, is essentially a being which is circumscribed by negation of absolute perfection; the perfection of the whole, which springs from the mutual communication of finites, cannot possibly be absolute and infinite. The finite and the infinite —and also relative perfection and infinite perfection—differ, not in degree, but in the whole of the intrinsic idea and essence of each of them.

The same idea of imperfection, which is necessarily included in composition of parts, has place also in *metaphysical composition;* even if those things which are conceived *as parts* are not distinct from each other in the object, as one thing is distinct from another thing.

It is not from the fact that the *simple* has no *parts* that absolute simplicity is formally a perfection. It is from the fact that God's *being* is all absolute perfection. Nothing, therefore, can be conceived of it, which is limited by defect of any possible ulterior perfection. Simplicity is a perfection, not inasmuch as the simple *has not* parts, but inasmuch as the simple *cannot be* a part or a quasi-part.

We suppose, as a truth which is manifest in itself, that there is in God that simplicity which excludes *substantial* parts, whether as constituting parts, or as integrating parts ; such as are in bodies, or are in those things which have in the composition of them at least some material part.

Apart, however, from this crass kind of composition—the exclusion of which contributes but little in the way of throwing light on the intrinsic idea of the Divine *simplicity*—there is a more subtle kind of composition, from which no creature whatsoever can be free. It is that composition which is founded in imperfection, with the possibility of ulterior perfection, that is to say— *in potentiality for the actual*. Every *essence* which can be conceived outside God includes an objective potentiality towards *being*, but it does not in its own intrinsic idea include *actual being*. Hence there can be conceived composition of *essence* and *esse* as of the *objectively potential* and the *actual*.

In like manner, *participated* being—since it is not absolute being in the, as it were, whole extent and idea of *being*—does not, inasmuch as it is somewhat of being, include that grade of *being* which is *life*, or *living* being. It is not life of the intrinsic idea of it. It is only a receptive potentiality for life. Hence a living creature is said *to have* life. It is not said *to be* life.

In the same way *participated* life is *potential* of the higher grade of *intellectuality*.

Further, a created living intellectual substance is not *absolute intellect*, pure and simple. It *has intellect* in some degree of its perfection; and so such intellect is potential for acts of understanding, and so for formal truth and wisdom. If this potential becomes actual, it can be actual only to some extent, along with a potentiality of farther perfection. It will therefore be actual in somewhat, and in somewhat else it will be potential. It cannot be a *pure act*, or in other words, it cannot be *absolutely actual*. Hence a created living intellectual substance will *have* certain acts of understanding and formal truth and wisdom, to a certain extent; but it cannot itself be *absolute* understanding, or absolute truth, or absolute wisdom. The same is true of the *will*, and of the perfection of the will.

There is here some, at least, *metaphysical composition* of the potential and the actual—or composition of that which is to be perfected, and that which perfects it. The created intellect remains indefinitely potential of farther perfection. The actual remains in that intellect indissolutely wedded with the potential.

The essence which is *absolute* Being, in the whole plenitude of *being*, is, formally as it is this essence, a *pure act*, without any potentiality, whether objective potentiality for *being*, or *receptive* potentiality for *more perfect* being. Hence this essence of itself, and without any addition—for to absolute perfection nothing can be added—but in its own *substance*, and not by reason of any quality which is not that substance, is, as it is Being, life also and intellect, and truth, and wisdom, and charity. It is all these, as these are absolutely actual.

Hence, in the inverse order, every one of these perfections, and all of them together, are really that one most simple essence, of which we have inadequate understanding, through the different conceptions which we derive from the perfections of creatures.

We cannot, therefore, conceive in God, as we conceive in creatures, *essence*, or *being*, or any perfection by whatsoever names it may be called, as something imperfect, and to be completed by some addition to it. We understand that every one of those perfections is *itself the plenitude* of absolute *Being*. It is that plenitude which, on account of the imperfection of our intellect, is conceived by us under different ideas; as different created perfections correspond to the infinite and absolutely simple pattern of them.

That Divine Being who has the singular name of *He who is* is spoken of in the Sacred Scriptures, not only as living, and as having life from Himself, and as having all wisdom and all truth, and as dwelling in inaccessible light, and as being the God of Charity; but also as *being* Life, as *being* Wisdom, as *being* Truth, as *being* Light, and as *being* Love. The Divine Being is, therefore, as it were, an infinite *form*, which of itself, and not through a quality which is distinct from it, is all these.

This is negation of all and every composition whatsoever; and that is the *simplicity* which, of the intrinsic idea of absolute being, is *necessary* in God.

The doctrine of the absolute *simplicity* of God is not merely implicitly contained in the Sacred Scriptures. They explicitly set forth the principles from which the metaphysical demonstration of God's simplicity is constructed.

The Fathers also argue, from the *absolute* perfection of God, that God Himself is at once *all and every* perfection to which we can possibly give name.

Hence it follows that the Divine perfections are not distinct either from the Divine essence—or one from another—but ought to be understood as being that one most simple *Being* who is truly conceived, but, at the same time, inadequately conceived by us, through various notions of perfections, and whom we call by various names. God *is*, in a word, that perfection which He is said by us to *have*.

What we conceive as *immanent acts* in God is really the Divine essence itself. God's Intellect, Will and active Power are not, and cannot be conceived as being *faculties* which are perfected by subsequent acts of understanding, volition, and efficiency. As the Divine *essence* or *substance* is itself infinite Intellect, infinite Will, and infinite Power; so also the *substantial act* which understands, wills, and effects, is itself the same Divine essence, without accession of anything in addition to that essence.

Will in God is not a faculty of willing which is at one time *actual*, and at another time *not actual*, or which is at one time actually *willing this*, and at another time actually *willing that*. It is *one act of willing* which is always the same in itself, since it is, in reality, the one Divine essence and substance. This Divine essence is itself infinite, substantial volition. In God, *essence* and *will* are not distinct one from the other, as a *subject* to be perfected is distinct from the *form* which perfects it—nor are *will* and *volition* distinct, one from the other, as a *faculty* is distinct from an *act* of that faculty. In God, essence, will, and volition are in reality *one*, and are distinct one from the other only in consideration of the mind. As Divine understanding is infinite *actual comprehension* of the Divine essence and infinite truth, with which that understanding is itself identified, and in which all truth is comprehended—so is Divine will infinite *actual love* and necessary love of the Divine essence, as of infinite good, with which that love is itself identified. Since the good, in which that love rests in the fulness of essential sufficiency and beatitude, is infinite; that substantial act does not necessarily have for its object any *participated* good. That same infinite act of volition can, however, have regard to participated goods, so that those goods should have existence *from* it, and exist *through* it, and be ordained *to* it as to the infinite good. This relation towards, and termination in finite goods cannot be through a superadded and accidental act of volition. That would involve contradiction. It would be impossible in volition which is absolute, substantial, and unchangeable. It is the Divine *substance* itself which, under the formal idea of that substance, as it is infinite will, can immediately and by itself— that is to say, without interposition of any other act of volition—have relation towards participated good, and, as it were, extend itself to participated good, without any change of itself. In the same way the Divine understanding of the Divine essence, an act which is one, is extended or extends itself to the understanding of all things which are intelligible.

It is clear, therefore, that in God—even as regards a free volition which has its terminus in an object which is outside God—there is not both a *potentiality* of acting, and an *act*. There is an *act* only. Of this act the termination may be in this or in that created object. This does not add anything to the Divine act itself; but only to the created object, or the object outside God, to which the Divine act is extended. There cannot, therefore, in short, be conceived in God composition which involves both *potentiality* of acting and a free *act*.

Hence we gather how great the difference is between God's volition and man's volition; and between the idea of the Divine freedom and the idea of our freedom, and indeed of all created freedom. Our volition is an accident, and a modification of a substance. When there is a determinate act of our will, the termination of the act in an object is intrinsic to it, and is necessary and not free. In so far only, therefore, are we free in will, as the volition is in our own power that it should either be or not be, and that it should either will this, or will that. An act of the Divine will, on the other hand—or Divine volition—is itself a *substance*; and is not either an accident, or a modification of a substance, and it is in reality the Divine essence. Divine volition is, therefore, in itself *one substantive act* of which the existence is necessary. The termination of this act of volition in its *principal* object, that is to say, in the *goodness* of the Divine essence, with which it is itself identified, is indeed absolutely *necessary*; but the relation of it to a *secondary* object, or *participated* good, is entirely *free*. The freedom of God, therefore, does not consist in this, that an act of Divine will can either be or not be, or that it can in itself will this or that. The freedom of God consists in this that infinite *substantial volition* of infinite good can, without any change in itself, either be, as it were, extended to goods which are outside God—so that they should exist—or can be not extended to the existence of these, and if so—they will not exist.

In other words, the same one Divine act which

wills, and which loves the infinite good of the Divine essence, and which rests in this good with the fulness of beatitude, *necessarily* indeed wills this good in itself; but it does not *necessarily* will this good either with imitation of it, or without imitation of it in participated goods, or creatures. The Divine will freely wills both imitation, and negation of imitation; and it freely wills one degree of imitation instead of another degree of imitation.

The reason or idea of the Divine *freedom* is in this, that to an infinite model, which is to be imitated, the actual existence or the nonexistence of an analogous imitation of it does not in the one case add to it anything of perfection; nor does it in the other case take from it anything of perfection.

The reason or idea of the *unchangeableness* of the Divine will is in this, that not another act, but one and the selfsame infinite *substantial act* which wills the Divine essence, wills also either the imitation of that essence, in and through participated goods, that is to say, through creatures, or the negation of that imitation. This relation to one or to another terminus in the creature, adds nothing to the *substantial act*. All diversity whatsoever concerns not the substance, but the *terminus* of the one unchangeable act.

The freedom of the intelligent creature is his

indifference of active will towards an act. This indifference is an accident and not a substance. The freedom of the Creator is indifference of *termination* in His act of will, which is itself a *substance*, and which is in itself necessary and unchangeable.

An *immanent act* of will in God is in reality the Divine *substance*, under the formal idea of that substance, as it is infinite substantial volition, with connotation of the object outside God which is willed by God. This connotation does not add anything to God Himself, or to God's infinite volition. From this connotation, however, it is that the will of God is said to be, for instance, a creating will. Since both that *substantial* will, or the Divine will as it is a *substance*, and this connotation of the creature as to be in existence at some point in the future of time, were from eternity; creative will, or creative action, is in God eternal.

There is not formally in God any *transient* act. All transient action is in the creature. Hence transient action begins in time, or with time. It is not less separate from God than is the creature itself.

Relation is an order of one person or thing towards another person or thing. When there are two persons or things, which are really ordained towards each other, their relation is a *real mutual* relation, such as is that of father to son, and of son to father. When, on the other hand, one of the two persons or things has a real ordination towards the other; while the other has not thence any new ordination of itself, through something real which has been superadded to it, but is only *conceived as* relative, because the other is *really* related to it—there is *real* relation in the one only, and relation *of idea* in the other. We conceive the relation *of idea* by reason only of the *real* relation.

Knowledge in a created mind has a *real* order of relation towards a thing which is actually known. The thing known has only a relation *of idea* towards him who knows it. There is nothing placed in the thing known, by the fact that it is actually known. The thing known remains the same, whether it is known or whether it is not known. In this way the creature, which is really dependent on God for the whole of its being, has a *real relation* towards God. God, on the contrary, is only conceived to have relation to the creature, because the creature is related to Him. God does not in any way depend on the creature, nor is there anything placed in God whereby He is ordained towards the creature. Hence, the relation of God towards one and all of

His creatures is not a *real* relation. It is a relation *of idea* only.

3

We speak of *truth*, and of *the true*, in three ways. First, and *formally*, truth is adequate correspondence of understanding with the thing understood. Secondly, that which is *fundamentally* true is the thing itself which is to be understood. Thirdly, the *morally true* has place in the *signification*, or manifestation, or imparting of truth. We may, moreover, make a distinction between *veracity* and *moral truth*. When the will, and the act which manifests the will, corresponds to the formal truth perceived, or to true knowledge, there is—veracity. In the manifestation itself by, for instance, speech or writing, which corresponds to the formal truth—a manifestation which has its origin from veracity—there is *moral* truth. *Veracity* belongs *formally* to the *will*, and *materially* to the *intellect*. *Truth* is related to the *intellect alone*. Hence, if the knowledge to be manifested should be false, there might, nevertheless, be habitual veracity in the will; that is to say, there might be a constant will to manifest the true. In the act of manifesting the *false*, veracity can be only *relative*. There cannot in any way be *truth* in manifestation of the false. He who says that which is false, but which he thinks to be true, is relatively *veracious*, but he is not in being veracious saying that which is *true*.

The *true* as it exists in objects is *being*, with connotation of an intellect, which either is or can be conformed to the true. *Truth* is, in this sense, the aptitude of a *being* for understanding in conformity with the true—or in conformity with *being* under the idea of its knowableness. *Knowableness* is as extensive as is the idea of *being*. In this sense St. Augustine says, "The true is that which *is*." The greater the perfection of *being*, the more ample is the *knowableness* of being.

The Divine essence is not only infinitely intelligible, but it is actually, of its own intrinsic idea, infinitely understood and comprehended. As God's *Being* is infinitely *intelligible*, so is God's Being also infinitely *intelligent*. God is the plenitude of the noble, throughout the length and breadth of being, or in the whole idea of *being*. The highest nobleness of *being* which we can conceive is *intellectuality*. This nobleness of *being* is in God, however, higher than is any conception of nobleness which we are capable of forming.

The Divine essence is so intelligible that it cannot be that that essence should not be comprehended in the whole of its intelligibility. The Divine essence is the primary object of the Divine understanding. God comprehends in His essence all *the true*, by the same act by which He comprehends that essence. Not only does the Divine *Being*, in its infinite knowableness, adequately correspond to God's infinite understanding; but the comprehended and the comprehension, the understanding and the understood, are identical and one. As *participated* and dependent *being* is *true*, in virtue of its aptitude for conformity of the understanding with it, so absolute, infinite, and necessary *Being* is itself *substantial Truth*. Of its own intrinsic essence, it is understanding and comprehension of itself.

Through consideration of the idea of objective *truth*, as that truth exists in created beings, we arrive at some understanding of the eminence of Truth in the Divine Being. Truth which is, or which can be conceived, outside God, may be considered in three ways—*actual* truth, in things which exist—merely *ideal* truth, in things which are only possible—and *formal* truth in created intellects.

The fountain and the measure of all this truth is the Divine Truth. This is truth in itself, and primal truth. Other truth is *participated* truth. This truth is derived from *primal* truth.

Things which actually exist are, in their relation of order towards the Divine intellect, in so far *true* as they correspond to Divine ideas. Those true things do not determinate the Divine intellect. The Divine *intellect* which comprehends the Divine *essence as imitable*, and which, in conjunction with the Divine *will*, is called the Divine *practical* intellect—is to created imitations of the Divine the cause of their actual existence. It is to them the cause also of their existence in that mode of existence which corresponds to the Divine idea of them. Those created imitations of the Divine do not give measure to the Divine intellect. The Divine intellect gives measure to them. In the Divine intellect all created things are, as all works of art are in the intellect of the artificer of them.

Hence that which is done, by a creature who is intelligent and free, in accordance with the moral order—the order which corresponds to the Divine ideas and the Divine goodwill—is, in the Sacred Scriptures, called a *truth*. That which is done contrary to this moral order, is therein called and is a *lie*.

As in the Sacred Scriptures it is said that all the commandments of God are *truth*—and God's law is *truth*—and all God's ways are *truth*, as a norm and measure; so are we also therein commanded to walk in *truth*—and to do *truth*. Of the devil, on the other hand, it is said that he stood not in the *truth*—and that *truth* is not in him—and that all those are excluded from the Heavenly Jerusalem who make a *lie*.

The metaphysical and ideal order of things which are merely *possible*, and all the *truth* which, properly speaking, is not *in them*, but may only possibly be at some time in them, depends on the fact that the Divine essence is imitable outside God in certain ways, and in accordance with certain laws. The whole of the metaphysical order, therefore, is constituted by the necessary laws of *essences*. These laws are *necessary*, because the Divine *essence* demands them. Hence the Divine essence is—not in virtue of free will, but in virtue of its own necessary perfection—the fountain and the measure of all *truth*, even truth of the metaphysical order.

Formal truth is, in created intellects, a participation of Divine *truth*. This it is, either through an immediate intellectual conjunction with the Divine essence and substantial truth—as in the case of the beatific vision in the light of glory; or through a supernatural light of another order, derived from the primal truth—a light which there is in all supernatural knowledge, in different modes and degrees; or through communication of a habit of knowledge, and of ideas—as in the case of the natural knowledge possessed by the angels, and as was the case in the natural knowledge possessed by the first man—or finally, through that which is the lowest of all communications of light, the intellectual light within us. From the conjunction of this light with the objective *truth* which is in existing things, there springs *formal* truth; that is to say, the adequate correspondence of our intellect with the reality of those things. There is a concurrence or confluence of the objective, and the subjective. The one is the counterpart of the other. The two meet and are wedded, and the offspring is *formal* truth.

The light of reason is itself a participation of the truth and wisdom of God. It is that which the Fathers call the "seminal word," by which man is constituted an image of God.

Finally, from participated *formal* truth, *truth* is derived to our words, and to the signs by means of which we manifest our meaning.

All *truth*, therefore, which is, and which can be conceived as being, outside God, depends from God as He is truth in itself, as from the principle —the pattern or model—and the measure of it. In the same sense in which God is primal *Being*, is God also primal absolute *Truth*.

4

The notion of *the good* is the notion of something *perfect*, which is *desirable*. In this definition the *perfect* is that which is in possession of all things which belong to it. *Desire* is the tending towards, and the rest of the will in that perfect, or that measure of the perfect, which belongs to him who desires. Every good in itself belongs to some one. Hence good is in itself desirable. Aristotle therefore defines *the good* as—that which all desire. This is not to be understood, says St. Thomas, as if every good were desired by all men, but in the sense that whatsoever is *desired* has in it the idea of *good*.

The good in creatures may be understood as that which is indeterminately perfect, in accordance with the *being* of creatures. In this sense, *the good* follows the idea of *being*. Along with being *the good* is transcendental. It is not contained within any genus, but transcends every genus. In another sense, *the good* is that which is perfect in a determinate essence. In this sense, likewise, whatever *is* is *good*. It is good with a metaphysical goodness. In a third sense, a thing may be *good* by reason of a perfection which has been superadded to the essence of the thing—whether in the physical order, or in the moral order. Lastly, *the good* may be understood as being perfection in final rest, and in the state of an ultimate end, beyond which there is no progress towards any farther good.

The good, in its relation to another is that which is good in itself, but as it is a principle of good in another, whether as an *efficient* cause—by action; or as an *end*—by fruition; or as a *form*—by the communication of itself.

God is infinite good in itself, and He is the "Good of goods," that is to say, He is the *principle* and *end* of all and every good which outside Himself can exist only by participation, and with absolute dependence on the Good which *He is*.

Being and *the good* are convertible terms, since being includes the idea of the good. Absolute Being is, of its essence, therefore, absolute Goodness.

The goodness of God in Himself may, for the sake of greater distinctness of thought, be regarded in a threefold order, the *ontological* order—the *moral* order—and the, as it were, order of the *final*.

God is goodness ontologically. Since God is, of the innermost idea of His essence, the actually existing plenitude of the whole of perfection, there cannot accrue to Him any perfection by means of which He should be good. *Necessary being* is the whole of essential and absolutely necessary being, because it is *being itself.* God is not, therefore, *good* with some other goodness, but He is good by His own essence. God is not *good* within some order or degree, beyond which He is not good. God is absolutely *good* in the whole idea of goodness. God does not *have* goodness, as an accident, which cleaves to His substance, but God *is* the whole of goodness.

Transcendental good is really identical with *being,* even in creatures; but being is itself *contingent* to the creature. It is not *necessary* with the necessity of an intestinal idea. Hence the *essence* of the creature is not *of itself* actual. It is merely possible. Essence in the state of possibility is only a possibility of good. The possibility of a thing being good has its only source in the idea of deriveableness from the underived. The *underived* is the Divine essence. Created essence cannot indeed be actual without its being good, with a metaphysical goodness; but this is a *relative* goodness, and demands many other goods which belong to it—both in the physical order and, in the case of intellectual creatures, in the moral order—if it is to be simply good within its own order.

Creatures are good within some finite degree of being and goodness, as a good *spirit,* or a good *angel,* or other good creature. God is good throughout the whole idea of the good. He is the "good Good."

Goodness in the *moral* order is called *sanctity* or holiness. It is chiefly on account of sanctity that rational creatures are called good. By sanctity alone are they rightly disposed towards the end, in the attainment of which there is the ultimate complement of goodness, beyond which there can be no greater goodness.

Sanctity in creatures, considered *negatively*, is freedom from sin, as from inordinate divergence from the eternal law in habits and acts. Sanctity in creatures, considered *positively*, is the conformation and commensuration of habits and acts to the rule of morals. This conformation is ultimately perfected by love of God, and conjunction with God as the Last End. As the law of love is the greatest commandment, from which depends, and towards which is directed, the whole law—so towards love of God, and union with God, every conformation to the law of God is of itself ordained. The Divine essence, as it is the foundation of all order, and of every order, is the foundation of the *moral* order. The Divine essence, as it is intellect and will, is the principle of eternal law, and the measure of all moral rectitude. God infinitely loves, with a *necessary* love, the fundamental rectitude which is His own essence. The same essentially right act, whereby He loves His own essential rectitude, is borne towards creatures who are outside Himself, as the law and norm of rectitude; a law which in part is necessary, and in part is free. Hence it is that every Divine disposition outside God is essentially right. It is as much a contradiction, and therefore impossible, that either a law of God, or a work of God, outside Himself should not fully correspond as the counterpart of essential rectitude—as it is a contradiction and impossible that the essentially right Divine act itself, and the Divine norm of all rectitude, should cease to be right.

The same essential love wherewith God infinitely loves rectitude in His own essence, and wherewith consequently He wills rectitude in His creatures, and loves that rectitude in them; is on the other hand and necessarily, rebuke and hatred of sin. Hence we see how not only identically, but also *formally*, so far as our manner of understanding is concerned, the goodness or sanctity of God, that is, the justice of God in punishing sin, and God's love of goodness, is God's hatred of sin. The distinction of the two is not in this Divine perfection, even as that perfection is understood by us. The difference is in the objects towards which the one Divine perfection is related.

The proper idea of the Sanctity of God comes then to this, that, in the first place and *positively* God is sanctity itself—secondly and *negatively*, God is sanctity, through essential and absolute opposition to every turning away from the norm of rectitude, which norm *He is*—thirdly, and from the point of view of *cause*, all participated or derived sanctity consists in, and is perfected by, love of God, and union with God. God is Himself the love of His own essence; and this love is adequate to the loveableness of its object. The same act of God's love, which loves His own substantial goodness, loves at the same time *in* that goodness, *with* that goodness, and *by reason* of that goodness, the participated sanctity and rectitude which exists in creatures. As God has knowledge of all things in His own essence, as in supreme truth; so does God love all things in His own essence, as in supreme goodness. He loves them in accordance with the different degrees of participated goodness which severally belong to them. Whatever there is of loveableness in creatures is a derivation from God's substantial and essential loveableness.

As whatsoever is not God has of necessity its ultimate end in God the Supreme Good, from whom and to whom every good is; so God, as He is Himself absolute good, rests in Himself, and in His own infinite plenitude of all good.

In this sense, God is to Himself *His own end*, that is to say, *negatively*, inasmuch as He cannot have an end which is distinct from Himself, but is Himself the end of all—and *positively*, inasmuch as in Himself He has the plenitude of good, or rather *He is* Himself that plenitude.

As in the perfection to which the intellectual creature attains in its rest in its ultimate end, the beatitude of that creature is placed; so God, in the plenitude of absolute good which He Himself *is*, is to Himself *His own* infinite beatitude.

In short, and to bring these truths to a focus, (1) God is Himself absolute Good, as He is the plenitude of the whole of absolute Being. He is, therefore, goodness *by essence*. (2) The goodness to which, as to its model and cause, the perfection, both physical and moral, of creatures corresponds, is in God *His essence*, and is not a superadded perfection. God *is* goodness in every order, and so God *is* sanctity. (3) Finally, the goodness to which there corresponds the ultimate perfection of the creature, in the attainment of its end, is in God *essential* beatitude. God *is* His own Beatitude. God *is* selfsufficing in the plenitude of all goodness; and He is necessarily the end of all, in whom all have, in their several orders, their ultimate perfection.

Although God is in Himself absolute and fully selfsufficing goodness, which cannot either be increased by any created goods, or diminished by the withdrawal of all of them, yet we mortal men are not capable of fixing the eyes of our minds on this truth by itself alone. In order to estimate the infinite amplitude of God's goodness, we must contemplate that goodness as it is also *our* supreme good, and the supreme good of every creature. God is the supreme good to all, as He is the exemplary cause, or pattern, as He is the efficient cause, and as He is the preserving cause of all good which is, or which can be, outside the Supreme Good. God's bestowal of good is perpetual and unceasing; for the whole idea of the existence of participated good, or its *raison d'être*, is derived from that bestowal. If God's bestowal were to cease for one moment, the whole of that which is, from the first elements of matter up to the highest of spiritual beings, and to the Sacred Humanity of Christ itself, would on the instant cease to be. As all of these created things are *good*, inasmuch as they are participations and imitations of absolute goodness, and are more and more good, the nearer and nearer they approach to that supereminent goodness, so is that Divine goodness the measure of all good.

As God is the "Good of goods," inasmuch as He is the principle and cause of all good; so is He also supreme good to all, inasmuch as He is the ultimate end of all. It is as impossible, as involving contradiction, that anything should not be *to* Him, as it is impossible that anything should not be *from* Him, "*Of* Him," says St. Paul to the Romans, "and *by* Him, and *in* Him are all things, *to* Him be glory for ever. Amen."

Besides God, the absolute good, there cannot be anything whatsoever which is good, unless formally as it is an imitation and a manifestation of the perfection of God. Hence the supreme eminence of the Divine essence, and the intestinal nature of things, demand that whatsoever is *from* God, as from the first principle of it, should be *for* God, as for its ultimate end. God would not be acting in accordance with the necessary norm of all rectitude, which is His essence, and so God would cease to be Holy, if He were to create any participated good which should not be directed towards Himself, as towards its ultimate end. Denial of this involves contradiction. It is intestinal to the very nature and essence of participated good, that it is ordained towards absolute good, as towards its own ultimate end— no less than is its entire dependence, throughout the length and breadth of its being, from that absolute good, as from its principle, essential to it.

Hence destination towards God, its ultimate end, may *immediately* be called the *moral essence* of the rational or intelligent creature, the only creature which is capable of *morality*. *Mediately* —or through and because of the rational creature —this destination towards God, as their ultimate end, is the *moral essence* of all other creatures, and so the moral essence of the entire universe. As the metaphysical essence of a thing is the reason and principle of all the *properties* of that thing; so from ordination towards God as the ultimate end, depend and flow forth all other *moral* relations.

Those creatures which have merely sensitive life can only by means of their senses have knowledge, desire, and feeling, and that with regard only to material things. Material things alone can be said to be *goods* to them. As regards intellectual matters, all creatures which have only sensitive life are in the same case as are things which do not have even sensitive life. Insensate things do not, *properly* speaking, *desire* any thing. They only *metaphorically* desire, and that inasmuch as by the very fact of their being they are ordained towards their own perfection. Hence there cannot be any good FOR them, as a beatitude. There can only be good *in* them, as belonging to the nature of them.

All irrational creatures, therefore, are ordained towards God, as towards the ultimate end *for the sake of which* they are. They are not ordained in virtue of knowledge and will—which together constitute rational appetite, or intelligent desire—towards God as towards an end which is *reasonably* desired by them, and which, when they have attained to it, they can *rationally* enjoy.

The ordination towards God of the irrational creature, through interposition of the rational creature, consists in this, that by man's making use of his irrational fellow creature, that creature helps man in his pursuit of the end for which he was himself created—and also and chiefly in this that, through its very being, the irrational creation is, as it were, a mirror and objective manifestation to the rational creation, of the Divine perfection. This, creatures which are destitute of reason are, not only to us mortal men, but also to the angels, and to the Blessed. We speak not merely of those of them which are actually in existence at this present, but of the whole creation from its first beginning, and throughout eternity; since at the end of time God's creation will not be annihilated, but will be renewed, in new heavens and a new earth, to endure for ever.

In a very far different way is God supreme good for the rational creature, as He is the ultimate end of that creature. Rational creatures, in all their perfections—in their natural perfections and also and especially in their supernatural perfections, up to their supreme perfection in beatific vision—are themselves *objective manifestations* of the Divine perfection. In this way the ordination of rational creatures towards God, as their ultimate end, is a good which is *in* those creatures. They are at the same time, however, so ordained towards God, as that He who is their ultimate end, and whom they shall enjoy, should be FOR them supreme good.

That is called the *supreme good* of man, by possession of which man is made blessed, or that for the sake of which other goods are to be desired and pursued; while that good is itself desired and pursued, not for the sake of something else, but for its own sake solely.

Hence that which is man's *supreme good* must necessarily be man's *ultimate end*. In it also must man's beatitude consist, since beatitude is none other than possession of supreme good. That is itself called supreme good, and the ultimate end, by possession and enjoyment of which we are made blessed. Possession and enjoyment of supreme good is also called supreme good. Similarly, beatitude stands for that by union with which we are made blessed; and stands also for that union. The former is called *objective* beatitude. The latter is called *formal* beatitude.

God who is in Himself supreme good could, even in a merely natural order of providence, be supreme good for His rational creature, beatifying that creature, through a knowledge and love in correspondence with its natural faculties.

In the present supernatural order, God presents Himself to His rational creature, as the ultimate end, and as the supreme good which will fully beatify it, not merely in accordance with the demands of a created rational nature but, beyond all demand of nature, in accordance with His own infinity of good—and in a way which corresponds not with the limitations and deficiency of the creature, but with the infinity of God, who has raised His creature above the level of its nature. God, as the infinite Good which He is, gives Himself to be *seen* by the intellect, which He has raised above its natural level, through the light of glory—to be *loved* with a love which corresponds to this vision of infinite good—and to be *enjoyed* with an everlasting beatitude. This beatitude is the connatural and necessary consequence of the infinite good, which is Divinely communicated through vision and love.

God is, therefore, *possessed*, through vision and love and unending joy, as He is supreme good, and the ultimate end of the rational creature. He is the supreme good of the rational creature, not only *causally*, as He is the supreme good of the irrational creature also—but by Himself as He is the Good which beatifies.

In order to the idea of perfect *possession*, no

more is required than that the thing possessed should be in the presence and power of him who possesses it, so that he has power to use it (if it is a means) and power to enjoy it (if it is an end) at his will.

Since God is, through the intuitive vision of Him, so made present, and so laid hold on, that he who beholds Him can enjoy Him, and draw from Him at will all manner of delight, the beatific vision of God is a true *possession* of God. To use an illustration, the hearing of a symphony is a possession of that symphony, since he who hears it can have from it all the pleasure and solace which it can afford.

Hence it is false to say that God in Himself is not immediately *our* good. In two ways God is said to be *our* good. He is our good, in the first place, *causally* or *effectively*, inasmuch as from Him, as from a source, all the good that comes to us flows forth. Secondly, God is said to be *our* good, as it were, *formally*, and by Himself. For this there is no need that God should inhere or cleave to us, as a *form* inheres in the subject of it. It is sufficient that God should be joined to us through intervention of *vision*.

God's necessary love of His own essential goodness is, by reason of this goodness, as it is worthy of infinite glorification, freely extended to willing the representation of the same goodness, and the recognition of it by His rational creature. In this consists the *external* glory of God, both objective and formal. The external glory of God, both objective and formal, but chiefly as *formal*, has its ultimate completeness in the beatitude of His rational creation. In the perfection of the Blessed, and in the whole of the heavenly City of God, there is a supreme expression and likeness of the infinite perfection of God. This representation constitutes God's *objective* external glory. The most perfect and unending state of vision, love, joy, adoration, and praise, of all the Blessed, constitutes the *formal* external glory of God, in the ultimate term of it. To this term God ultimately directs all His external operations, the whole order of creation and sanctification, of nature and grace, of natural and of supernatural providence.

In short—God, in His own infinite essential goodness, is the ultimate end *for the sake of which*, and *to* which, are all things. The glorification of God is the ultimate end which is *to be obtained*. This glorification is completed by the exaltation and beatitude of All Saints.

God is not, and God cannot be, to any one *formal good*, in the sense of His communicating Himself to, and uniting Himself with, the creature as if He were a *form* properly so called. All *informing*, in the proper sense of the word, implies the essential imperfection of the *form*. A form both perfects and is also itself perfected. It has, therefore, the idea of a *part*, and as such it is in a manner dependent on the whole, of which it is a part.

God, nevertheless, in a supernatural and marvellous way, so communicates Himself to, and so unites Himself with, His intellectual creature as, —by this communication of Himself after the manner of a *formal cause*, apart from all its imperfections—to raise His creature to that most sublime state and dignity, to which the Fathers give the name of *Deification*.

The highest of all such communications of Himself by God to His rational creature, after the fashion of a *formal cause*, is that in which a created human nature was made to be the Eternal Word's own nature; and so much a nature of His that the man Jesus Christ was and is true God.

Although this good, which is of an infinite dignity, belongs immediately and formally to the human nature of Christ, and to that nature alone, yet *morally* and *by extension*, if we may say so, it belongs to every creature which has in Christ, who is the Firstborn of every creature, been raised above the level of its nature. It thus belongs to the intelligent or rational creation, angelic and human, of which He the Firstborn is

Head. Most of all does it belong to human nature, and so belongs to human nature as that this mystery is the fountain and origin of all the subministration from the Head to the members of Him from whose plenitude we all receive, and grace for grace.

Consequently, and with, as it were, a still farther extension, this dignity belongs also and lastly even to the irrational creation; which is related towards the rational creation, as is a means towards its proximate end.

There ought also to be considered the marvellous exaltation of corporeal nature in the Body of Christ, which is the Body of a Divine Person—and by reason of His Body, in the bodies of all the just, which are called by St. Paul "temples of the Holy Ghost," and are bodies which are one day to be reformed, and made like to Christ's Body of glory.

We ought not, moreover, to lose sight of the elevation of corporeal nature to be instrumentally efficacious of sanctification in sacraments, or of the consecration of corporeal nature, in its widest range, in instruments and aids of Divine worship.

Finally, there is the deliverance of the creature from the bondage of corruption, into the freedom of the glory of the sons of God. Up to the day of that deliverance, every creature groaneth and is in travail.

All these are consequences of the mystery, and flow forth from the mystery, that the Word was made flesh—that God appeared in flesh—and that the flesh of a virgin became the flesh of the Son of God.

We discern a second, as it were, *formal* communication of supreme good to the creature, in the beatific vision. Through its will, a soul which is Blessed is borne, with an impetus of the whole of its being, towards the good which its intellect conceives, so as to unite itself thereto in a new way by love, and to be, as it were, transformed into it. Through those two powers, the intellect and the will, the soul enters into divinity, and divinity enters into it; and there is made, so to speak, a mutual penetration, and intimate vital union between the soul and God.

A third, in a manner, *formal* communication of God, the supreme good, is found in all the just. Although the just are not *formally just* with the justice of God, wherewith He is just, but are formally just with the justice, charity, and sanctity which, shed abroad in their hearts by the Holy Ghost, inheres or cleaves to them; yet this inhering gift of sanctifying grace is, as it were, a spiritual bond, whereby those souls are in a singular manner united to God their Sanctifyer through the Holy Ghost who is given to them, who dwells in them, and who remains in them.

5.

With the *true* and the *good*, the *beautiful* is in intimate connection. As God is essential *Truth*, and essential *Goodness*, so is God also essential *Beauty*.

The beautiful is defined by St. Thomas, from its *effect*, when he says—"Those things are called beautiful which please, when seen." This statement does not declare what the *beautiful* is in itself. It does not give the intestinal idea and essence of *beauty*. Things are not beautiful because they delight, but they delight because they are beautiful.

The elements of beauty are unity and variety. It consists in the oneness of the manifold, with conformity to an intellectual type. Manifoldness, or variety, is by way of *matter*, and oneness is the *form* of beauty. The greater the variety or manifoldness is, so long as there is a corresponding intensity of oneness, the greater will be the beauty. Where oneness and proportion are absent, there will be an absence of the *formal* idea of beauty.

There are several kinds of beauty. There is the physical beauty which is an object of the senses. There is the physical beauty which belongs to spiritual beings. There is also moral beauty.

Since in creatures beauty is finite, one beauty can be greater or more perfect than is another beauty. The excellence of one beauty over another may be either in the nature of things, or from the pleasure which it produces in him who beholds it. Hence, as regards this relative beauty, that may be more pleasing, or may be regarded as more beautiful, which is not in itself more really beautiful.

Since we are much affected by means of the senses, and have a very vivid perception of the objects of the senses; the beauty of the senses appears to many men, who do not abstract from sense, to be greater than is moral beauty.

Looking to the nature of things, the beauty is there more excellent, where the elements of beauty are not only more perfect in themselves, but there is between them a more perfect harmony and oneness.

The intrinsic beauty of God may be demonstrated, both from its effects, and from analysis of the Divine essence. Looking to the effects of the Divine beauty, all the beauty in creatures, whether material or spiritual, along with the moral beauty to be seen in free intelligences, is a beauty which is not selfexistent, any more than is finite being. The ultimate reason or idea of created beauty is in God. God is the efficient cause of it. God is also the exemplary cause, or pattern of it. The first cause of all order acts through His understanding. Hence supereminent types of all and every beauty exist in the Divine mind. Those types of created beauty, which are *formally* in the Divine intellect, *virtually* exist supereminently in the Divine essence, by reason of which created beauties are possible, and of which those beauties are a created participation. Inasmuch as God virtually contains in His Divine essence all possible beings in a supereminent manner, He is Supreme Being, and the most perfect of all beings, in the idea of *being*. Similarly, inasmuch as God virtually contains in His Divine essence all possible beauties, He is to be said to be supremely and most perfectly beautiful. His beauty is infinite, and it is self-existent. God not merely has beauty, but God Himself *is* His own beauty.

Apart from effects, the Divine beauty is evident on analysis of the Divine essence. Therein we find an infinite variety of perfections, as we conceive them, along with the utmost oneness. This supreme oneness includes that perfection which is proper to the order which is free from all imperfection. There is there the greatest oneness with the greatest virtual variety.

God's beauty is also such as it ought to be in

accordance with the conception of the most perfect essence; and this Divine essence the Divine intellect apprehends. To the Divine intellect which contemplates this variety in unity it must be pleasing. If it is proper to God-given reason to take delight in perfect unity in variety; most of all must this delight belong to God's contemplation of that beauty in Himself.

This is that *physical* beauty of God, of which we find imitations and objective manifestations in God's creatures which, all of them, in their measure and degree, are made after the model, and to the pattern of Him who is not only the efficient, but the exemplary cause of them.

The beauty which delights the senses is only analogous to that beauty which enchains the mind. There is an intellectual beauty in those abstract truths of the intellectual order which, when beheld in their marvellous connection, and in the unity and simplicity of their principles, and in the variety and concord of their consequences, fill the mind with the purest of delight.

We discern the oneness of the manifold, and in it that beauty which appeals to the mind, in all life and living things. From created life, and as effects and harbingers of its interior beauty, there present themselves to the senses, the most beautiful phenomena in animal bodies, and in vegetative structures.

From this we pass to better understanding of how far more noble is the beauty in a rational soul, and how more noble still is the beauty in a pure spirit. In pure spirits there is the greatest oneness, and the simplicity of the most noble of substances; and along with it a wondrous variety of faculties, of forces, and of powers. Through its intellect, the soul conceives the whole world, and paints in itself invisible pictures of all objects. Through its memory, the soul preserves these pictures, and on occasion produces them for use. Through its will, the soul has power to employ them, or to enjoy them, at its pleasure. A rational soul is a substance of such marvellous beauty and perfection, that if it were clearly and fully known in itself, and as it really is, there would be discerned in it a divinity, and the contemplation of it would flood the mind with delight in its beauty.

The most sublime of all created beauties is that of a soul or spirit which has been raised to the supernatural order, through sanctifying grace, through the habits and virtues which have been Divinely infused into it, and through its participation of the Divine nature. This is that beauty which will attain to its completeness, in the final consummation in beatific glory.

All these created beauties are, singly and together, but as shadows, or as a feeble image in the dark, as compared with the beauty that is in God.

God's one and most simple essence comprehends in its simplicity all the ideas of all perfections, which it is possible for our minds to conceive. The Divine essence comprehends also all the ideas of all things, not only of those which exist, but of those likewise which are only possible. It comprehends in one infinite cogitation, which is itself the Divine substance, all the ideas of all the *true*. It comprehends in one substantial volition, all the ideas of all the *good*. This is God's physical beauty.

We may reason in the same way with regard to God's moral beauty. It consists in God's justice and sanctity. God is infinitely upright and holy, not as if He conformed Himself to an extrinsic rule of rightness; but as He is Himself the subsisting rule or norm of all moral order.

By reason of His Beauty, both physical and moral, which He not merely *has* but *is*, God is infinitely loveable, and is infinitely to be desired.

CHAPTER V.

The negative properties of the Divine Essence.

IF we were to conceive *eternity* simply as *duration* without beginning and without end, we should not have a true idea of the eternity which is proper to God, as belonging to Him alone.

It is possible to conceive duration, taken as a whole, as without end to the continuance of it, although there is an end in the various successive parts, of which it consists. There might be an indefinite series of years, although every one of those years had its end. A duration which consists of parts could not possibly be without a beginning; but it is possible for a duration which consists of parts, to be without an end, or without cessation of the continuous succession, by which time is constituted.

Duration of this kind falls very far short of absolute perfection. In it that which is actual would be always very small, while the rest of it would either no longer be, or would as yet not be at all. Such duration would never form one simultaneous whole.

There is no permanence which is of the intestinal essence of a finite being. As a finite being has beginning through creation, so the duration of the existence of a finite being is due to the preserving power of God. If that were to cease, the existence of the finite being would come to an end. All this betokens imperfection.

We derive our understanding of the Divine duration, from the perfection of the Divine *essence*. That essence is, of the very idea of it, not *contingent*, but *necessary*. It not only, therefore, has no beginning and no end—no first terminus and no last terminus—but it is as essential to it that it should be without either terminus, as it is essential to it to *be from itself*, or to be self-existent. It is as impossible, as involving contradiction, that there should be in the Divine essence beginning or end; as it is impossible and contradictory that the Divine essence should not necessarily exist.

The Divine *being* is, of the innermost essence of it, the plenitude of absolute being. This Divine being must consequently be always *actual*, without any potentiality, or possibility of farther perfection. In the absolutely and necessarily *actual*, there cannot be any succession. There cannot be anything which is not always, and always in the same manner of being. There cannot be anything which is *more*, or anything which is *not yet*. There cannot be *before* or *after*. All is perpetual *now*. The whole plenitude of being is there, *at once* and *always*.

To the Divine *being*, as it is in the perfection of the actual, we may give the name of *life*—as it is permanence, it may be called *possession*—as it has no terminus, or either beginning or end, it is possession of LIMITLESS life—as there is no succession in its actuality, it is a *simultaneous whole*—and as succession in it, as it is a pure act or entirely actual, involves contradiction, and so is absolutely impossible, it may be called *perfect possession*. This is the absolute and perfect eternity, which Boethius rightly defines when he says—Eternity is the simultaneous whole and perfect possession of LIMITLESS life.

The character which is proper to the Divine *eternity*, regarded formally, is the perfection which of its own idea excludes *possibility* of succession. This is a *negative* perfection, as excluding imperfection. Moreover, God is His own eternity. The eternity of God, says St. Augustine, is the substance of God. In it is nothing changeable. In it there is nothing past, which no longer is, and nothing future, as if it were not yet. Whatever is there, it IS.

When there was as yet no creation, and consequently no *time*, there was what is called *The beginning*, that is to say, there was duration which was not preceded by anything. In this Beginning—God was. Whithersoever thought may carry itself, there cannot be conceived anything which is *more first*, if we may use the term, than is perpetual beginning, and in this *Beginning* God already was, and therefore always was.

2.

Whatsoever begins to exist, and whatsoever does exist *with* time, and *in* time, necessarily *co-exists* with the eternity or eternal duration of God. This eternity, alongside of which lies time, is His Divine *being*, as it is, changelessly and endlessly, one simultaneous whole. An object in time, regarded from the point of view of its *actual existence*, co-exists with the eternal being, or eternal duration of God, for that time only in which its existence in time endures. It co-exists either permanently or successively, as its duration is itself either permanent or successive.

Successive co-existence is not to be understood as if it implied succession in the eternal duration, but only as there is succession in the co-existing time. The several parts of its duration co-exist in *actual reality* with the eternal duration, for that time only in which they actually exist.

As regards actual reality, those things which now at this present exist, co-exist with the eternity of God. Those things which have passed away, and are now no more in existence, did co-exist with the same changeless eternity, at that time when they were in existence. Those things which are not yet in actual existence, but which will one day exist, will then co-exist with the same eternity; in that day when they shall begin to exist, and so long as they continue to exist in their actual being.

It is not as if the past co-existed with one part, and as if the present co-existed with another part, while the future co-existed with yet another part of the eternal duration. The Divine eternity does not consist of parts.

If we regard a created being, which exists in time, in its relation to the Divine vision and knowledge of it; that knowledge, from the very fact of its being eternal, and of its having in it no succession whatsoever, is always the same. The Divine knowledge is always the same, whether the created being is as yet in the future, or whether it is actually existing in the present, or whether it is already in the past, and exists no longer. All things, therefore, which at any time exist, co-exist, so far as the actual being of them is concerned, with the whole of the Divine eternity, although *not from eternity*. The knowableness of them is, however, present to the gaze of God *from eternity*. It is not because things in the future of time are eternally seen, that they will at some time be. It is because they will at some time be, that they are seen from eternity.

3.

As the Divine *eternity* is to *time*, so is the Divine *immensity* to *place* and *space*.

As with everything that endures, *time* can co-exist, and as it is possible for time to co-exist indefinitely with the eternal; so also with everything that exists, it is possible for another thing to co-exist, with that relation to it, to which we give the name of *presence*.

Hence to one who is without limit in his presence, it is possible for others to be present; or, conversely, he who is without limit to his presence, can be present to others, and that indefinitely. He to whom such a mode of presence belongs is rightly called unmeasured, or *immense*.

As the first and obvious notion of eternity is conceived by comparison with co-existing time without limit; so is the notion of *immensity* which first presents itself to the mind, conceived as—presence without limit of place and space.

The presence of a spirit is not, in the manner of it, the same as is the natural presence of a body. Those things in which there are parts outside parts, and which, in order to signify this, are called *extended* things, can be naturally present to other "extended" things, in this way only, that part should correspond to part, and the whole to the whole, in that space which is constituted by the "extension" of the corporeal or material thing. If a man falls flat on plastic clay, the impression which he leaves upon it is that of his head in one place, and his body in another place, and the several members of his body in the places which correspond to them, in the clay on which he has fallen, and of which "extended" clay, his "extended" body has displaced a portion.

A spirit, on the other hand, in which there are no parts, can be present to several wholes simultaneously. It can be present also to extended objects and spaces, in such a way as to be at once as a whole in the whole, and as a whole also in every one of the several parts of that whole.

This force of presence in a spirit is, without doubt, a perfection. The perfection is, moreover, greater, the greater the number of objects to which this force of presence reaches. In a finite spirit, this force of presence cannot possibly be without its limit. It must necessarily have its limits. It may not always, perhaps, be actual in the whole of its efficacy, and may to some extent be potential only. All such limitations are absolutely impossible, as involving contradiction, in an infinite spirit.

God could not be an infinitely perfect spiritual

substance, without His being able to be present to other existences. In God there cannot be conceived a force or power of presence, which is partly actual, and partly potential. The whole of that power is always actual, since it is in reality none other than the absolutely perfect intellectual substance which, whatever it is, is always in act. Power of presence cannot in God be restricted to any limits whatsoever, beyond which God is not actually present.

Immensity, so conceived as that God is intrinsically determinated to intimate presence indefinitely in all existences, is a perfection which is included in the perfection of God, as that perfection is *absolute* perfection.

Omnipresence is a *relative* attribute; which connotes and has relation to actually existing creatures. Omnipresence is a necessary consequence of absolute perfection of being.

Presence, as it is an *absolute* perfection in God, is the absolute Divine being itself, which is limitless in presence. This Divine presence presents itself to the mind, through the thought of the indefinite possibility of the co-existence with it of creatures. No creature is possible, and so no place and no space is possible, with which, if it were to exist, God would not be intimately present, and that without any change in God Himself.

We are not to conceive the Divine *immensity* as if it were infinite extension or diffusion—any more than we are to conceive the Divine *eternity* as if it were infinite time and infinite succession.

When we think of objective truth in the metaphysical order, or, what comes to the same thing, when we think of the absolutely *necessary laws* to which is subject, and by which is ruled, whatever is or can be; we see at once that those truths and laws are ontologically prior to, and independent of, all relations of place and space. Where there is no place and no space, nothing can be said to be *here* or *there*. When we think of place or space, we cannot conceive either of them as existing anywhere, without that *objective truth* which is God, being also there. God does not begin to be there, where He was not before. The *change* from the not present, to the present occurs in the thing created, in the place or in the space, which before was not in being. Before place and space were in existence, there was no either *here* or *there*. They cannot, however, begin to be, except *in* God, and *with* God. God, therefore, is not anywhere *locally*, by limitation to *anywhere* beyond which He is not, but He is *everywhere*.

4.

When we say that God is in all things *by essence*, we are abstracting from His operations in His creatures, from the mode in which He manifests Himself, from the gifts which He bestows, and the like; and we are looking simply and solely to the existence of His essence in itself. From this point of view God is necessarily both everywhere, and everywhere in the same manner.

With God's existence in all things *by essence*, is bound up His being in all things *by power*—since all things, in the whole of their being, in their every perfection, and in their every act, are dependent on the Divine preservation and action.

From God's existence in all things by *essence*, it follows that He should be in all things *by presence*. He is present, both generally as He is the beholder of all things, and specially through the singular presence, whereby He exhibits Himself as present, through singular manifestations and gifts.

Hence we say that God is present everywhere, and everywhere in the same manner by *essence*, but we do not say that God is present everywhere *in the same manner* by presence, and by power.

When God, who is necessarily present everywhere, is nevertheless said to *come to*, and to *depart from* His creatures; this refers to presence not simply through His *essence*, but through His *operations* in those creatures.

5.

That which is called *imaginary* space, and imaginary time, has no reality outside conception of the mind. We form the conception of imaginary space, *negatively*, when we abstract from the existence of bodies, or rather from the real existence of any creature which is limited in the mode of its presence; and when *positively*, we conceive the possibility of bodies, or other "extended" creatures, existing in indefinite number.

As God is not subject to any limitations of *real* place or space, so neither is He subject to the limits of things, the existence of which is only possible. God is not present to anything where nothing exists.

Similarly, we form a conception of *imaginary* time, *negatively*, by abstracting from all really existing successions of time; and *positively*, by conceiving the possibility of continuous successions of time in indefinite number.

Hence we see the absurdity of imagining the Divine *immensity*, as if it were indefinite presence in imaginary space—and the similar absurdity in imagining the Divine *eternity*, as if it were indefinite duration in imaginary time.

Immensity is absolute perfection in the order of presence, in its utmost simplicity, and always the same, whereby God is exempt from all local limitations.

Eternity is absolute permanence, in its utmost simplicity, which is without any possibility of succession, and is always the same.

Spaces and places to which God, as He is immense, would be present, and successions of time which would co-exist with the eternal God, might be multiplied indefinitely, without ever arriving at an ultimate end.

CHAPTER VI.

God's Knowledge.

BY the word *spirit*, we mean a substance which has no real *parts*, which either constitute that substance, or complete it in its entirety. A spirit is *simple*, and one in itself. *Simplicity* in a spirit, however, is to be understood not merely *negatively*, as simplicity is negation of parts—but also *positively*, as simplicity is an essential nobility of being.

This nobility of being, in a spirit infinitely, in a sense at least, exceeds the grade of being which belongs to substances which have their perfection *in* composition, or *from* the composition of their parts. That perfection in those substances, in whatever degree it may exist, cannot possibly attain to the natural perfection, in nobility of being, which essentially belongs to a spirit. The perfection is of a different order.

A spirit is an *immaterial* substance. *Negatively*, a spirit is not inert, nor does a spirit act only outside itself, nor is its action restricted as is that of composite beings. *Positively*, a spirit has in itself intellectual life. Of its own essence, a spiritual being has been so constituted as, by a vital act, to understand the *true*, and to have within it *formal* truth—and also by a vital act, to tend towards *good* which is recognized by it, or comes before it under the idea of the good—to embrace the good with love—and in the good to find its blessedness.

In all these most interior vital acts, a spirit has at the same time an intimate and vivid consciousness of their being its own acts; and a consciousness also of itself, as the substantial principle of them, that is to say, as the substance which is the source of those acts.

From the simplicity, nobility, and intellectuality of its being and life, a spirit is, of its own nature, *immortal*. A spirit is changeless in the substance of it. As regards *place*, a spirit is exempt from, and is superior to those modes of existing, to which bodies are subject in space. The more perfect the simplicity and the intellectuality of a spirit is, the more perfect is its nature as it is a spirit.

God is, as we have seen, a most "pure act," or *absolutely actual*, and in God, by reason of His essential perfection, not only physical composition of real parts, but also metaphysical composition of ideal parts, is absolutely excluded, as in Him involving contradiction.

God is not only an *intellectual* substance, which has the faculty of embracing the true and the good, by vital acts of its own, but He is essentially *one substantive act.* This act is at once and identically both the absolute *true*, and infinite *understanding* of the true—both absolute *good*, and infinite *love* of the good—and so in Himself, and in the plenitude of His own perfection, God is absolute infinite Blessedness.

As God is absolute changeless truth, goodness, substantial active power, and purely actual, without any mingling of the potential; so is all succession of time—and all limitation of presence—in absolute contradiction with God's perfection. God is Himself His own Eternity. God is Himself His own Immensity.

This life of infinite understanding, of infinite will, and of infinite blessedness, is not only an intimate act of the Divine substance. It is itself the eternal and immense Divine substance.

Hence the Divine understanding, along with the Divine will, is not only independent of all things which are, or which can be excogitated as being, outside itself; but it is the principle, and pattern, and cause on which is dependent all the true, all the good, all life, all understanding, all love of good, and all beatitude.

God is therefore an infinite spirit, because He is intellectual life of infinite perfection. He is a Spirit in a supereminent sense. Of Him created spirits are only images and likenesses.

Hence, the nearer creatures are to the image and likeness of God, the more properly are they spirits. In the Sacred Scriptures the human soul in view of its intellectual faculties, is called a *spirit*. In view of its sensitive faculties, whereby the selfsame substance informs and animates the human body which it tenants, it is called a *soul*.

Hence again, those intellectual substances which are not ordained to inform and animate a body, through sensitive faculties, belong to a more noble order, and are pure spirits. There is nothing material in their being, they are purely spiritual. Further, a soul which has been raised to the supernatural order, through supernatural gifts, which are called and are *spiritual* gifts, is itself called *spiritual*; in comparison with its merely *natural* condition, in which that soul is called *carnal*. The human bodies also which shall be transformed in the Resurrection, are, on account of the supernatural properties which shall then belong to them, called by St. Paul *spiritual bodies*.

God is called and is a *Spirit*, in the most proper of all senses, although as regards the name "spirit," that name was first applied by us to creatures, and is then from them transferred to God; as in the case of nearly all other names by which we designate Divine perfections.

2.

Since God is a perfect Spirit, He is a *substance*, the life of which is *understanding*. Since God is most *simple*, His understanding is itself the Divine *substance*. Further, God neither is, nor can He be conceived as being, in any way *potential*. He is always and necessarily *actually* intellectual.

Since, however, the conception of *essence* is one thing, and the conception of *understanding* is another thing, essence and understanding are in idea distinct one from the other. Absolute being has, besides understanding, the idea of a *knowable object*. Since absolute being is *being* of infinite perfection, it is infinite also in the idea of the *knowable*, or of the *true*. To an infinite knowable it is only infinite understanding that can be perfectly adequate.

The Divine act which understands is as equally infinite as is the infinite object of Divine understanding. It is itself the Divine *essence*. The Divine act of understanding is, therefore, in perfect proportion with its own infinite object, or that which it understands.

Since *understanding* is adequate correspondence of the intellect with its object, where infinite actual understanding is identical with an infinite object, under every idea of its infinite knowableness, there is there a perfectly adequate correspondence of the intellect with the object, as the object is knowable. This adequate correspondence is called and is *comprehension*. God, as He is an act of infinite understanding, which is adequate to Himself, as to the infinitely knowable *true*, is perfect comprehension of Himself. Since this act of understanding is itself the Divine *substance*, it is *substantial comprehension* by God, of God Himself.

We apply to God abstract names, which serve in a manner to express the Divine perfections, both in order to signify plenitude of perfection—and in order to set forth God's simplicity. Thus God is called Wisdom—because in God wisdom is not restricted to any degree or limited extent of wisdom, but is the whole idea of absolute wisdom—and because wisdom in God is not, as in created beings, something which is superadded to substance and essence. God's essence itself, of the intestinal idea of it, is wisdom.

In the same way we apply to God those abstract names which, in creatures, denote immanent action. Thus God is infinite understanding infinite volition, and infinite efficiency. We signify by these names, intellect and will, and omnipotence, in the perfection of the *actual*—and not by way of a *faculty*, which proceeds to an act of understanding, of willing, or of effecting. When God, therefore, is said to be *substantial comprehension* of His own essence, it is meant that the Divine Essence IS the Divine Intellect—and that the Divine intellect is essentially in the perfection of the *actual*—and is therefore ever actually understanding. Hence it is that infinite Divine understanding adequately corresponds to the infinite Divine essence.

Divine understanding, considered as distinct in idea from its object, which is the Divine essence, may, by way of analogy with our knowledge, be compared to *direct* knowledge. If, on the other hand, Divine understanding is regarded as it IS the Divine essence, and so as being to itself its own object; there analogically corresponds to it the *reflex* knowledge wherewith we recognize our own act of knowing, or know that we know.

3.

The Divine essence, in its relation to the *true*, and to *understanding* of the true, may be regarded in three ways. In the first place, the Divine essence is absolute *being*, and it is the absolute *true*, from which all things whatsoever, which have the idea of *being*, and of the *true*, depend. By analogical participation of that essence those things ARE.

When absolute *being*—which is the absolute

true—is understood with perfect comprehension, then necessarily, through that comprehension, all things are understood which, in dependence on the absolute, either actually are, or possibly may be. God, in comprehending His own essence as absolute Being, and the primal True, from which all participated *being*—and all the participated *true*—is dependent, does necessarily, by the same act of understanding, comprehend all the *true*.

The Divine essence may, secondly, be considered more expressly, as it is an idea and pattern which is *imitable* outside God, and this throughout all the degrees, ideas, and relations of participated being, and participated objective truth.

This Divine pattern may be considered from the point of view of the shadows of it outside God, which are not as yet in actual existence, but are only possible. It is evident that comprehension of the pattern is at the same time comprehension of all the possible shadows of that pattern—or comprehension of the whole of participated *being* in the metaphysical order, and in the region of the ideal. This *imitableness* of the Divine essence, an imitableness the actuality of which is possible, is as *necessary* as is that essence. The *understanding* of this imitableness, and of the whole of the *being* through which the

Divine essence is imitable, is also *necessary*. It is necessary, because the *terminus* of Divine understanding is a necessary terminus.

If the Divine pattern is, on the other hand, regarded from the point of view, not of the possible, but of the actual, the actual imitation of that pattern outside God is not *necessary*. It is *contingent*. The Divine understanding cannot, however, comprehend the Divine pattern—from which the created imitation depends with a real, continual, and essential dependence—without at the same time comprehending all the actual expressions and imitations of it, which are in dependence upon it.

The Divine essence is, in the third place, infinite also as it is an ideal representation of the *true*, or of the wisdom which, after the manner of an objective idea, represents the true. It would not be an infinite representation, unless there shone and were represented in it all the objectively true, both in the order of *essences*, or ideal order of the possible, and in the order of *existences*, or actual order of the whole of participated *being*.

All that which God knows besides Himself is a *terminus*, indeed, of the Divine knowledge; but that which God knows does not *effect* knowledge in God by any real inflow. It does not determine the Divine knowledge, as if it were a cause or principle.

. Although God would not, for instance, know the world *as existing*, unless the world did at some time really exist, because God has the objectively *true* as the terminus of His knowledge; yet the existing world does not exercise any action or inflow on God. The Divine knowledge is only *terminated*, as by all the *true*, by this *true*, as included therein. Of its own intestinal perfection, the Divine knowledge is determinated to comprehension of all the true.

4.

Form and matter are properly spoken of in connection with composite substances. In these the *form* is that which gives the essential perfection of order and species; and so constitutes an order or species as distinct and different from other orders or species. The *matter*, on the other hand, does not give specific perfection, or perfection which distinguishes from other orders. The matter is common to many, or rather to all orders of material substances.

These names—matter and form—are transferred from their original meaning, to the *object* of knowledge, or that which is known, when we speak of the *material* object, and of the *formal* object of knowledge. In accordance with this analogy of matter and form, the *formal object* of knowledge is that by which the proper perfection of a knowledge is constituted, as distinct and different from that of other orders of knowledge. From this that the object gives to a knowledge the perfection which is proper to it, the object determines it; and that knowledge is known by itself, and by reason of itself, and not by reason of something else. The *material object*, on the other hand, is subject to a knowledge which, not from it, but otherwise, has its own proper perfection; and a perfection which is different from that of other orders of knowledge. The material object does not therefore determinate the knowledge, and the perfection of it; although the knowledge, through its perfection otherwise determinated, has this knowledge also for a *terminus* of it. The material object therefore is known not by itself, and by reason of itself, as a motive of knowledge, but through something else, and by reason of something else.

From these the proper ideas of the *formal* object and the *material* object, it follows that the formal object, in comparison with the material objects which are subordinated to it, is at the same time the *principal* object of knowledge, while the material objects are *secondary* objects of knowledge.

The Divine knowledge and understanding is in reality the Divine substance and essence. The Divine knowledge has therefore from the Divine substance, that is from itself, a perfection which is proper to it—and it differs from every knowledge whatsoever of another order. This is the proper idea and perfection of the Divine knowledge and understanding, that the infinite act which understands is the Divine *substance*, and infinite substantial truth, to which nothing of perfection can possibly be added.

If we distinguish in idea the infinite *true* from the infinite act of understanding, that infinite true is not only *knowable* but, of its own innermost idea, it demands that it should be *actually known* by the infinite understanding. It is therefore with a foundation in reality, that we conceive the infinite *true*, or the Divine *being* as determining the Divine *intellect* to the comprehension of itself.

The substantial act of understanding—or, in other words, the act of understanding which is itself a *substance*, being itself the Divine substance or essence—in the comprehension of the Divine essence, is determinated so as at once in the Divine essence, as in absolute *being*—and as in an infinite pattern, or as in an actual representation of all the true—to comprehend whatever has the idea of the true.

The Divine essence is, therefore, the *formal*

idea under which God comprehends the *true*, wherever the true exists. An object of knowledge which is distinct from God, does not act on the Divine intellect, nor does it induce any modification of that intellect. This would be utterly subversive of that substantial act which is God's understanding. Hence an object which is distinct from God neither perfects God's knowledge, nor determines God's knowledge. It is through His *essence*, and in His essence, as through a *formal object*, that God is determinated to knowledge of all the true, even when the objectively true is distinct from Himself.

It is most clear then that the *formal* and *principal* object of Divine understanding, whereby it has the perfection which is proper to it, whereby it is determinated, whereby and in which it knows all the true, is the *essence* of God. Every *true* whatsoever, on the other hand, which is distinct from God, is a *secondary* and *material* object of one and the same act of God, whereby He understands Himself. This object does not give to that Divine act the perfection which is proper to it. The secondary and material object is known in another, and through another, that is to say, it is known through the *principal* and *formal* object.

Hence we see how faith, and theology, and

mystical contemplation, and much more how the beatific vision, are imitations of the Divine knowledge; while all created things, and every truth, are considered in God, the supreme Truth, as in their cause, as in their principle, and as in their end.

In like manner we see how Divine understanding is the only *adequate* Theology, in the most sublime meaning of that word. As the faith, and exposition, unfolding, and understanding of the faith by mortal men, which constitutes our theology on earth, corresponds to the theology of the Blessed, as does a beginning to a consummation; and corresponds to the infinite Theology of God Himself, as does a shadow to its archetype; so is God the *principal* object of Divine understanding, to which all other objects, considered in their relation to God, are subordinate, and hold the second place.

If God were to know the *being* of things, only as those things are "eminently" (as theologians say) in God, He would not be knowing created *being itself*, or possible *being itself*. He would be knowing only His own essence in which that being is mirrored. This "eminent" *being* in God is not the created or possible being itself, but is the Divine essence.

If God were not perfectly to know the *being*

itself of things as they are in themselves, or as they may one day be; He would not be comprehending His own essence, as it is the *cause* and *pattern* of all things. Perfect comprehension of the *cause* includes knowledge of *effects*, whether possible effects, or actually existing effects, as they are *in themselves*.

Although, therefore, God does not know the *secondary* objects of His knowledge in themselves as in a cause which determinates and perfects His knowledge; yet God does know them, not only as they are "eminently" in the Divine essence, but also as they are now, or may one day be, *formally in themselves*.

5.

If, therefore, we consider knowledge from the point of view of the *termini* which it connotes, and which are subject to it; there is not only a foundation, but a necessity, in accordance with our inadequate conceptions, for making a distinction of several different ideas in one and the same knowledge.

Although Divine understanding is in itself so simple, and beyond all multiplication of acts and forms; yet the objects of Divine understanding—and the attitudes of these objects to the Divine understanding—are not of one and the same idea with that understanding, but are of a very different idea.

It is possible for us to distribute the secondary objects of the Divine knowledge, so as to consider it either as comprehending *actual existences*, or as comprehending the *essences* of things, in the mere *possibility* of those things. The Divine knowledge under the first of those two aspects is called —knowledge *of vision*. The name is taken from our knowledge of things through the sense of vision. By vision we have knowledge only of *actual* existences, since these alone can possibly be seen by the eye of the body.

The Divine knowledge under its second aspect, as the knowledge of the *essences* of things, in the mere possibility of those things, is, to distinguish it from knowledge of vision, called—knowledge *of simple understanding*.

Things which do not exist may be considered either as in a state of mere possibility—and in this case they are the object of *simple understanding*—or in the existence which they do not have as yet, but which they infallibly will have, if a certain condition is verified. In this second sense, the object is not known as at some time really existing; but neither is it known only as an essence, or mere possibility of existence.

Rightly, therefore, and by reason of the diversity of objects, there is made a third distinction. It is that of God's knowledge of things which *under condition will be*.

This knowledge agrees with the knowledge of *simple understanding* in this, that the object is not beheld absolutely as in actual existence. It differs in this, that it is related not only to necessary essence, but to *contingent existence;* or existence which, given fulfilment of a condition, will infallibly have place.

In an inverse order, this knowledge of *contingent* existence so far agrees with knowledge *of vision*, that it is related to *existence*, and not only to necessary essence. It differs in this, that it does not regard an existence which absolutely will actually be.

This object of knowledge, therefore, stands *midway* between the object of *vision*, and the object of *simple understanding*. With both it agrees in somewhat, and in somewhat it differs from both of them. Hence, theologians, since the sixteenth century, have given to this knowledge a name, derived from the properties of its object, and called it—*mediate knowledge*. It is intermediate between the other two.

The essences of things in the state of possibility, and the objective truth of essences, consist in this alone, that the Divine essence is in this way *imitable* in analogous beings and perfections, and in their mutual relations. This imitability is natural to God, it is necessary, and it is independent of free will. It is in reality none other than the essence of God itself, under the idea of primal and absolute *being*—under the idea of the absolute *true*—and under the idea of it, as the *pattern* of all perfection. Hence the objective *truth* of essences in the state of possibility, is an absolutely necessary truth.

Divine understanding necessarily comprehends all truth. God's knowledge of *simple understanding* is therefore absolutely necessary, throughout the whole of its object.

Existence, on the other hand, is *necessary* in God alone. Every created existence is *contingent*. The actual existence of all things which, besides God, at any time exist, is *an objective truth;* in such wise as that absolutely the non-existence of them might also have been true. That they should actually exist depends on the free will of God, either as operating by itself alone, or as operating through a creature.

It may depend on the Divine free will, and on, at the same time, a free created will. There are some things of which God is the whole cause, such as those things which are created—some things of which the creature, or the creature's will, is the sole cause, such as defects and sins—and some things of which God and His creature are simultaneously the cause, or are con-causes, such as natural and moral operations, since in these operations God co-operates.

The *principal* object, therefore, of God's knowledge *of vision* is absolutely necessary, as it is the necessarily existing *essence* of God. A *secondary* object of His knowledge of vision might possibly not be. If, however, it actually is, it is necessarily subject to the Divine intuition. The same knowledge which, looking to the existence or the non-existence of its objects, is distinguished in the threefold division which we have given; is, looking to the *necessity* or to the *contingence* of the same objects, rightly distributed into *absolutely necessary* knowledge, and *only hypothetically necessary* knowledge.

God's knowledge *of simple understanding* may be regarded, either as it is simple knowledge of an objective truth; or as it comprehends the natures, ends, goodness, order, and relations of all things, formally as those things are such that it is fitting that they should receive from God existence.

God's knowledge, considered in this second way, follows the idea of those objects which are made in the exercise of an art. It is not merely *theoretical* knowledge of essences, and of objective truth. It is the *practical* knowledge of an artificer, who has knowledge of that which he is to make, before he makes it. It is as having the

Divine Will along with it, that this Divine knowledge is the *cause* of things. With the Divine will, the Divine knowledge is effective, directive, and creative.

Approbation, and disapprobation, belong properly not to knowledge, but to the will. That which is called God's knowledge *of approbation* is His knowledge of good objects, which are pleasing to the Divine Will. God's knowledge *of disapprobation* is His knowledge of evil objects, which are displeasing to the Divine Will. All God's *practical* knowledge is knowledge *of approbation*, since God's works cannot be otherwise than good.

Since evil is privation of good, and since God knows every good, and the measure of every good, He knows also every evil. As it is negation of knowledge *of approbation*, God's knowledge *of disapprobation* is sometimes called in the Sacred Scriptures—an ignorance, or ignoring. "I never knew you." "I know you not whence you are, depart from Me, all ye workers of iniquity."

No evil actions are *predefined* by God, in the proper sense of the word; not only as regards the moral depravity in them, but even as regards the physical *being* of the acts. That which God forbids, under threatening of His wrath and eternal punishment, is a physical act; although the reason why He forbids it, is the moral depravity which is inseparable from that act, either in itself, or under the circumstances of it. It involves contradiction, that there should be in God a will of complacence that this act should be done—or that God should will to effect that a man should determinate himself to such an act. The sinner himself does not will the moral depravity of his action, except in so far as he wills the *act* from which the depravity is inseparable.

God nevertheless *permits* sins; and with prevision of sins He wills certain effects of sins. His permission is not an antecedent will that the action in which there is the depravity of sin should be done. *Positively*, God preserves in being the natural faculties, and the freedom, of His creature; and He extends His concurrence and inflow—on which every second cause is dependent in its acting—to all the actions to which the freedom of the creature extends. God, at the same time, does not *will*, but, on the contrary, forbids the created will to choose an action in which there is moral perversity. God offers also and gives sufficient aids—whether of the natural order, or of the supernatural order—so that His creature, by availing himself of these aids, has power, at least here and now, not to sin. *Negatively*, if the creature will not make use of those aids, God may not give other aids; either on account of previous demerits—or because His wise and well-ordered providence does not demand other aids—or because He is not bound, in the distribution of His graces, to accommodate Himself to the wickedness of His creatures.

While God sees, and although God sees, His creatures in their freedom willing to abuse His natural gifts of preservation of their faculties, of their freedom, and of the Divine concurrence, on which the natural action of all creatures is dependent—He, nevertheless, wills not to withdraw these gifts; although He may will at the same time not to grant other aids. This is His decree of *permission* of sin.

In this decree God is not regarding sin. While He has knowledge of a future act of sin, in the objective *truth* of that act, He decrees not to hinder it, and, what comes to the same thing, to *permit* it. Consequently to His knowledge of the act, in the objective truth of it, God does indeed absolutely will to *permit* it; but this permission is not at variance with His not willing it, or with His forbidding it.

Very different is the idea of good acts, and especially of supernatural acts. These acts God wills, with His will of approbation, to be done by His free creature. With His will of *efficiency*

God anticipates, and by His grace so aids His creature, that he will be able to do, and will do such acts. Hence, as St. Augustine says, God *foreknows* both good and evil actions; while He *predestines* not evil actions, but good actions.

The order of thought in this matter is as follows. First, there is the objective *truth* of the *possibility* that, if to such and such a free creature there should be granted such and such a prevenient grace, that creature would have the power, through the forces of grace which he has received, to determinate his will to a particular good act; while he would at the same time have power, with his own natural forces, to resist the grace, and to sin. Here we have God's knowledge *of simple understanding* of all things which are possible. Secondly, there is the objective *truth* of a *hypothetical fact*. The free creature, among all the acts to which it is possible for him to determinate himself, would choose such and such a good act, with the forces of such and such a grace, if that grace should be given to him. Here we have God's *mediate* knowledge of the objective *truth* of this *hypothetical fact*. Thirdly, there is the will in God, or God's decree, really to bestow the grace in question. Fourthly, there is the objective *truth* of an *absolute* fact, when the creature, out of the number of all acts which are possible to him, chooses, and determinates his will, with this aid of grace, to the doing of that particular good act. Here we have God's knowledge *of vision* of this *absolute* fact of the future.

It is true, therefore, to say that God *predefines* all the good free acts of His creatures, in this sense that, first, He by an antecedent will wills those acts to be done, if the free creature, in the exercise of his freedom, does not resist. Secondly, by this will God bestows the aids, with which He knows that His creature will freely consent. Thirdly, foreseeing the consent of the creature, God, not with a merely conditional will but, on the condition being verified by the creature, with an *absolute* will, wills those acts to be done.

Thus we see how very different is *predefinition* of good acts, from *permission* of evil acts.

Acts which are morally evil are not foreseen in a cause which antecedently determinates them; the *terminus* of the Divine prevision is—the free acts, in themselves, as at some time in existence. A free act, when it is actually done, is in itself, and in the objective *truth* of it, a *terminus* of God's knowledge *of vision*.

Of the very idea of *eternity*, God's knowledge and vision does not begin to be otherwise in time, than it was before time; but remains always the same in the manner of it. Hence God has knowledge of an act of the future, before it is done, in the objective *truth* of the *existence* of it, as distinguished from the *essence* or possibility of it.

Moreover, the Divine essence would not be the infinite pattern and representation of all the *true*—nor would the Divine knowledge be an infinite act—unless the Divine *essence* should represent to the Divine *intellect* all the objectively true, and the Divine intellect comprehend all the true. Although, therefore, an act, in the real existence of it, begins in time, it nevertheless constitutes a foundation of its eternal knowableness, in the case of infinite knowledge. Things of the future are present to the eternal gaze. The objective *truth* of an act of the future comes first in idea; while the termination of God's knowledge in that act, is subsequent in idea to the knowableness of the act.

6.

The whole of the difficulty in reconciling the freedom of intelligent creatures, with the infallibility of the Divine foreknowledge, has its origin in the imperfection of the way in which we conceive God's eternal knowledge. We ourselves do not have knowledge of the future, except in an antecedent disposition of causes which is present to us. Hence we have knowledge of the future with certainty, only inasmuch as we have understanding of causes which have been determinated in one direction. We always, therefore, conceive an act which is infallibly foreknown, as if that act had been antecedently determinated in the cause of it; and consequently as if that act were not free. We can have intuition of an act itself, when it is in the present; but we cannot have intuition of an act itself when it is as yet in the future. We find no difficulty in reconciling the freedom of an act, which we see being done in the present, with the infallibility of our own vision of it. The reason is, because we understand that our vision is not the *cause* of that act. There would be no greater difficulty about foreknowledge of the future, than there is about knowledge of the present; if we could distinctly conceive vision of the future, as if it were vision of the present. Prevision is no more the cause of a future act, than is vision the cause of a present act. When we see a man stealing, our seeing him steal does not make him steal; it is not a cause of his stealing. In the same way, God's foreseeing a man stealing does not make him steal, or determinate his will to steal.

The objective *truth* of the *existence* of a free act, which is at some time done, is prior in idea, and it is presupposed as a terminus of the Divine vision. The action is present to the eternal gaze as if being done, in the same way in which it is actually done in time. Prevision of the act is not the cause why the act is done; nay, our free determination of our wills, in the doing of the act, is the reason why God should foresee this particular action rather than another action. Infallible knowledge, which supposes as the *terminus* of it the free determination of the created will, does not hinder freedom; nay, the more infallible that knowledge is, the more certainly is it a sign and proof of freedom. The infallible foreknowledge of God supposes the free determination of the created will, as a *terminus* of that knowledge; and so it not only does not interfere with freedom but, as it is foreknowledge of free acts, confirms freedom. As man's memory does not *effect* facts of the past, so neither does God's foreknowledge *effect* facts of the future.

7.

Among things which only *under condition* shall one day be, absolutely *necessary* objective truths cannot be numbered. There can only be *contingent* truths. There cannot be the *essences* of things, regarded in themselves. There can only be the *existences* of *contingent* things. Contingent existence is not in the sphere of the merely *possible*, for that belongs to the idea of *essence*. Contingent existence is not in the sphere of the already *actual*. It is that which will infallibly one day be actual, if something else shall be actual. This, on account of the *bond* between the one as antecedent, and the other as consequent, is what is called a *condition*. If there is no such bond, there will not be either *condition* or *conditioned*. In that case we cannot speak of a thing as to be in the future *under condition*, since there is in reality no condition.

If the bond is something which itself is *necessary*, then knowledge of the *conditioned* is reduced to knowledge *of simple understanding*.

Knowledge of the existence of free acts of a created will, acts which under condition will be in the future—with this bond that, given that condition, the acts will be done, and failing that condition, the acts will not be done—but without a *necessary* bond, or a bond which in its results is infallible, of the very nature of the condition itself, so that the act cannot, given the condition, not be—is the kind of knowledge which we are now considering.

That under such a condition the act will be, rather than not be, is not infallible otherwise than as it is true, that the will under such a condition will determinate itself to this act, rather than to other acts; although it is equally in the power of that will not to determinate itself to this act, and to determinate itself to other acts. Hence, not only is the *condition*, under which the act will be, something which is ontologically contingent; but the *bond* between the existence of the act and the condition is also contingent. There is here no *necessity* of existence of the act, other than that which is consequent, not only to supposition of the *cause*, but to supposition also of the *fact* of existence. That comes to this, that an act which *is*, cannot at the same time *not be*.

8.

To re-state the same truths in different words, and from another point of view, may serve to make more clear a subject which, of the very nature of it, is somewhat abstruse.

God's knowledge is *an act*, and an act which is *necessary* in God. Knowledge is a simple perfection, and every simple perfection is necessary to God. Moreover, God is the *first cause* of all things; and the first cause must be an *intelligent* cause. The first cause cannot be *necessitated*, but must be *free*. A cause which is necessitated is not independent in its action. Given due conditions, it necessarily acts. It is, therefore, dependent on those conditions. Again, a necessitated cause either acts to the full extent of its power— or it is determinated by its adjuncts to the doing of this, rather than to the doing of that—or it determinates itself. If the first cause were to act to the full extent of its power, all things would at once actually exist. If the first cause were determinated by its adjuncts, there would not be in it the *ultimate reason*, and the *adequate* reason of the existence of its *effects*. This reason should include the existence of those adjuncts, on which the existence of its effects is dependent. Those adjuncts are, however, *supposed* by a necessitated *cause*; and so that cause would not be the cause of all things that are, and would, therefore, not be the first cause.

If, on the other hand, a cause *determinates itself*, it is a *free* cause, and cannot be a necessitated cause.

A *free* cause is an *intelligent* cause, and the first cause must be an intelligent cause. This intelligent cause must also be ever *actually* understanding. Were it otherwise, it could *never* actually know; because it is changeless, and incapable of change.

God's knowledge is not distinct from God's *essence*, because in God there is no physical composition. A being who *necessarily* exists, is *self-existent* and independent. Every compound being is a *dependent* being, since it depends on the parts of which it consists. Every compound being is of itself a *contingent* being; because, since it consists of parts, it can be dissolved, and then it thereby ceases to be.

A being who necessarily exists is an *infinite*

being, and an infinite being cannot emerge from finite beings. God's knowledge not only is an act, or ever actual, but that act is itself a *substance*. An act of knowledge may be either accidental or substantial. An *accidental* act of knowledge— whether it is something which is really distinct from the substance of him who knows, or whether it is a modification of that substance, it matters not—is an act which can be either present or absent; and nevertheless the whole substance of him who knows remains in its entirety. An accidental act of knowledge is not therefore of the intrinsic idea of him who knows; and the presence of it involves some at least *metaphysical* composition. It will be remembered that metaphysical composition (see pages 58, 77) which is called composition after the analogy of physical composition, consists of ideas which, although not parts as in *physical* composition, are conceived after the manner of parts; and, like parts, those ideas perfect each other.

A *substantial* act of knowledge, on the other hand, is an act which is so identified with the *substance* of him who knows, that it cannot be separated from that substance. It is so much of the intrinsic idea of that substance, as to exclude even metaphysical composition. Such is God's knowledge, as that knowledge is a substantial act.

It is a necessary perfection of infinite being

that it cannot be conceived as capable of perfection, through another perfection. The Divine *knowledge* is essentially the Divine *substance*. God's being IS God's knowledge.

The Divine knowledge is an *infinite* act, that is to say, the capacity of that knowledge has no limits. If the Divine *knowledge* had limits, it would be finite. Since it is the Divine *essence*, that essence would also and necessarily be finite. The idea of this is absurd.

The Divine knowledge is an *independent* act. God, as a selfexistent being, is an unproduced act, and cannot have in another any reason of His being. The Divine knowledge is, finally, *one* act alone. It cannot consist of several acts, whether these are simultaneous, or whether they are successive. A plurality of simultaneous acts would involve composition in God. A plurality of successive acts would imply some change in God. If there were a plurality of acts, either simultaneous or successive, God's knowledge would not be infinite. The infinite is incapable of multiplication.

God's knowledge cannot be conceived as proceeding from a *faculty* of knowledge. This would again imply composition, and dependence, in God. Not even in idea can there be distinguished in God a faculty of knowledge; as if that faculty were a *potentiality*, with knowledge as an *act* of that potentiality. In God there is nothing of the potential, all is ever actual. A potentiality of knowing is, moreover, distinct from an act of knowledge; and indicates imperfection. A potentiality is, of the nature of it, perfectable. It is perfected by the act which issues from it.

When an act is selfexistent and independent, no possibility is left of conceiving a *faculty* for eliciting it.

Where there is *reasoning*, there is a plurality of acts ; and a knowledge which is begotten by reasoning is a knowledge which is dependent on previous knowledge.

It does not follow that in God there should be no act of *judgment*. Whatever we apprehend through several ideas, God apprehends by *one act* of knowledge; and with this an act of judgment is identified. His one act of judgment both apprehends and judges. It supereminently contains every perfection which is contained in our apprehension, and in our judgment. Divine judgment comes to this that it is—knowledge with certainty.

The Divine knowledge is necessarily comprehension of every object of knowledge. If the object of knowledge is infinite, the Divine knowledge is also infinite. As infinite, it is adequate to the knowledge of an infinite object. If the object is finite, God's knowledge may be said to be more than adequate to the knowing of it, in all its knowableness.

The *formal principle* of knowledge is that which *determinates* the intellect towards knowledge. Since our intellect is indifferent as regards the knowing of this, or the knowing of that knowable object; it requires something by which it shall be determinated towards the knowing of this, or of that object. In God there should be some *reason why* the Divine knowledge should be determinated to the knowing of all the knowable. This reason can be none other than the Divine *essence*. Were there in God any other principle of His knowledge, that principle would be not a substance, but an accident. The existence of accidents is, as we have seen, absolutely impossible in God. The Divine knowledge would, moreover, be dependent on that accidental principle of its determination. God is, therefore, to Himself the sufficient reason why He knows both Himself, and all things outside Himself which are *knowable*, or objects of knowledge. The Divine knowledge cannot be *indifferent* towards knowing; because indifference involves both potentiality and change.

The *terminus* of knowledge is that which is known; and so every *object* of knowledge is a *terminus* of knowledge. An *extrinsic* condition of knowledge is a condition which in no way inflows to the physical act of knowing. It inflows only to the *termination* of the knowledge. It is the reason why the knowledge is terminated at this object, rather than at that object. It does not effect, but presupposes the object which is perceived.

In order that God's knowledge should be *terminated* at this, or at that object, it is required that this or that object should be *knowable*. The knowableness of it, whether in a state of mere possibility, or in a state of actual existence, is the condition of the *termination* of the Divine knowledge. This condition is an extrinsic condition. It cannot be an *intrinsic* condition, because it does not in any way inflow to the physical act of knowledge. It cannot possibly inflow to that act, for that act is God Himself. Hence we see how it is that the Divine knowledge is changeless, as regards all things outside God which are knowable. All change is in the *termination* of the Divine knowledge in the *objects known*. Since God's knowledge is not determinated by the created objects which are known by Him, it cannot receive from them anything by which it should be perfected. His knowledge is of itself determinated to the knowing of all things knowable. That knowledge is necessarily *terminated* by the sum of all things that are *possible*. If a thing the existence of which is possible, should exist, it is known by Him *as existing*. Things which exist, God knows as existing, because they exist. Things which do not exist, God does not know as existing, because they do not exist.

The *necessary* object of the Divine knowledge is that which, by reason of its perfection, the Divine knowledge requires—and this is God Himself. God's knowledge is necessarily a knowledge which is absolutely the most perfect. This it could not be, unless it were knowledge of the most perfect of knowable objects.

In the case of an *intellect*, when there is the *presence* of a knowable object, and a *reason* which determinates the knowledge of it, then that object is necessarily *actually* known. All these there are in God. There is the Divine *intellect*, there is the *presence* of a knowable object—the Divine essence—and there is the *reason* which determinates the knowledge of that essence. This reason is none other than the Divine essence itself. Hence God necessarily knows His own essence, and He knows it with an absolute necessity.

A *principal* object of knowledge is that which is of itself and primarily understood; and by reason of which other things are understood. The Divine *essence*, and it alone, is the *principal* object of God's knowledge. All other things He knows by reason of His own *essence*.

Since God is His own knowledge, He, in understanding Himself, understands His own knowledge of Himself. He understands that He understands. This is a reflex knowledge. God's knowledge of Himself is, therefore, at once a *direct* knowledge, and a *reflex* knowledge. It is not, however, a *double* knowledge. One and the same act is formally direct knowledge, and is formally reflex knowledge. It is direct knowledge, because it knows the object—the being of God. It is reflex knowledge, because this object is—itself knowledge.

Another *necessary*, although *secondary* object of the Divine knowledge, consists of all things which are *possible*. That is possible, which can exist. That which can be, but, nevertheless, does not exist, is called *purely possible;* to distinguish it from that which actually exists, and the future existence of which was of course possible, before it began to exist. The *impossible* is that which cannot be. It neither is, nor can it be. That which is purely possible is not quite the same as *nothing*. It has in it somewhat of *being*, since it is capable of existence. *Nothing* is incapable both of existence, and of possibility of being. It neither was at any time capable of being, nor can it be conceived except as negation of being. *Being* is either real or possible, and since the possible is not quite the same as *nothing*, it is conceived as having some idea of *being* in it. The idea of *being* in the *possible*, consists in this, that it is something which can in itself be conceived. It is somewhat in the order of the intelligible. The *possible* is, therefore, in itself *a terminus of knowledge*, and that not a fictitious, but an objective terminus. Further, the possible has a relation towards actual existence. It is potential existence.

The *extrinsically* possible is that which can be, because the cause of it has power to produce it.

The *intrinsically* possible is that which has in itself the formal idea of its own possibility; although it is not from itself that it has this possibility.

Intrinsic possibility does not depend on actual *existence*. That which now exists either could be, or it could not be. If it could not be, it would not now exist. If it could be, the possibility of it in the past was something, apart from the actual existence of it in the present. Actual existence, is, therefore, not the reason of the possibility of things.

The intrinsically possible does not depend on *human understanding*. The reason why a thing is in itself possible, is not because it is conceived as possible by the human understanding.

The intrinsically possible does not depend on

the *Divine power.* The terminus of the activity of power is the actual existence of a thing; and not the possibility of it. Possibility in itself is not in the order of the real; neither is possibility producible. Possibility is presupposed to action, for that which is made, is that which was possible to be made.

Neither does the intrinsically possible depend on the *Divine will.* If the possible, and the impossible, depended on the Divine will, God could effect that the possible should be impossible, and that the impossible should be possible. This is absurd, as involving contradiction.

The possible is an *essence,* which is capable of existing. Every essence, as an essence, is capable of existence; and to essences alone can existence belong. In order that any thing should be capable of *existence,* all that is required—besides the *cause* of it, if it is something which is producible—is that it should not contain contradiction in the idea of it.

The intrinsic possibility of things is prior to the existence of them, to our knowledge of them, and to exercise of the Divine power, and of the Divine will, with regard to things which are outside God. The *essences* of things do not depend on those, but are supposed by them. The possibility of things is necessary—it is unalterable—and it is eternal.

The Divine power is the adequate reason of *extrinsic* possibility; but it is not the reason of *intrinsic* possibility.

Every thing is possible, only inasmuch as it is in some way an imitation of the essence of infinite being. In infinite being, whatever can be is supereminently contained. It is therein contained as in the pattern of it. The Divine essence cannot possibly be the *formal* pattern of finite essences. It does not *formally* contain those objects which are possible, such as a man, or an animal, or a rock. The Divine essence is, however, the radical or virtual pattern of all the possible, as containing all of them in a supereminent manner. The infinite Divine essence is the ultimate reason of all objects, of every order whatsoever. It is the ultimate reason, not only in the order of *existence*, but also in the order of *essence;* since nothing except God can be self-existent. The Divine essence is presupposed as an object of the Divine knowledge. The Divine *intellect*, comprehending the Divine *essence*, and knowing it to be *imitable* outside itself in manifold ways, necessarily conceives manifold *termini* of this imitability. The Divine intellect thus, as it were, *determinates itself* to conceiving the essences of objects which are *virtually* contained in that infinite essence. As our intellect, from its knowledge of a singular or individual thing, is determinated to the conceiving of the universal, which is virtually contained therein; so also we may, in our manner of understanding, conceive the Divine *intellect* as determinated, by its knowledge of the Divine *essence*, to the conceiving of the *possible*.

The Divine intellect does not see created essences in the Divine essence, as if they were *modes* of that essence. It sees them as they lie outside that essence, although it is IN that essence that they are seen.

God knows all the possible, not confusedly, or generically, but every one of them separately, distinctly and clearly.

It is through this knowledge that all things which are possible are constituted formally in the order of the ideal. Apart from supposition of God's *knowledge* of them, they exist only virtually and fundamentally in the Divine *essence*. They are, therefore, not yet distinct, nor has every one of them its own proper form, nor are they proximately knowable objects. By the Divine *knowledge* they are, as it were, unfolded from the Divine *nature;* every one of them determinated, and distinct with its own notes, and its own proper form. It is thus that they become, in their proper form, an object of the *intellect*. This object is conceived as other than the Divine essence, or as outside that essence.

The Divine knowledge of all things which are possible, as that knowledge is a *terminus* of *reflex* knowledge—or of knowing that it knows—has the character of an *idea*. This idea is one in itself, but is manifold by reason of the different relations which the things that are possible have towards it. They are not all in the same measure, or in the same way, imitations of the Divine essence. An *idea*, or mental model or pattern, is the form of a thing existing in the intellect— a form which the effect imitates or resembles— and that by intention of the agent or maker of it. God is here the agent, and God is intelligent, and to God it is proper to determinate for Himself the end, and the appearance, of the things to be produced by Him. This cannot be done without an *idea* pre-existing in the mind. Hence the *ideas* of created things must be somewhat *in* God Himself; since God cannot work after the pattern of anything outside Himself.

The *extrinsic* possibility of created objects depends on the efficient cause of them; and that is the Divine omnipotence, on which every second cause is dependent.

The multitude of things which are possible is not confined to those things only which at any time exist. All objects are possible, in the constituent notes of which there is not found contradiction. It is clear that besides those things which now are, or which have been, there are many more which do not in themselves, or in the notion of them involve contradiction; such as other bodies, other men, other worlds, and these either more perfect, or less perfect than are those which now actually exist.

The number of the objects which are possible is not *infinite*, for the created cannot, of its nature, be infinite. It is, however, *indefinite*, since it is without end or limit.

God's knowledge embraces, as its *secondary* object, all those things which at any time exist; and that whether they are necessary, or whether they are free.

The *future* is that which will be, as the past is that which was. Things of the future are said to be *future* in their relation to God, not as if they will be after some instant of the Divine existence, but inasmuch as at one time they were not, while God was. The things of the future which are said to be *necessary*, are so called, not because they will necessarily be, but because they are effects of a necessary cause. The things of the future which are called *free* are those which are effects of a free cause.

God from eternity knew all future things.

The formal principle of God's knowledge is His Divine *essence*. That exhibits to the Divine *intellect* all things which are *knowable;* and, since that intellect is changeless, whatever it knows it ought eternally to know. As our knowledge is measured by the present in which it is elicited, so is God's knowledge measured by the eternity which is one simultaneous whole, without beginning and without end.

God has, therefore, from eternity that same knowledge of things, which He has when those things are in the present of time. Again, God's knowledge is of itself determinated to the knowing of whatsoever is *true*, and from eternity it was true that this or that thing was to be.

There is no interference of God's foreknowledge with created freedom. Although God knows from eternity all acts of created will, yet the freedom of that will, and of those acts, remains in its entirety. God's knowledge stands to our acts, as our knowledge stands to objects which are present to us. His knowledge, therefore, is not antecedent but consequent. We see things because they are. They do not exist because we see them. God knows our acts of the future, because they will be. It is not because He knows them, that they will be. They are *future* as regards passing time, but they are *present* to the Divine eternity. It is true that an event must happen which God foresees as at some time to happen; but this is not as if God's knowledge laid necessity on that event, but because God, who is infallible, saw with certainty what would occur by free determination of a created will. That must happen which God's knowledge foresees as happening; but the necessity of its happening is not *antecedent*, in the Divine sight, but *consequent* to the free determination of the created will.

Conditionated events of the future are those which will occur, given certain adjuncts. Those adjuncts are the *circumstances* of the thing or action—who?—what?—where?—with what aids?—why?—how?—and when? Under the circumstance *with what aids*, is to be included the Divine co-operation or concurrence in order to the doing of the action as a physical act. This is a condition which is always required, and which is, therefore, always supposed, in every act of every creature. It is as necessary as is creation itself.

Without these circumstances no act is done; and they are circumstances which belong to the *action itself*, as it is in the future. These circumstances can contribute more or less to the action, as an *occasion* of it, or even as a *moral cause* which allures the will to act. This connection is, however, always *contingent*. The opposite of that which happens, could have happened.

Between the circumstances and the act, or the absence of the act, there is, as matter of fact, a bond of co-existence. This bond is the simple fact of the co-existence of the act—or the absence of the act—with certain circumstances. This co-existence depends causally on the free will itself. That there always is this bond, is clear from this that, given certain determinate adjuncts or circumstances, it is impossible that the will should neither act, nor abstain from acting, or at once act and not act. Either action, therefore, or non-action, will co-exist with those circumstances.

That God infallibly knows *conditionated* free acts of the future, is evident from the infinite perfection of His knowledge, wherewith He knows all the *knowable*. The will, constituted in certain adjuncts, will either act or not act, and either fact is determinately *true*. It is objectively true, with a truth which is unknown to us, but which is not unknown to that intellect which is of itself determinated to the knowing of everything which is in any way objectively true. Of God's knowledge of the future, and of *conditionated* events of the future, men are themselves convinced. They are in the habit of praying to God to place them in those adjuncts in which He sees that they will act as they ought. They beg God also to bestow upon them the goods of this world, if He sees that those goods will be for their welfare, and to withhold those goods if He sees that they will be for harm. They thus give testimony to the truth that God knows what men will do under various circumstances.

The will, considered as it is a *power*, remains always indifferent towards acting or not acting; and so it is not from the will alone that it can with certainty be known what it will determinately do. Moreover, there is no necessary bond of inference from the circumstances of the act. It can only with probability, therefore, and not with certainty be known, looking to the inclinations of the will, what it will do.

The *being* of those events of the future is objective. It is not imagined, but is supposed by him who knows. It is real, with the reality not indeed of an existence that *is*, but of an existence which *will be*. This reality which will be, or this act which will be—for whether the will wills, or does not will, there is an act of will—is not entirely *nothing*. It is something which is more determinate than possible, and even the possible is not entirely *nothing*. That is most certainly something knowable, which consists in a determinate truth; and whatever is *knowable* is *known* to the Divine intellect.

When those *conditionated* events or acts of the future become *absolute*, God's knowledge of them is not posterior to His knowledge of them as possible; since the Divine knowledge of everything is eternal. God's knowledge is also a most simple act, and it is a changeless act of knowledge. God does not then see anything new, for He saw all from eternity. He sees something which is *better* than something else; but He does not *better see* the one than He sees the other.

The knowledge which may be called the cause of *absolute* acts of the future, is that which directs the Divine *will* in making the Divine decree, that free created wills shall exist, and shall exist in certain adjuncts, in order that a certain end intended by God should be obtained. For this decree there is required that knowledge which exhibits possible wills, and what these will do in all possible adjuncts whatsoever—and do of themselves; not as determinated by God, but as determining themselves.

Given the divine decree, that becomes an *absolute* fact of the future which was, in our idea, previously known as *conditioned*. It will absolutely be; and the will of the created agent will freely determinate itself. God has knowledge of that will, as a will which is to be *actually* determinated. This is the knowledge wherewith God from eternity sees *absolute* acts of the future. He sees them because they are to be; although of course, they would not be, unless He had some preceding knowledge of them.

It follows that God's knowledge may, by reason not of itself but of its object, be distinguished into His absolutely necessary knowledge, and His hypothetically necessary knowledge— and into His knowledge of simple understanding —His knowledge of vision—and His mediate knowledge. His knowledge of His own Divine *essence*, and of created *essences*, that is, of all things which are intrinsically possible, is *absolutely necessary* knowledge. His knowledge of things which are *contingent*, is necessary only on the hypothesis that they will actually exist.

God's knowledge of the *purely possible* is rightly called His knowledge *of simple understanding*. Understanding is wont to prescind from the existence of the object which it contemplates.

God's knowledge of Himself, and of *absolute* events of the future, is called his knowledge *of vision*. It is knowledge as of a real object which is present. God's knowledge of *conditionated* events of the future, as standing midway between the two, is called *mediate* knowledge. Those things which under hypothesis will be, are intermediate between the purely possible, and the actually existing.

That which is true of God's knowledge is true also of God's volition. The *necessary* object, which is also the *principal* object of God's will, is God Himself, as He is infinite good. The *secondary* object of His will consists of finite good.

God's will, by reason of the *terminus* of it, and of the *mode* in which it is borne towards that terminus, may be distinguished into His absolute will, and His conditionated will—His antecedent will, and His consequent will—His prescribing will, and His effecting will—His will which only prescribes, and His will which at once prescribes, and sanctions His law—and finally, His efficacious will, and His inefficacious will.

God's *absolute* will is His will of a thing which He wills, without reference to any condition which is extrinsic to it. Such is His will of the existence of the world, the constancy of the physical order, His obtaining His own glory, and the like. God's *conditionated* will is His will of a thing which He wills under a condition, to be fulfilled by His free creature. Such is His will to bestow on man eternal glory, on condition that man meantime keeps His law.

God's *antecedent* will is a will, the whole reason

of which is the Divine goodness or bounty, as antecedent in idea to His knowledge *of vision*. Such is His will of creation, and His will of man's destination to eternal blessedness.

God's *consequent* will is a will, of which the adequate reason includes, as an element of it, a free act on the part of His intelligent creature. This will is therefore subsequent in idea to His knowledge *of vision*; which is His knowledge of that which actually exists. Such is His will to punish the wicked, and to reward the good. His will is, in this case, consequent on His vision of the free and actual wickedness of the one, and the free and actual goodness of the other.

God's *prescribing* will is His will as *Lawgiver*. This will decrees what free created causes ought to do, and what they ought to refrain from doing. To this will the natural law, and positive Divine laws, belong.

God's *efficient* will is His will, as He is the First Cause, in producing an effect; whether by Himself alone, or through second causes.

A will which *prescribes only* is the will wherewith God wills a law, laid down by Him, to be observed.

A will which at once *prescribes* and *sanctions*, is the will wherewith God wills observance of His law, and at the same time decrees reward to those who keep it, and punishment to those who transgress it. This is God's *adequate* will as Lawgiver. From this will no man has power to withdraw himself. If a man withdraws himself from the will which prescribes, he falls under the will which sanctions by threatening and inflicting punishment. This *adequate* will of the Divine Lawgiver is always fulfilled.

Looking to the bond of consequence, between God's will and the object willed by Him, His *efficacious* will is the will which attains to the *terminus* of it; whether by itself alone, or through the free co-operation of a created will.

An *inefficacious* will is a will which does not obtain the *terminus* to which it is borne; and this by reason of absence of a requisite condition.

These distinctions, in our idea, of the Divine will, are derived from the diversity of the *objects* of God's will.

It is not unworthy of God that, in regard of some objects, His will should be conditionated and inefficacious. It is certain that not all of those things which God truly wills are, as matter of fact, done; such as observance of the natural law in countless cases. It is certain also that God's will to reward those who do well, supposes fulfilment of a condition, the determination of which ultimately depends on a created will.

Further, it is not unworthy of God to will

something *under condition*, for [in this there is no dependence of the Divine will on the condition. The dependence on the condition is that of the object willed. God wills that object to be dependent on some thing, as on a condition of it. God wills objects, in that way in which He intends those objects; and so with that dependence which they have on a condition.

Finally, it is not unworthy of God, that His will should sometimes be *inefficacious*. The inefficacy is not from lack of power in Him, but from failure of the condition under which alone He *intends* the object. If that condition is absent, there will be a real absence of the *object* of His will. It would indeed be unworthy of God if His *absolute* will were ever inefficacious; but this it never is, and this it cannot be.

God's inefficacious will, moreover, when it is His will as lawgiver, is inefficacious in part only. It comes to this, that either the free created will shall observe His law, or will be punished for transgression of His law. One or other of these the Divine will always obtains, and so it is always efficacious.

When it is said, therefore, that the will of God is always fulfilled, this is to be understood of His absolute will, and of His will as lawgiver, when He both prescribes, and punishes transgressions of His law.

CHAPTER VII.

God's sincere will of man's salvation.

THE Divine Will cannot be conceived as a *power* which elicits diverse acts, since it is one simple act. It is itself the Divine essence, regarded under the idea of *volition*. This volition has for its principal and necessary object, infinite and essential good. Towards other good objects, and in order that those objects should be, it is freely determined, without any change in itself.

The same infinite volition is, in a supereminent way, equivalent to many acts; inasmuch as it, in its oneness, is *terminated* to many diverse objects, towards which a finite will could not possibly be borne, except by distinct and diverse acts.

While in the Divine volition all *real* distinction must be denied as impossible, we must, in our inadequate mode of conception, make use of *virtual* distinctions with regard to that volition.

A distinction which is common among the Fathers, is that between God's *antecedent* will and God's *consequent* will. Antecedent and consequent are relative terms. A thing is understood to be *antecedent*, in its relation to another thing which is posterior to it; and to be *conse-*

quent, in its relation to another thing which is prior to it—either in reality or in idea.

The question therefore is—What is the *terminus*, with relation to which God's Will may be said to be *antecedent*, and to be *consequent*? On the answer to this question depends, as from a principle and foundation, a right understanding of nearly the whole of the true doctrine with regard to God's will of man's salvation, and God's predestination of man to eternal glory. God's will of man's salvation is *antecedent*, as in idea preceding, and not yet supposing, God's prevision of the free acts of His intelligent creature. God's *consequent* will is that which in idea follows on prevision of those free acts, and supposes them.

God's *antecedent* will is that which God, of Himself, and of His own innate goodness, conceives. His *consequent* will is that which He conceives provoked, as it were, by free acts of ours.

By *antecedent* will God, Whose nature is goodness, wills communication of His own goodness, although in different degrees of it; and does not will anything which is not in every way good for His rational creature, who has been created to His own image.

By *consequent* will God, supposing evil acts of His creature, wills some things which are good in themselves; but which are to the sinful creature evils, as being privations of great goods.

On prevision, therefore, of *good* acts of His free creature, God by *consequent* will, wills goods which He also wills by *antecedent* will. On prevision of *evil* acts of His free creature, God sometimes wills things which are not good, except as *consequent* to those evil acts; and those things God does not will by *antecedent* will.

God's will of man's salvation includes will to place within men's reach—at least antecedently to hindrances which have been interposed, either freely by man, or otherwise, but not directly by God—all those aids without which salvation cannot be obtained; and which are of themselves sufficient in order that man, if he rightly uses them, should be able to attain to his salvation, and should in fact secure it. That God has, of His antecedent will, prepared all these aids for men, so that men by means of them should be saved, is asserted when we say that there is in God a *sincere* antecedent will of man's salvation. There cannot be in God a will which is not sincere.

The reason why God wills all men to be saved is, as St. Paul argues in his Epistle to the Romans, because He is the God of all men. No one is excepted, unless there should exist a man of whom God is not the God. The apostle further argues, that for a man to be comprehended under the mediation of Christ, and consequently under God's will of man's salvation, it is sufficient that he should have specifically the same human nature which Christ has; and that he should be of that human race from which Christ assumed His human nature.

The will with which God wills all men to be saved, is not *mere complacence* in the goodness of the object, as God has complacence in every even possible good. It is a will that the salvation of all men should exist as a fact, although not absolutely, but under a condition of dependence on the co-operation of men. This will is, on the part of God, an *active* and *operative* will. From God's universal will of man's salvation proceeded the economy of Christ, and His universal redemption. " He gave Himself a redemption for all." As St. Augustine says, sufficient grace is within the reach of all men, whereby they may be saved, unless they are their own enemies.

2.

God's antecedent will, by which He wills all men to be saved, extends not only to adults, who are capable of actual grace and free action, but also to infants.

The question here is—what is the *terminus* with relation to which, God's will of the salvation of all infants is called *antecedent ?*

It must be a terminus whereby an *antecedent,*

conditionated, and universal will is distinguished from a *consequent, absolute, and particular* will of the salvation of those only who, as matter of fact, are saved.

Speaking generally, the *terminus*, in the case both of infants and of adults, is the same; namely, the final state of grace, or the final state of sin, in which death finds them. If, however, we look to the *mode* by which it is that a man perseveres in grace, and whereby the antecedent will of God, so far as is in it, wills the justification, the perseverance in grace, and the salvation of all, there is a great difference between the two cases, of infants and of adults. There cannot be justification, and active perseverance in justice, in adults without their free co-operation with the aid of grace; failure in perseverance, on the other hand, and a final state of sin, is due to their free sins of commission and omission. These God does not *will*, but only *permits*. Hence God cannot be understood as, by antecedent will, and so far as concerns Him, willing the salvation of all; unless He offers to all the possibility of justification, of perseverance, and of salvation, by granting to them the necessary graces without which there is no possibility of salvation. As regards adults, therefore, the *terminus*, regarded in its entirety, with relation to which God's universal will of man's salvation is said to be antecedent, includes also prevision, and so foreknowledge, of the good use of free will through grace—or foreknowledge of the bad use of the same free will, notwithstanding the graces which have been offered. It is far otherwise in the case of infants.

With the justification and perseverance in grace of infants, their free will has not, and cannot have, anything to do. Infants are incapable of an exercise of will, as they are incapable of an exercise of reason. The means whereby their justification is effected is—if we except the privilege of martyrdom—baptism, which is bestowed without any free co-operation on their part. Their perseverance in grace is merely passive. It consists in the grace of death after reception of the sacrament of baptism. This death, in itself and ontologically, is natural, as *death in the state of grace*. It, nevertheless, includes grace which is *intrinsically* supernatural. The death is also of itself an *extrinsically* supernatural benefit, as ordained towards the securing of a supernatural end.

Hence, as in the case of adults, where there cannot be antecedent will of their salvation, unless there is at the same time antecedent will of the graces and means, without which salvation is impossible; so also in the case of infants, there cannot be an antecedent will of their salvation unless there is at the same time an antecedent will that the merits of Christ should be applied to them through Baptism.

In the same way, therefore, is the will of the salvation of all infants *antecedent* and *conditionated*, as the will that the merits of Christ should be applied to all infants by means of baptism is *antecedent* and *conditionated*. It is certain that God does not will the application of baptism, in the case of all infants, by antecedent *absolute* will, and in all the amplitude of His omnipotence. It is also certain that He does not will the baptism of all infants, by *consequent* will, since what He should so will would undoubtedly be done; and that all infants are not actually baptised is manifest. It is equally manifest that by *absolute* will—whether antecedent or consequent—God does not will the salvation of all infants.

If, therefore, God wills the application of baptism to all infants only under some condition, *prevision* of the verification, or of the frustration of this *condition*, will be the *terminus* with relation to which His will of the application of baptism is divided into *antecedent* will, and *consequent* will. The condition is contained in the actions of those second causes which are required for, or which hinder, the bestowal of baptism. These actions are, in the first place, those which, either immediately or mediately, depend on the free wills of other men; or which, secondly, are effects which naturally flow from physical causes in the present order. The present order was introduced by original sin, and has been constituted by God for various most wise ends. The *condition*, therefore, is in this wise—God wills the application to all infants of the merits of Christ through baptism, *in so far as second causes*, moral and physical, *do not hinder* the baptism of them. The effects of these second causes, so far as they hinder application of baptism, God does not directly *will*, but only *permits*. God's will of the salvation of infants, therefore, in the case of infants who die without baptism, is a will which is *antecedent* to prevision of hindrances. *Consequently* on prevision of those hindrances, God does not *will to change* the natural order. He, therefore, *permits* the death without baptism which follows from the laws of nature. On prevision of death in original sin, God, by *consequent* will, does not will the salvation of those infants.

The order of thought is as follows. Consequent on prevision of original sin, and the infection of the whole human race therewith, through the free transgression of Adam, its progenitor and head, God in His mercy wills the restoration of the whole human race. To this end He destines from eternity, and promises, and sends in the fulness of time, His Incarnate Son, with a nature assumed from the same human race. He wills that this Incarnate Son, who is the Christ, should exhibit full satisfaction for all sins. This satisfaction, as foreseen, He accepts. At the appointed time, the Christ actually offers it for all human sins. "God sent His Son that the world should be saved by Him." "He is a propitiation for the sins of the whole world." In the restored human race all are comprehended—even those who die in infancy, before use of reason. In the will of redemption, all those infants, therefore, are comprehended. In the Divine will which accepts the satisfaction, and in the human will of Christ which offers satisfaction for all human sins, there is also an acceptance and offering of satisfaction for the original sin wherewith all those infants are infected. Hence, in view and in virtue of the merits and bloodshedding of Christ, God institutes for all those infants a sacrament, by means of which there might be applied to every one of them the merits and satisfaction of Christ. All these provisions have, of their nature, been ordained by God for the salvation of infants.

A will of salvation, which is such as this is, is no mere *complacence* in the goodness of the object regarded by itself; and, in this case, complacence in the goodness of salvation. It is, on the part of God, an active and operative *will* of the salvation of infants. To all and every one of them this will of redemption is related.

God wills to effect application of the sacrament of baptism, not by Himself immediately, but by means of second causes; and through these second causes not to all infants by *absolute* will, but to all infants in so far as second causes, disposed in accordance with His universal and ordinary providence, do not hinder it.

Among these second causes are, in the first place, the free wills of human beings, on which application of the sacrament, in the case at least of very many infants, is dependent. These human wills God anticipates, excites, and inclines by His precepts, counsels, and aids, both of the natural order, and of the supernatural order. He thus provides that through the diligence and solicitude of those concerned—through their obedience and co-operation with grace received —through congruous merits and good works— through the alms-deeds and the prayer especially of the parents, and of those to whose guardianship the little ones have been confided—and through the apostolic labours of His ministers— the infants should be brought to the grace of baptism. As in the natural order, so also in the supernatural order of sanctification and eternal salvation, God wills to provide for infants through other human beings, and in accordance with the demand of the general laws of His Divine providence.

In this way the Divine will of salvation acts on the wills of men, to procure the salvation of at least many infants who, nevertheless, by fault of men, are not saved. With regard to these infants the antecedent will of God is an *active* will, that they should be saved; although it is not *absolute*, but *under condition* that men, on their part, should second the Divine will, as they can and ought to do—and although, consequently on contrary action on the part of men, God permits death in original sin, and on prevision of this does not will, with a *consequent* will, the salvation of those infants.

Besides the wills of human beings, which are in the *moral* order, and are free; there are also second causes of the *physical* order, and these are not free. These causes contribute, in accordance with the common and ordinary laws of providence, to render bestowal of baptism either possible or impossible. The course of these causes, and the universal laws by which they are governed, God, consequently to original sin, wills to remain such as they now are. God has not restored the preternatural state of immortality, even after the redemption of the human race by Christ had been decreed and effected. Hence, in accordance with the ordinary course of those natural laws, there follows the death of many infants before use of reason; and this sometimes independently of all exercise of will, and free action, of human beings.

With this natural course of events there is thoroughly consistent an *antecedent conditional* will in God, of the salvation of all those infants. The *condition* under which He wills the application to them of baptism is—*so far as the general order*, which has been wisely and justly instituted, *permits*.

If God had willed this order of physical causes of itself to the end that infants should die in original sin, He certainly could not be said to will the salvation of those infants. God has not, however, instituted that order to this end, nor does He so direct it by His will. He wills it for other ends, and those most wise ends.

Hence, God does not *directly intend* the consequent death of infants in sin. He only *permits* it, inasmuch as He does not will to hinder, for all infants, the natural demands of physical laws, by a change of the general order, or through continual miracles.

Such a *permission* proves only, that there is not in God an *absolute* will of the salvation of those infants. It in no way proves that there is not in God a *conditioned* will of the salvation of all of them.

In short, God wills the salvation of all infants

who die in original sin, by an *antecedent* will, in accordance with His *common providence*; but He does not will to provide for the salvation of all of these by a *special providence*. In His common providence God predefines for everything a certain end—He conceives and prepares sufficient means in order to the obtaining of that end—He leaves everything to use those means, in accordance with the demand of its nature; that is to say, He leaves natural and necessary causes to act naturally and necessarily—contingent causes to act contingently—and free causes to act freely.

3.

Predestination, in the generic meaning of the word, includes every counsel of God, whereby from eternity He disposes and wills the existence of any one of His works. A Divine counsel is a *destination* in the Divine mind; and since, both in the order of duration, and as a cause, the counsel precedes from eternity the work in time, this destination is called PREdestination.

In the common meaning of the word, which is a more restricted meaning, *predestination* is God's disposition of His works, in order to the eternal salvation of His rational creatures.

God's decree of punishment and damnation, consequent on His prevision of the final impenitence of His free creatures, is called *reprobation;*

and the term *predestination* is reserved for God's disposition of those of His works which conduce to eternal life, and also for eternal life itself.

Among these works are some which, by themselves and ontologically, are natural; and are gifts of only *external* grace, which are presupposed to supernatural gifts. Among these external graces are creation itself, time of birth and place of birth, condition of parents, good natural disposition, and the like. Hence *predestination* is again commonly restricted to those goods alone which are *intrinsically* supernatural, and directly ordained to eternal salvation.

Further, the graces to which *predestination* refers, may be considered either as, in the first place, they are *prevenient*, prescinding from the effect for which they are given, whether it is obtained, or whether it is not obtained, through fault of man—or, secondly, as those graces are conjoined with the effect of them, that is to say, obtain the result for which they were given.

In the first of those two senses, all graces may be said to be *predestined*, since all graces are gifts of God, and have been destined from eternity. Since, however, the graces which are not conjoined with their effect—although by the antecedent will of God they are ordained towards salvation—do not, through the fault of man, in reality conduce to salvation; we use the term *predestination* with reference to that grace only which obtains its effect, and with reference to those goods only which are bestowed through that grace. This restriction of the meaning of the word, is also prompted by the scriptural distinction of the *called* and the *chosen*.

As is every external Divine operation, so also is predestination by God—the Divine intellect and will, with connotation of certain *effects* in the creature. If, therefore, it is asked, *Is there*, and *what is* the meritorious cause of predestination? the question has in view those effects.

In this that one merits a predestined effect, he merits that God should *will* that effect. Christ, in meriting for us grace, merited that God should *will* to bestow on us grace. The foreseen merit of Christ is the meritorious cause, that God from eternity should *will* the grace for us which He bestows in time; and so that God should *predestine* this grace for us.

Those gifts which God bestows in time, without any preceding merits of ours, He also prepared from eternity, as to be bestowed in this way, that is to say, without prevision of any merits. If any one were to deny that grace, taking it universally, as the *whole* of the grace which God has bestowed, or as the *first* grace which God grants to any one, was predestined by God *gratuitously*, and without prevision of any merits of ours, he would thereby be asserting that grace is rendered to human merit, and so is not *grace*, but is *reward*.

We not only say that from gratuitous *bestowal* is necessarily inferred gratuitous *preparation* from eternity; but, in inverse order, we also affirm that from gratuitous *preparation* we rightly arrive, by way of conclusion, at gratuitous *bestowal* in time —and so that all the benefits which are bestowed in time on antecedent merits, were predestined from eternity on prevision of those merits—and so that God does not *bestow* His gifts in time, whether from merits, or wholly gratuitously, in an order which is other than that order in which He *predestined* them from eternity.

The predestination of all gifts, and the bestowal of them, do not differ otherwise than does one act of the Divine will, regarded in its eternity with connotation of a future work of grace; and the same act, with connotation of the same work of grace, which is done in the present of to-day. The same work, which was subject to the Divine will from eternity, is not in another order when it is effected, and begins to exist. Preparation and execution are not in inverse order. The order is the same. The predestination and the bestowal of grace do not differ, except by connotation of the *future* and of the *present*, in one and the same effect. Where the bestowal of grace does not produce its effect in the present, unless for *merit;* God in predestination does not will the same effect, unless from *prevision* of merit. The predestination and the bestowal are one effective will, related to one and the same effect. The distinction is only as regards the *time* at which the effect exists, and not as regards the *mode* and *order* in which God wills the effect.

Predestination is wholly gratuitous, as regards the *first* grace that is bestowed, and through it the idea of gratuitousness extends to the *whole series* of graces; inasmuch as every subsequent merit has its foundation in that first grace.

With that *first* supernatural grace, a man can by congruous merit impetrate other and more abundant graces, which would not be granted but for that antecedent impetration. Those graces, therefore, were not predestined except on *prevision* of the merit of that impetration.

When, therefore, it is said that predestination to grace is *gratuitous*, this is to be understood in the same way in which the bestowal of grace is gratuitous. Grace is not predestined from prevision of any merit of *nature*; and so predestination of the *first* grace is antecedent to all merit whatsoever. Manifold graces can, on the other hand, be predestined, and are predestined from prevision of *supernatural* merits. Justification is never predestined for adults, unless on supposition and prevision of congruous supernatural dispositions.

It is possible for men to impetrate for other men manifold graces; and so to contribute towards obtaining those graces, as instruments of God, and fellow workers with God. The graces which are given to a man in view of the impetration or co-operation of others, are predestinated also in the same way, in view of the impetration or co-operation.

From man's freedom either to receive grace in vain, or to receive it not in vain, it follows that it was in the free power of a man who resisted the grace which he had received, to have cooperated with that grace, and so to have received farther graces—and by a good use of these to have arrived at justification—and through grace to have persevered to the end in justice; and so he would have been *predestinated*.

It also follows that he who actually persevered to the end had it in his power, by resisting grace through badness of will, not to persevere. If he had done so, he would not have been *predestinated*.

But from this it does not follow, that the effect of predestination is in the power of man's free will as *naked*, or destitute of grace, and left to its own *natural* forces; nor is it in any way in the power of a man to *begin* the way of salvation. Grace necessarily precedes every *beginning*, and itself bestows the *power of entering on* the way of salvation.

Hence the first effect of predestination is not on the part of the man predestinated. The *first* effect predestinated is not the *consent* of the free will under grace; but is the prevenient *grace* under which the future consent is foreseen. It is not the *co-operation* which has the idea of merit, but the *grace* of which the co-operation is the *fruit*.

The reason and cause, on the other hand, why the *first* grace, granted and resisted, does not belong to the order of *predestination*; but only to *common providence*, is in the free will of the man who resists, and rejects that grace.

From all that we have said, there follows doctrine which is most certain, and is of supreme moment, not only for theoretical theology, but also, and much more, for practical spiritual life. In the order of execution, it is in our power freely, through wickedness of will, to fail from the good will of God; and so sins are our own. It is not in our power to will, or to do, any thing that is saving, except by means of grace offered and given to us in our unworthiness; by the mercy of God who operates in us that we should freely both will, and do, good in the way of salvation.

As these principles are certain, and without question amongst Catholics, as regards the order of execution; so also is it certain, in the order of predestination, that if a man is not predestinated, and therefore is *reprobate*, it is the fault of that man. That a man should be predestinated, whether to a saving work, or to the whole series of gifts in its completeness, up to the result of them in eternal life, is a grace of God. He, apart from any preceding merits, and with preceding demerits on that man's part, predestines in His foreknowledge both the *first* grace—and subsequent graces, which He foresees will be conjoined with their effect in the man's free co-operation— and in those graces, the great gift of perseverance, and eternal life itself, as "grace for grace."

The predestination of God is, therefore, to all men a cause of their standing, and to no man is it a cause of his falling.

If, in defence of free will, the grace of God should seem to any one to be denied; or if, when the grace of God is brought into prominence, the freedom of the will should seem to be undermined, it must be borne in mind that, as in the order of *execution* all saving good, and no evil, is to be referred to the grace of God—but not in such wise that either the antecedent will of God to give to all men the grace which is truly sufficient, or the freedom of man's will, should be interfered with; so, in exactly the same way, in the order of *predestination*, all saving good, and no evil, must be referred to the predestination of God—but not in such wise as that either the antecendent will of God to save all men, or the freedom of man to attain to salvation through the grace of God, should be denied or interfered with. The one truth cannot lawfully be defended in such a way that the other truth should be denied, or called in question.

CHAPTER VIII.

God, the one Creator.

CREATION, if we take the word in its active sense, is an *effecting* or *producing*; since by creation something is *made*.

Within the genus of *effecting*, there is more than one species of effecting. One species of effecting is the production of an effect from something which is already in existence. This production might take place in two ways. The agent might be giving to matter new *modes* of existence, and a new *form*. His action in doing so might either, retaining the generic name, be called *effecting*; or, in accordance with differences in the character of the effects, it might be called *fashioning, moulding, fabricating*, or the like.

Again, a living agent might so modify matter which was existing in himself, and which was part and parcel of himself, as to produce something which should be similar to himself in *species*. This kind of production has its own proper name of *generation*.

There is another species of production, or it is possible to conceive another species of production, which is—the production of an effect from nothingness. This we call *creation.*

Creation may be defined to be—the production of a thing from nothing of all those things which belong to the constitution of that thing. When something is already in existence, of which a thing is made, then the making of it is not creation. That thing is not made of nothing, but of a pre-existing something.

That which belongs to the constitution of a thing, and from which, as already existing, the thing is made, is the *subject* of the effect which is brought about in it. If that from which a thing is made is not already in existence, then the operation which effects that thing, has *no subject.* It does not suppose anything *in* which it operates, or *of which* the thing is made.

Hence another definition—Creation is production of a thing from nothing of its subject. This definition comes to the same thing as the one we have already given. We may add a third—Creation is bringing from *not being* to *being.*

Since that which already is, is not being made, but that is being made which was not; so the *nothingness*, or the *not being*, of the thing which is being made, is presupposed to the effecting of it. This is what is called the *nothingness of itself*, as distinguished from the *nothingness of its subject.*

A *substance* has no *subject* in which it is; nor

has it any *material cause* of which it might be made. That production therefore, of which the terminus is a *substance*, is production from nothing of all those things which belong to the constitution of a thing—and it is a bringing from the *not being* of the thing, to the *being* of it.

Hence St. Thomas defines creation as—the production of a thing in the whole of the *substance* of it, with nothing presupposed. The last three words are merely declarative. The sense of them is contained in the words which precede them.

The *formal object* of creation is *being*. The formal object of any *effecting* is that to the producing of which, the effecting is of itself ordained. This is, therefore, the reason also why one *effecting* is discriminated from other effectings, and is called by its own proper name. Creation makes that to be, which was not. Hence, another definition—Creation is the production of *being*, as *being*.

Creation is not conversion of nothingness into reality. By creation, the nothingness of the thing ceasing, the thing is made. Creation is not a passing from *essence*, or pure possibility, to *existence*. It is a passing from negation of existence to existence. It is, therefore, a bringing from *not being* to *being*.

To be created is proper to *substance*. This is

so, both because, if substance is to be made, it can be made only by creation; and because other things, even if they are made at the same time, and along with substance, are nevertheless made of that substance, because it is through the reality of the substance that they consist.

2.

God's *dominion* is a dominion not only of jurisdiction, but of *ownership*, through right of property. God is the Lord or Master of all things, because God has made all things. Universal and independent dominion of ownership necessarily supposes God's *creation* of all those things of which God is Lord.

If God had not *created* all things, but had only *formed* them, He would not be Lord of all that is in them. In all that is in them there would certainly have been contained the matter or substance, of which the natures of the things were made. That would not be subject to God's dominion of ownership, because the title to *dominion* is *production*. If matter or substance were *not made*, and were, therefore, *selfexistent*, they would not be subject to the dominion of *any one*.

Again, God would not be *independent*, as regards the natures which He had made, in the sense that nothing could resist Him. In those natures the substance, whereby the natures consist, would be *unproduced;* since substance cannot be *made,* except out of nothing. The whole reality of substance would, therefore, be independent of God. A thing, the whole substantial reality of which is independent of the agent, necessarily puts limits to the power of the agent. He cannot do whatsoever he wills with it; but that only of which there is a potentiality in the substance. Even if the agent had power to alter the dispositions of the subject, yet if the subject were, of its own nature, master of its own acts, and so of its own dispositions; there would necessarily be conflict between that subject and the agent, and there would not be any sufficient reason why the agent should prevail. There is, therefore, contradiction between the two propositions—God has dominion of ownership of all things that are; and—all the reality of the substance of all things was not *made,* and is independent of God.

If matter was not made, but was selfexistent, God was destitute of the power to impose on it a particular order; and is powerless to preserve that order. God would not be Maker and Master. The proposition—God is Lord of all things, because He made them—would be false, in all the parts of it. When, therefore, it is simply asserted that God is Lord and Maker of all things, it is implicitly asserted that God is *Creator* of all things.

3.

The ancient pagan philosophers, who were destitute of the light of revelation, were either ignorant of, or they denied, the production of things from nothing. Their ignorance or denial was, however, a departure from right reason. The function of faith is not, in this matter, to supply the principles of demonstration. It is only to direct the mind, so that the mind, more accurately reflecting on its own native principles, and making a more full analysis of them, can arrive at the knowledge contained within those principles. All the elements of the demonstration are derived from reason; and they do not exceed the natural force of reason, as is manifest from the arguments themselves.

Every being is either *being* which subsists *of itself*, and is therefore the whole plenitude of being, and is infinite being; as it is *participated* being, that is, it has *in part* the perfection of *being*, and is finite. Being which is self-subsistent is *one*, while other beings have their being from it, or must be produced by it, in order that they may be.

Every finite can BE, and can NOT BE, and so every finite is *contingent*. The infinite alone is *necessary*. The contingent has not in itself, but in another, the reason of its own existence. Every finite being can exist, only as produced by another being. This other being, which is the reason of existence to all contingent beings, is *necessary* Being—which is necessarily *one*—and is God.

Either Creation, or Pantheism, or Dualism, or Atheism must be admitted. Either there is no necessary and infinite being—and we have Atheism; or, if this being exists, it is either really identical with us, and with the world, or it is distinct from other things. If identical, we have Pantheism. If distinct, either the things distinct from it, are from themselves, or they are from it. If they are from themselves, we have Dualism. It matters not whether there are one or many subjects which, outside God, are from themselves. If they are from the infinite and necessary Being, then again they are from that Being, either by an *immanent emanation*, or by an *effecting*. If by immanent emanation, then the distinctness, which was supposed, is in reality removed, and we return to Pantheism. If they are from the infinite and necessary Being, by an *effecting*, either the infinite Being is the adequate reason of the whole of their reality, or something real is supposed from which that Being produces them. If the latter, we have Dualism again. If the former, we have—Creation.

The demonstration of Creation is in reality a completing of the demonstration of the existence of God. There is no God, unless God is a Being, who is distinct from all other beings, and is infinite. This He cannot be unless, through Creation, other beings are distinct from Him. Creation is therefore a fact as certain as is the existence of God. To be *created* is proper to every substance, except God alone. It is of the intrinsic idea of it, as it is a finite and contingent substance.

4.

The creative act is an act which is formally immanent, but virtually transient. The *formally immanent* is that which, in the whole of its reality, remains in the same subject from which it proceeds, and perfects that subject. Such are acts of feeling, of understanding, and of willing. By these acts a created agent modifies and perfects himself. In this operation *life* consists. The formally immanent may also be defined as an operation of activity, the intrinsic *terminus* of which, whereby the exercise of it is constituted and completed, remains, throughout the whole of it, in the agent.

A *formally transient* operation is an operation

which is not—at least as regards the whole of it—in the agent, or in the subject who is acting; but which is completed outside the agent. It is an operation of activity, of which the intrinsic *terminus* whereby the exercise of it is constituted and completed, is in part at least *outside* the agent.

On analysis of a formally transient action, which is essentially distinct from immanent action, two things are manifest. First, outside the agent something is done, and this of the very essence of transient action. Secondly, transient action supposes some subject outside the agent, in which something is done by the agent. This subject is —in nature at least—prior to the operation of the agent. If no subject, outside the agent, is presupposed to the action of the agent, that action will not have place, and will not be completed, except in the agent himself. Such action is formally *immanent*. A formally transient action, therefore, presupposes some subject outside the agent, in which his action is received.

An act which is *formally immanent* and *virtually transient* is an act which, in the whole of its reality, remains in the agent; or the *intrinsic terminus* of which is in the agent, but is, however, of so great an efficacy that the *extrinsic terminus* follows, as a consequence outside the act. The extrinsic terminus in no way belongs to the *constitution* of the act. It is only an existing effect of the act.

Creation, in the active sense of the word, is an act of God which is *formally immanent*; that is to say, Creation is an act of the Divine will, which presupposes Divine knowledge.

In the Sacred Scriptures it is written that the Lord spoke, and they were made, He commanded, and they were created—by the Word of the Lord the heavens were established—God said, Be light made, and light was made—Thou, O Lord and God, hast created all things, and for Thy will they were, and have been created—we trust in the Almighty Lord, who at a beck can utterly destroy both them that come against us, and the whole world.

The created universe existed because God spoke, because He willed, because He commanded, and by the same beck of His will was the world made, as that by which the world could be destroyed.

This is the nature of the Divine activity, that God by speaking, willing, and commanding should make things to be, even when matter is already in existence, as when light was made—so that nothing should intervene between the act of the Divine will, and the existence of the effect. The adequate reason of the existence of the world was, therefore, an act of Divine will.

Active creation cannot be other than a formally immanent act. The creating act is formally *in God*, for God is truly said to be creating.

Reason itself declares that active creation in God must be an act which is formally immanent. The act which creates is formally *in God*. God is truly creating, inasmuch as, by His own omnipotent virtue, He is the cause of the existence of creatures. This virtue in God is, in its intrinsic reality, entirely *actual*. In other words, it is an *act*. It is not merely a *power* of creating. It is a creating act, which is formally *in God*. A *transient* act supposes a subject, in which the agent operates. Creation does not suppose any subject. Hence a creative act is most certainly an act which is formally immanent.

An immanent creative act is either an act of knowledge, or an act of will. Knowledge is demanded as *directing;* but the act which is immediately *efficacious* cannot be other than an act of *will*. Knowledge is indifferent, with regard to objects which are opposed to each other; and it holds an even balance between the *being* and the *not being* of things. The will can determine either the one or the other. Knowledge draws towards itself objects which are outside it. Will inclines towards objects which are outside itself. An *effecting* principle involves inclination towards something outside itself. Hence if in thought we remove, from him who creates, action which is formally transient, there remains only command, or volition, that things should be.

We cannot excogitate in God *power* which is distinct in idea from God's intellect and will— that is to say, power as distinct from will, as will is distinct from knowledge—as the *immediate principle* of creatures. An act of *power*, apart from intellect and will, could not be conceived as *immanent*. Power, as distinguished in idea from will, cannot be conceived otherwise than as a principle of the execution of a work, which follows the *intellect* which directs, and the *will* which commands. A principle of execution which is subsequent to knowledge and will, is a principle which is acting by action which is *formally transient*. Essentially, that principle does not do anything more than to effect something which is outside itself. An act of it, therefore, cannot be conceived as being a *vital* act, which modifies the subject who is acting, as does every immanent act. Creative action cannot be formally transient; because there is *no subject* in which it operates.

Divine power is the Divine will, as that will is efficacious outside itself. Not only when God produces things out of nothing, but also when God modifies things already produced, His *effi-*

cacious act is none other than an act of *will*. God's will is the principle of every effect outside Himself. When God modifies a thing, He must in acting be wholly independent of the subject on which He acts. He will, most certainly, be absolutely independent, when the effect exists at the beck of His will.

An *immanent* act of our will—as it is a volition of things which are not itself—has a relation of order towards objects which are outside it. As this act of will is a command—while the will itself is an imperial principle, which moves the faculties towards operation—it is a principle of execution and production of those effects which proceed from an active faculty, which is itself subject to the command of the will. There is, therefore, in this act of the will, a relation of order, and an efficacy towards something which is outside itself. This efficacy in a finite will is limited, and it is only mediate. But if the act of will is of infinite perfection, the efficacy of it will be also infinite. It will not need other intermediate forces, in order to production of the effect. It will of itself be efficacious. It will therefore be an act which is formally *immanent;* although *virtually* transient, inasmuch as it is efficacious outside itself. There would be contradiction in an immanent act being *formally* transient. There is no contradiction in an immanent act being *virtually* transient.

When it is said that God *makes*, there is signified not volition solely, but *efficacious* volition. Those two—volition and efficacious volition—are not convertable terms; since there is also a volition of God which is inefficacious. Although God's will, and God's power, are one and the selfsame thing, since the power of God is the will of God; yet it is not every will that is power. There is one which is simply a mode of will, and there is another which is a mode of *efficacious* will. Two different things, therefore, are signified by the words *makes* and *wills* in the proposition—God makes that which He wills. The first signifies the *efficacy* of the Divine virtue. That virtue does not less belong to God, because it is itself the will of God. The other signifies a *counsel* of His will. There is no tautology therefore in the phrase—God makes that which He wills; as there would be, if it were simply equivalent to—God wills that which He wills.

God's will in creating was and is a free will. The phrase—God makes that which He wills—indicates the independence of the agent from all external pressure—his freedom from all intrinsic necessity—and the election or choice of His will.

There are many things which might possibly be made by the Divine agent, and He by His will determines which of them are to be made, and which of them are to be left unmade. This determination is an act of choice. A will that *chooses* is a *free* will. "God worketh all things according to the counsel of His will."

It would have been easy for God to produce any number of worlds. To will, is of all things the most easy. To will, is most easy in us; but in us faculty does not always follow will. In God faculty and will are co-extensive; and so God can do all that He wills to do.

The existence of the world which God willed was in no way necessary to God. The motive of His willing it, which was the Divine goodness, in no way imposed necessity on the Divine will. The character of the Divine *goodness* is such that it can diffuse itself outside itself, by producing objects which bear the likeness of it; but actual diffusion outside itself is not necessary to it. Even without this diffusion the Divine goodness would remain most perfect; since it does not through diffusion receive anything in itself.

It is in this way *becoming* to God to communicate Himself outside Himself, that His not communicating Himself would not be *unbecoming*, apart from some free decree of the Divine will. Becomingness in God is to be regarded in connection with the total independence from creatures, which the Divine nature demands. Becomingness in God is not in this, that a perfection would accrue to God if He communicated Himself to others; but in this only that, prescinding from His other attributes, communication of Himself attaches to the nature of *goodness*, regarded by itself, more than does non-communication. To communicate Himself is becoming to God immediately, as God is Good. Not to communicate Himself is also becoming, as becoming to the fulness of God's self-sufficingness and independence.

5.

A *principal cause* is so called, both by reason of the relation of it to an effect; and by reason of its relation to another cause which acts *along with* it, and *under* it, and is called an *instrumental cause*. This relation is not, however, absolutely necessary, in order that a cause should be a *principal* cause. Even if there is no concurrence of an instrumental cause, another cause may be, and even with much greater reason, a *principal* cause. We are speaking at present of a principal efficient physical cause; and of an efficient physical instrumental cause. That which is a principal cause is not of itself principal, as regards all effects; but only as regards certain determinate effects. The notion of a principal cause comes to this, that the cause which, in relation to some effect, is called a *principal* cause, can in virtue of its own form determine the existence of that effect; whether it acts along with another cause, which is subordinate to it, or not.

An *instrumental* cause is, as regards an effect, that which concurs to the production of it, in virtue of its own nature, indeed, but as moved and applied to acting by another. It does not, in virtue of its own nature, determine the existence of a perfection which is proper to that effect. The perfection of the effect is determined by him who *moves* the instrumental cause.

An artificer, by reason of the art which he bears with him in his mind, and the power which he possesses to move bodies, and to moderate their movements, can determine the existence of a work of art, for instance, of a vase. The fire which is applied may, indeed, in virtue of its own form, determine combustion, or liquefaction, or the like; and so, as regards those effects, the fire is itself a *principal* cause. The fire, however, cannot determine the existence of that work of art; towards which it only concurs by effecting, in virtue of its own nature, something which is less. The force of a principal cause can be from itself, and independent, as in the case of a *primal* cause; or it can be from another, and dependent, and preserved in being by that other, as in the case of second causes.

The Sacred Scriptures not only do not attribute the work of creation to any other than to the one God; but they so attribute creation to Him as to exclude every other cause. They set forth creation as proper to the one true God.

The Fourth Lateran Council sums up and confirms, with its own authoritative testimony, the universal teaching of the Catholic tradition, when it says—We believe that there is one true God, one principle of all things, the Creator of all visible and invisible, spiritual and corporeal things. The Fathers not only deny that an angel, or any cause whatsoever other than the only God, has as matter of fact created anything; but they also affirm that the angels could not and cannot create, and that no creature whatsoever can create. They give as a reason, *because it is a creature*. It is characteristic of the creature, that it cannot create. They not merely deny to the creature a power of creating which is independent of God, as the first cause, but they deny the possibility of any creature creating. They give as a reason, because the creature is an image, and not the archetype, because to create is singular and proper to the Divine nature, and belongs to the supreme glory of it, and because a creature cannot create itself. The Fathers deny the possibility of creative power, not only to creatures that now exist, but to all possible creatures.

The most universal of causes, as regards efficacy, must necessarily be one, namely God. The reason is evident. No cause except God can have force to produce all the possible. A cause which produces *being* as *being*, or being *from nothing*, whether it produces one being or more, is the most universal of causes. He who can produce being *as being*, can produce whatever has the idea of *being*. Every faculty can extend itself to all material objects which are contained under its own formal object. The formal object of creative power is *being as being*, or *being* produced from *nothing*.

There is contradiction in the idea of a cause which is able to *create* some things only. No sufficient reason can be given why a cause which is able to create *some* things, should not be able to create *all* things; nay, there is sufficient reason why, if it is able to create some things, it should be able also to create all things. Such a cause acts at the beck of its own will, and so has an infinite efficacy. It follows that it is the most universal of causes, that is to say, it is God.

The true conception of creation excludes the possibility of the concurrence of an *instrumental* cause. God spoke, and creatures were made. The existence of them followed of itself from the beck of the Divine will; and that was an immanent act. With such an act, no act of another cause could be conjoined. An instrumental cause should have its own act, which is proper to it, and wherewith it subserves the principal cause. It cannot have, as the terminus of its own proper act, productions from nothing; for if it had, it would be the principal cause. It cannot be in touch with the principal creating cause, which is God, by modifying Him; and it cannot be in touch with the createable subject, because that is not as yet in existence.

Whatever is attributed to God, and does not express a relation of origin in God, is said of God, as He is regarded *absolutely*, as He is the Divine *essence* or nature. Creation belongs to God, and it does not express a relation of origin in God, since it is a production of objects which are outside God. Everything that is said of God as He is the Divine *essence*, is as equally common to the three Divine Persons, as is the Divine nature. The principle of creation is indeed knowledge and will, but these are absolute properties, which are equally common to the three Divine Persons; and so the one God—who is the Father, the Son, and the Holy Ghost—creates.

The Divine Persons create as they are one; because that which is common to them, and absolute, is one, namely, the Divine essence. Since, however, this one principle is the principle of creatures, inasmuch as it is infinite directing knowledge, and infinite efficacious will—and it is under these formal ideas, that this principle is conceived by us as creating—we say that the Father, the Son, and the Holy Ghost *create*, as they are that one directing knowledge, and efficacious will. The principle *which* creates, is the three Divine Persons, since to operate belongs to a subsistence or person; and in God there is a threefold subsistence, and no other subsistence. The principle *whereby* God creates, is the Divine nature, or the Divine knowledge and will. There is one Creator, but there are three who are creating. Every one of the three Persons *immediately* creates; because to every one of them that efficacious act belongs, in the whole of it, of which the created effect is the immediate consequence.

The words *from*, *through*, and *in*, applied in the Sacred Scriptures to the external operations of Divine Persons, cannot indicate different activities or causalities; although they may signify a different *mode*, in which the same activity belongs to those Persons.

By way of *appropriation*—whereby, on account

of a certain affinity between a particular Divine work, and the personal characteristics of one Divine Person, this particular work is specially attributed, or "appropriated" to that Person, although it belongs at the same time and equally to the other Divine Persons—*from* is specially attributed to God the Father, *through* to God the Son, and *in* to God the Holy Ghost; especially when the three Divine Persons are connumerated, all of them together. God the Father is said to create *through* the Son, *in* the Holy Ghost—and *from* Him, and *through* Him, and *in* Him are all things. A different causality or efficacy is not thereby signified, or a different mode of causing. There is signified only the attitude of the Persons, one towards another; and the different way in which they individually obtain, or have derived to them, the one creative force, which is identified with the Divine nature. The Father has the Divine nature from Himself, the Son has it by generation from the Father, and the Holy Ghost has it by spiration from both the Father and the Son. The three Divine Persons are, all of them, required in order to the causality of creation; inasmuch as that God is required, to whom a trinity of persons is essential, so that without this trinity He would not be God.

6.

When an effect represents its cause, it represents that cause, as the principle *whereby* it was effected; and not as the principle *which* effected it. It represents the *nature*, and not the *person*. It tells of what nature the cause is which operates. The reason is because an effect represents its cause, in accordance with that perfection which it receives from its cause. It represents the perfection of the cause which corresponds to itself; and the perfection of a cause belongs to the *nature* or *essence* of it. Hence, when we see a work of art, we gather that it has proceeded from a human intellect; but who could form a judgment as to who made the work, or whether one or more persons had a hand in the making of it?

There may be representation of a cause in two ways—either by way of trace, or by way of image. Representation by *trace* is so called from the footprints left by animals on the earth. It may be defined, generally, as correspondence of an effect with its cause in this, that the effect exhibits in itself that from which knowledge of its cause is necessarily deduced.

Representation by *image* is so called from pictures, in which—looking to external appearance, which alone is represented—there is true likeness to the type. This representation may be defined as correspondence of the effect with the cause; through which the effect exhibits in itself elements, by which distinct knowledge of the cause is informed.

When there is representation by *trace* alone, the effect is said to represent only the *causality* of the cause. When there is representation by *image*, the effect is said to represent the *form* of the cause.

Representation of *causality* comes to this, that the effect signifies the existence of some cause.

When the existence of a cause is signified through a determinate effect, there must necessarily be indicated also, at least confusedly, some note of that cause. Representation of *causality*, therefore, is not to be understood as if the only thing signified by it were, that there is a cause. There is in some manner signified also what the cause is. This representation is of its own nature ANALOGOUS.

When an effect so represents its cause, that the specific properties of the effect are, in their own formal idea—although in a different way—found in the cause; then the effect is said to represent the *form* of the cause. There is an agreement of *form*, or of nature, between the effect and the cause.

Representation by way of *image* may be either

univocal, or analogous. It is *univocal*, when the *form* is found in both *termini* in the same way. It is *analogous* when the *form* is found in both *termini*, but in different ways. Further, an analogous representation may be such that through it the principal analogue can be found, and conceived with the aid of the light of reason alone. There is another analogous representation, through which the principal analogue can only be conceived by us, at the instigation of the faith.

It is certain, that there cannot be in created things a representation of the Trinity, in the proper and formal idea of three Divine Persons; both because it is not as they are three, that the Persons create, but as they are one—and because an effect signifies, not the person or persons who act in producing the effect, but the *nature by which* the person operates—and also because the mode which is proper to the existence of infinite being, cannot formally exist in finite beings.

It is also certain, that there can so far be a representation of the Trinity in created beings, as there are more or less represented in them those attributes through which processions of persons have place in God.

Some sort of representation of the Trinity is common to all created beings. In every being there are indications, from which we are led to knowledge of the attributes through which processions of persons exist in God. Every thing, as it is a created thing, leads to knowledge of an *efficient* cause; and of a cause which acts through *intellect* and *will.* Every thing represents, or signifies, an artificer, who conceives his work, and imparts order to his work; or, in other words, who is endowed with *power, understanding,* and *goodness.* A created thing represents the artificer of it, inasmuch as it leads to knowledge of that artificer, even if it does not in itself exhibit the characteristics of one who understands, who wills, and who is able to operate, through understanding and will. This is a representation of attributes in God, by way of *trace.* It is through such attributes, however, that processions of persons exist in God.

There is another, and a more perfect representation, which belongs to *rational* creatures. A distinct conception of the *nature* of the Triune God is contained in the notion of a spirit, who, because he is a spirit, both understands and wills. This conception is still more distinct, when it is found that in the intelligence there is a *word* which proceeds from the mind, whereby the mind apprehends itself; and a love, by the intelligent being of itself, which proceeds from this knowledge. In this way rational creatures represent in themselves those attributes, in accordance with which there are processions in God. They also in themselves represent in some manner that which of itself belongs to the Divine Persons. It is proper to God the Son to proceed, as the Word, from God the Father's knowledge; and it is proper to God the Holy Ghost to proceed as Love, from the mutual loving of the Father and the Son.

This representation is *analogous*. Analogous representation is the only representation of the infinite that can possibly be in, or by, the finite. Both kinds of analogous representation have place here. The *word* in us, and the *love* in us represent, in the first place, that essential knowledge, and that essential volition, in God, in which they are supereminently contained. They represent also that essential demand of both of them for an immanent *terminus*, which should of itself subsist.

The first of these representations is clear; and that which is represented can be discerned by the natural light of reason.

The second representation is so obscure that, apart from the instigation of the faith, that which is represented cannot be discerned by reason.

When it is discerned through faith, there is seen in a creature who understands, and who wills, a demand for an immanent terminus; but not for an immanent terminus which *subsists*.

Such a terminus is proper to God alone. All therefore that can be gathered by reasoning from the word in us, and from the love in us, is the existence of infinite *essential* knowledge, and *essential* will, in God.

The trinity of Divine Persons, therefore, is represented in created beings, either by way of *image*, or by way of *trace*, in those attributes through which there is procession of persons in God; but not in those attributes which are "appropriated" to persons.

There is not in created beings any representation of the Trinity *formally* as there are three distinct Persons in God, from which, by force of the light of reason, the Trinity could be discerned.

There is, however, in created beings a representation through which the intellect, enlightened by the light of faith, can analogically perceive the Trinity. This is sufficient in order to the idea of *analogous* image.

7.

Creation of beings demands, as a norm, an exemplar; that is to say, a pattern or model of them existing in God.

The *idea* of a thing is the form of that thing which exists in the mind of the artificer; and in accordance with which he makes the thing. It is proper to this *idea*, to be in the intellect as an idea which is *known;* since it is that which the artificer contemplates, in order that he may operate. From this it follows that the *idea* of a thing is also an objective principle of *knowledge* of the thing of which it is the idea. When the *idea* of a thing is known, the *thing itself* is known. The reason is, because the thing is made to the likeness of the idea of it.

It is also proper to the *idea* of a thing, to be a principle of *operation,* as directing the will of the artificer in his work; since the thing should be made to the likeness of the idea of it. These are *practical* ideas. They are ordained towards the work, which it belongs to the will to command and execute.

The *ideas* of things have, therefore, the character of a CAUSE, in so far as the *will* is conjoined with those ideas. The *ideas* are not properly *acts of will,* but are only a principle which *directs* the will. The *intellect* of the artificer contributes to the work of his hands, which his will commands, inasmuch as the intellectual idea exhibits the norm, or form, of the thing to be made.

God executed the work of creation in accordance with *ideas* of it. Those ideas were not outside Himself, but in Himself. When God said, Let us make man to our image and likeness, this saying of His signified that, before His work existed, He had conceived that work in His mind. He had conceived it, not confusedly, but determinately. His conception of it was the *idea* in accordance with which He was to work.

Both revelation and reason represent God as creating all things *freely*, and with entire *independence* of everything that is not God Himself. He who *freely* executes a work, which is outside himself, is operating *through ideas*. He, moreover, who in operating is wholly *independent* cannot be receiving the *ideas* of his works from outside himself.

A *primal* or first cause ought to be such a cause as to determine what effects, out of any number of possible effects, are to exist. A first cause should also be such as to determine in what *modes*, out of any number of possible modes, those effects are to exist. Things which are *possible* cannot be from themselves; nor can they be all together, or at once, in all the modes that are possible to them. There is, moreover, no greater reason in one possible thing, why it should be, than there is in another possible thing. All this a primal cause can determine only by acting with *freedom*. If he is acting by *necessity* of nature, and if, not determining himself in his action, he is being determined by another, he is not the primal or first cause. A *free* cause is a cause which has understanding, and freely produces effects; inasmuch as from among the number of those things which he apprehends with his mind, he chooses one for production, instead of another. That which is apprehended by the mind of the producer, and after the norm of which the effect is produced, is the *idea* of the thing produced.

The Divine wisdom could not receive *ideas* of things from outside itself, because there is nothing outside God, which is not made by God; and because the Divine wisdom, as infinite, is wholly independent. With the *efficient* causality of creation, therefore, there is bound up *exemplary* causality, as an element of it. As there is a first *efficient* cause, so is there also a first *exemplary* cause.

Ideas in God are in reality the Divine essence itself, since whatever is in God *is* God. The idea of a thing ought in itself distinctly, and properly, to represent the thing to be made; and therefore to represent it *formally*, and with that representation which, by priority of nature at least, precedes the knowledge wherewith the idea is apprehended. The knowledge supposes the *idea*. The Divine *essence* does not *formally* exhibit in itself any thing which is to be made; and can only be called a *virtual* exemplar of created things, as it supereminently contains all things. God's *knowledge*, on the other hand, expresses distinctly, and properly, all *essences* or possible beings. This expression, as it is an object of *reflex* knowledge, has the character of an *idea*. Although in God both direct knowledge, and reflex knowledge, is one most simple act, yet *reflex* knowledge, in its own formal notion, can be attributed to God; because God not only understands Himself, and all things outside Himself, but He also understands that He understands.

There is in reality one idea in God, as there is in God one essence, and one knowledge. This one idea is manifold, in the relation to it of the various things to be made. All of these it distinctly expresses by one act. An *idea* in God is *essential*, and not *personal;* just as in God His knowledge is essential, and not personal. The Divine *idea* of creation is a necessary element of the *efficient* causality of creation. This causality is *essential*, and not personal. It is, therefore, equally common to the three Divine Persons.

8.

There is no *final cause* of the Divine *will*; but there is a final cause of the *effects* of that will. The final cause of those effects is the Divine *goodness*.

A final cause, as regards *the will*, is that which, by reason of its goodness, allures the will to love, or desire, of it. A final cause, as regards *the means*, is that which, when loved or desired for itself, is a reason why other things should be loved or desired, and ordained towards it.

An end, as regards a created will, can be the cause, both of an act of will, and of the will being borne towards this or that object. If we understand the final cause, in the proper sense of the term, as meaning something which is distinct from God, and which, through perception of the goodness of it, morally influences God's will, so that He should will that thing, or will something else for the sake of that thing, we must say that there is not any *final cause* of Divine volition. The primal Being, who is wholly independent, cannot be subject to the influence of any thing. If, as St. Augustine says, the will of God has a cause, it is something which precedes the will of God.

Divine works have necessarily some cause, by reason of which they are done. They are the works of one who acts through intellect, and intellect has always an end in view. Although the Divine will has no cause, yet, since it acts reasonably, it must prescribe an end for its effects, and ordain those effects to that end, and will them to be effects for the sake of some end. There must be an *ultimate end*, to which all creatures are ordained. This end is the Divine goodness, which the Divine will necessarily loves.

The Divine *goodness* is here to be understood ontologically, as it is plenitude of being, the infinite ocean of perfections, or, as it is the *essence* of God, who is good. That the ultimate end of Divine effects, and so the *ultimate final cause* of created beings, is that which is the first *efficient* cause of them, is evident. The dignity of a final cause belongs necessarily to God; and it should belong to Him in the most perfect way. If the ultimate end, to which things are ordained by God, is something other than God, there will be some being, other than God, which is the ultimate end of the Divine works. Such a being must be either equal to, or greater, or less, than God. That it should be equal to, or greater than God, is absurd. If it is less than God, it is either ordained towards God, or it is not ordained. If it is so ordained, then it is not an ultimate end. If it is not so ordained, then it is independent of God; and so it is not less than God, but is equal to God. The ultimate end of all things must therefore necessarily be God Himself, the Creator of all things.

The Divine goodness is the final cause of all things, for it is that which, loved by God, is the reason why they are; and it is that towards which they are ordained. God wills the effects of which He is the efficient cause, to be ordained towards ends which are fitting for them; for He wills order in all things, and He wills all things for Himself, or His own goodness, which is the ultimate end of all.

A *reason* differs from a *cause* in this, that a cause requires distinctness of being between itself and its effect. A cause requires also real dependence of the effect upon it. A mere sufficient *reason* can be in reality the same as that of which it is the reason; as, for instance, infinite perfection is the *reason* of the necessity of the existence of infinite perfection. Between a reason, and that of which it is the reason, there is not required *real* distinction. A real *foundation* for distinction *of idea* is sufficient. The mind can then conceive one of two formalities as necessary, in order that the other should exist; and can conceive one of them as really existing, or at least as possible, if the other is in existence. The thing is, by objective affirmation, said to *be*, inasmuch as it *is*; and not because it is *conceived* to be. In this way, the sufficient reason of freedom is—intelligence. An adequately sufficient reason why the will is determinated to this or to that embraces also free determination of the will. Prescind from this, and all that remains is the existence of sufficient reason why it can, if it wills, be terminated to this, or to that, object.

It is manifest that the Divine goodness—or

God's love of His own goodness—is the reason why the Divine will wills things outside God. Unless God loved Himself, that is to say, loved His own goodness, He could not love other beings. Creatures are none other than finite participations of the Divine goodness; by reason of which alone it is that they are good. When God loves Himself, He can, if He so wills, love other beings also, which are likenesses of Him. Comparing two things, which are in reality identical, but can be distinguished in idea, namely, the Divine goodness, and the Divine love of creatures, or the Divine will to create, the first is the *reason* of the second; in that way in which infinite perfection is the *reason* of the necessity of the Divine existence.

The Divine *goodness* is the end to which the world is ordained; and the world is an effect of its efficient cause. An *effect* cannot be ordained towards its *cause*, as towards an *end*, unless as either to perfect it, or certainly to manifest and glorify it. Either both or one of these reasons must be intended, when an effect is directed towards its cause, as towards an end. No other reason, besides these, can be excogitated of final ordination of effects towards their cause. Either the intrinsic good of the cause is sought, or it is its extrinsic good that is sought. Intrinsic good is a perfection of the cause. The extrinsic good of a cause cannot be other than the glory of it, which the effect of itself begets. God, it is clear, cannot be perfected. The world, therefore, exists for the *manifestation*, and *glorification*, of the Divine goodness. This manifestation can be made only to intelligent natures. It is of itself ordained to the love, and praise, of the perfection which is manifested. The world exists in order that God may be known, loved, and praised. This knowledge, love, and praise constitute what is called the *extrinsic* glory of God; as that differs from the knowledge, love, and praise, wherewith God from eternity knows, loves, and praises Himself.

We may make a distinction in this extrinsic glory, between *objective* extrinsic glory, and *formal* extrinsic glory. God's *objective* extrinsic glory is the excellence, and beauty, of His creatures. God's *formal* extrinsic glory is the knowledge and love of Him, and the praise and honour which are given to Him; from the knowledge of Him derived through creatures, and also and especially from the vision of Him. The *objective* glory is given to God by all things, in their manifesting the goodness of God. *Formal* extrinsic glory is given to God by rational creatures alone.

This extrinsic glory may be called one of the *extrinsic goods* of God; because it is ordained towards God, and is due to God.

Although the Divine goodness poured itself forth, in the creation of the world, for the good of rational creatures, yet the ultimate end, which was to be obtained through the creation of the world, was the GLORY of God Himself. From created perfections, both the existence of God, and His divine perfections, can be rightly gathered, and declared—by reason of them, man is bound, as of debt, to recognize, and worship God—and men cannot otherwise than through creatures come to knowledge of God. It was defined by the Vatican Council that—God, by His goodness and omnipotent power, not for increase of His own beatitude, or for acquiring it; but for the manifestation of His perfections, through the goods which He imparts to creatures, made the creature out of nothing.

If the question is asked, Is it not contrary to the law of morality, that God should have made all things for His own glory; since a man who seeks his own glory, and makes it the end of his works, and wills to be great in the eyes of others, is a vain or ambitious man? we answer that—the ultimate end of God is, as we have said, not His glory, but His *goodness*—and that to seek honour is then evil when *undue* honour is sought, or when honour is sought in an *undue way*. As, moreover, we men must seek the honour of God, because the Divine perfection demands it; so also the Divine will, if it wills to operate outside God, ought to seek the honour of God, because the Divine nature of itself demands this honour.

If, again, it is asked, If God stands in no need of extrinsic goods, why does He seek this extrinsic glory? We answer that—the idea of pleasure, and advantage, is one thing; and the idea of glory, praise, and honour is another thing. Pleasure and advantage are sought, in order that, by means of them, the subject of them should be intrinsically perfected. God cannot be perfected; and so God cannot will created goods for His own pleasure or advantage. Glory, praise, and honour, on the other hand, can be sought simply because the subject of them is worthy of them. These goods are, moreover, so extrinsic that there is no need that the subject, to which they are ordained, should be *perfected* by them. They are in themselves a sign of already existing perfection. They are not a cause of perfection. God could be without extrinsic glory, without any detriment to His own happiness. It was not, therefore, necessary for Him to will it. God could, however, will extrinsic glory, because the Divine goodness is *worthy of* that glory. The ultimate reason, which determinated the existence of extrinsic glory, was the free will of God.

In the ultimate end of intelligent creatures— the extrinsic glory of God, which consists in their knowledge, love, and praise of Him—is constituted their own greatest good. In the knowledge and love of God is constituted the happiness of the *rational* creature. God, in attaining that end for which He made the rational creature, obtains also that His rational creature should be blessed. The end of God, and the end of His rational creature, are one and the same, under different aspects. The Divine goodness, as to be known, loved, and enjoyed, is the end both of the rational creature, and of God. It is the end of the creature, as a good to be *obtained*. It is the end of God, as a good to be *communicated*. If, comparing God's works one with another, we look to His intelligent creatures, on the one hand; and to His irrational creatures, on the other, and to the order which exists between those two classes of His creatures; we see that all irrational creatures were made *immediately* for the sake of intelligent creatures—and that intelligent creatures are the *immediate* end to which all irrational creatures are directed. All knowledge which can be had of irrational creatures, and the pleasure which is a consequence of this knowledge, are goods which God has prepared for his rational creatures. God is in such wise the end of intelligent creatures, as to be their *proximate* end. Since the intelligent creature exists in the supreme order of created beings, he cannot be ordained for the benefit of another creature, as his proximate end. God is in such wise the end of His inanimate and irrational creatures, that the proximate end of them is the intelligent creature who, through the use of them, gives praise and honour to God.

Since the last end of man is the glorifying of the Divine Majesty, the principal norm of man's actions ought to be the glory of God. Although man, by attaining to his own beatitude, procures God's glory, so that the two ends come to be *materially* the same; yet the two ends of man differ *formally*, as God's good, and man's good. When, therefore, there is question of the supreme rule of human actions, it is to be placed in the supreme end, as it is the glory of God, and not as it is the beatitude or eternal happiness of man.

9.

In considering Divine action, we must bear in mind the distinction which exists between the terminus of an act—the formal idea of an act—and the formal motive of an act.

The *terminus* of an act is that which is attained to, by the faculty which is acting. The *formal idea* of an act is that idea under which the terminus is attained to, by the faculty which is acting. The *true*, or the *knowable*, is the formal idea for the *intellect;* while the *good* is the formal idea for the *will.* This idea is in the thing which we will, and it is that which we directly intend, or have in view and aim at, when we will something for the sake of it.

The *formal motive*—as it is a *motive*, and not simply an *idea*—is that which *determines* the faculty to the act, or to attain to the terminus of the act.

As regards Divine acts, there cannot properly be any *motive* of them; for acts of Divine knowledge and love are selfexistent, as is the Divine essence—and the Divine act of knowledge is of itself determinated to the knowing of all the true. In like manner, the Divine act of volition is of itself determinated towards the loving of infinite goodness. The same act is wholly free, with regard to all other goods. Active termination of Divine volition to certain extrinsic goods has the *idea* of termination in the *act*, and not in the *objects* of the act. This the freedom and independence of the Divine act demands.

It cannot, therefore, be that created goodness should be the *formal motive* of Divine love.

There is no formal motive, properly so called, of the Divine will. As regards the *formal idea* under which God loves His intelligent creatures, no creatures whatsoever are loveable to God, unless with relation to His infinite *goodness*. The *formal reason*, therefore, for which intelligent creatures are loved by God, is the Divine goodness, as that goodness is loved by Him. God cannot love created goodness, except as it is related to His own goodness. God wills, however, beings other than Himself; and does not merely will His own goodness. He wills the good of creatures, and effects it; and so He wills good to them, and loves them. The reason, however, why He wills the existence of creatures, and their good, is His own Divine goodness, which through them, and in them, is both *manifested* and *glorified*. Creatures are, therefore, regarded by God as *means* for the glorifying of His goodness. They are not empty means, but means which contain perfections, *from* which, and *in* which, His goodness is glorified. All these perfections are loved by God, under no other idea than as they give glory to God; and this glory is loved, under no other idea than as there is loved the infinite goodness which is glorified.

10.

God's created universe, so far as concerns the *genera* or kinds of things which it contains, is absolutely the best of worlds. We mean by *absolutely* that, not only by reason of order towards an end freely chosen by God, but by reason of itself, as compared with other possible worlds, this world or universe of worlds is the best of worlds. It cannot be more perfect as regards the genera of things which it contains. It contains matter and spirit. No possible creature is more excellent than is a spirit. If it were, then God, who is a Spirit, could not contain the perfection of a spirit *formally*, but only supereminently. The faith teaches us that God formally understands and wills, and, therefore, is *formally* a Spirit. As nothing can be conceived higher than a spirit, so among the things of which we have knowledge, nothing can be conceived which is lower than matter. Besides these two extremes —spirit and matter—there is the synthesis of the two, which is man. There is matter which is inorganic, and matter which is organic. There is life which is vegetative, life which is sensitive, life which is rational, and life which is purely intellective. Besides the natural order, there is the preternatural order, and there is the supernatural order. In the supernatural order, there are not only adoptive sons of God, and the intuitive vision of God, but there is the Godman, and there is the Mother of God. As regards the moral order, there are moral goods, justice, and holiness, and exercise of virtues. There is also the struggle of the good with evils, and the splendour of virtue in adverse circumstances, the war against the evil, the victory of the good, and the final triumph, and the manifestation of the

Divine liberality, and mercy, and justice. Besides these genera, no genus more perfect can either be excogitated, or can exist.

Since, however, it is only by confining our consideration to the perfection of the genera which the existing universe contains, that it can be called absolutely the best of worlds; by reason of this limitation, it can only relatively, and in some way, be called the best of worlds. That world is not simply and absolutely the best of worlds, in comparison with which another, and yet another, can be conceived as more perfect, not only materially, but also formally. It is certainly possible to conceive another world, which would formally be more perfect, than is this world or universe.

By the *material* perfection of the universe, we mean here the number of its perfections. By the *formal* perfection of the universe, we mean its perfection in manifestation of the Divine goodness.

One world would be only *materially* more perfect than another world if—the manifestation of the Divine goodness remaining in both worlds the same—it were to contain more creatures. If the manifestation, and so the glory of the Divine Majesty, were greater in the one world than in the other; then the world which afforded the greater manifestation and glory, would be the more perfect of the two. The manifestation of the Divine goodness which is got from this universe, whatever it may amount to, or arrive at, is and always must be finite. In the case of every finite there can always be a greater finite; and so there can always be a greater manifestation of the Divine goodness. In every genus of the things that are, farther degrees of perfection can be added. Prescinding from the Divine and uncreated holiness, the created holiness of the Sacred Humanity of Christ, and the holiness of the Mother of God could, each of them, be greater than it is. With the increase of perfection in any genus, there is necessarily increased the manifestation of the Divine Majesty, which is manifested by these perfections. There could certainly be created spirits more perfect in the degree of their intelligence, than is any created spirit now existing. In the event of their creation, there would be a greater manifestation and glorification of the Divine goodness; since there would exist a more perfect knowledge, and so a more perfect love and praise, of the Divine goodness.

Again, prescinding from God's essential and infinite knowledge, the knowledge which belongs to the Sacred Humanity of Christ, as bestowed upon, and contained within His Human Soul, as well as the knowledge which belongs to the Divine Mother, is ontologically finite. There could therefore be instituted an order of intelligences, such as that the knowledge which now belongs to those two would belong to many other spirits; whom Christ as man, and the Mother of God, would excel in the same proportion, or in greater proportion, than that in which they now excel the spirits that actually exist. There could be also such an institution of intelligences, that the knowledge of the Blessed in heaven should be much greater than that which has been established in the present order; and so the glory of God would be the greater.

There could have been a greater number of species of animals, and of plants, than the number which exists. The human body could have been furnished with senses more acute than are those which it possesses; or with other senses, wherewith we should have been able to perceive things which are hidden from our present senses. In these ways there would have been a greater real or objective manifestation of the Divine wisdom.

God, in freely decreeing the creation of the existing universe, set before Himself a certain end, which was to be obtained thereby; and that end, since it was the ultimate end to be obtained, He willed with an *absolute* will. If the perfection of the universe, which we find in parts of it, or in it as a whole, be compared with that certain degree of manifestation of His goodness which God freely chose, as a means with reference to an end to be obtained, the existing universe can again be called the best of worlds. As regards that particular end, of God's choice, it is the best means; since it most fittingly contributes towards that end for which it was made. This we know *a priori*, from what we know of the Divine wisdom and power. When God has freely chosen a certain degree of glory to be obtained, He truly wills to obtain it, and He really does obtain it. Nothing resists His power. The most wise Ordainer employs the most fitting means towards the end which He has set before Him. By His *absolute* will He wills and effects the ultimate end, which is His glory. The existing universe, therefore, is perfect in its contribution to the glory which is intended by God. The perfection of the universe, moreover, remains always greater than is our knowledge of it; and in this sense also it may be called a most excellent world.

Moral necessity, begotten of the fittingness and rightness of an action, is in God a physical and metaphysical necessity. It involves metaphysical contradiction, that God should do anything unfittingly and unbecomingly; and so, if it is necessary that some particular thing should be done by God, if He is not to be acting unfittingly and unbecomingly, the doing of that thing will be metaphysically necessary to God.

If God were necessarily bound to choose that which is objectively the *better*; since the existence of the created universe is certainly objectively better than is its non-existence, God would have had necessarily to choose the existence of the world.

Since that which is *absolutely* the best is not to be found within the sphere of the possible—for in comparison with any *finite* thing, there can always be a greater finite thing—God cannot be bound to create that which is absolutely the best, or even the better. Supposing that the absolutely best were within the sphere of the possible, God would, nevertheless, not be bound to produce it; even on the hypothesis that He willed to create. This the absolute independence of God, and His most perfect self-sufficingness, demands. Hence nothing extraneous to God is in any way necessary to God; and God was entirely free to determine Himself to the creation of the universe. Of all manifestations of His Divine goodness, so long as they are simply *good*, and *positively* becoming—that is to say, so long as they do not contain anything which is contrary to His attributes—God can choose one manifestation instead of another.

As regards the sufficient *reason* of a choice which should pass over that which is the *better*, it is not only the principle of a sufficient reason which has to be kept in view, in our contemplation of God's action, but also the idea of the Divine independence and freedom. In considering the free action of the will, an adequately sufficient *reason* of the existence of an effect, or a reason which necessarily involves determination of the will, is never to be sought before determination, or outside determination, of the will—for this would be to destroy freedom. There is to be sought only a reason why the will can exercise itself, and why it can choose this or that object.

A sufficient reason of the Divine choice in the creation of the existing universe, is because such a world is of the number of good and fitting manifestations of the Divine goodness; and so is one of those things which are possible, and eligible by God. In other words, such a manifestation of the Divine goodness, as is obtained through the created universe, is *good*—and that which is *good* suffices to allure the will.

Exercise of Divine will is not to be demanded after the norm of the exercise of a created will. A created will is either bound by the law of perfectibility, properly so called; or it has a natural desire for being perfected, and it is perfected through acts, and through the objects to which it tends. It may therefore be that it should morally be either necessary, or exclusively fitting, for a created will, that it should choose the *better* among those things which it has power to choose. God, however, is wholly free from that law, or from any natural desire of perfectibility, which in Him would be impossible, as involving contradiction. Moreover, since God gains nothing for Himself *intrinsically* by operating, He could have abstained from creation of the world. For the same reason, God could in creating refrain from making an objectively *better* world, and rest content with a world which is objectively good.

Further, God was not bound to create such an universe as He has actually created, as *best* from the point of view of the *genera* or kinds of things which it contains. The creation of the world was, in every detail of its creation, free to God. Uncompelled by any necessity, He freely chose the creation of the universe, and through it a certain determinate degree of manifestation, out of any number of possible manifestations of Himself, represented to Him by His Divine knowledge. God chose that series and synthesis of created beings, which is the existing universe.

II.

That which begins at any time to be, at one time was not. This time during which it was not, is not necessarily *real* time, preceding that which began to be. *Possible* time is sufficient. In accordance with possible time, the thing could have been, before it actually was.

The beginning of the world comes to this, that at one time the world was not. This time was not real, or actual, time, included within eternity, which is absurd. It was an indefinite possibility of time, when the world could have been, and actually was not.

Since the world is dependent on the *free will* of God, as on its efficient cause; it is not necessary that the world should have existed simultaneously with its cause. It was then when God willed the world to be, that the world ought to have been. From eternal action on the part of God, there does not follow an eternal effect. Although God was from eternity the sufficient cause of the world's existence, yet the world was actually produced by Him in accordance with the predefinition of His will. God's will was that the world should have *being*, after *not being*. There was in this Divine determination no change, on the part of God. It is not as if God first willed the world not to be, and afterwards willed the world to be.

God, the universal cause of all *being*, is the cause also of *time;* and so no real time is presupposed to His effect. When an effect of His is said to be produced *in time*, this is not meant in that way in which the effects of natural causes are produced *in* time. In the case of these, *real* time precedes, accompanies, and is subsequent to them. Creation is said to have taken place *in time*, in the sense that *real* time began *with creation*. Before real time, there was only *possible* time. This was indefinite, in the possibility of it. Hence we may, with St. Augustine, say that the world was made *with time*, rather than made *in time*.

The *now* of time is the boundary line between the past, and the future. As soon, therefore, as the world was created, there existed a boundary line between an *imaginary* or possible past, and a *real* future. This was the beginning of *real* time.

The possibility of the existence of the created universe, or of any contingent being, from eternity, is an idea which intrinsically involves contradiction. There underlies this chimerical idea a confusion of mind between the *indefinite* and the *infinite*.

CHAPTER IX.

God, as the Author of Nature.

DIVINE revelation declares not only the *fact* of creation, but also the *mode*, and *order*, in which the world was made.

By the *world*, we mean the synthesis of all the created natures which are contained in heaven and earth. When we speak of the *mode* in which the world was made, we mean the formation of the several natures, whether living or inanimate—the allocating of them in space, and in their own proper places—the connection, and harmony, established between them—the laws of activity, and duration, implanted in them, and the like. When we speak of the *order* in which the world was made, we mean the relation of earlier and later, among the works of God, in the making of the world.

In the Book of Genesis there is given not only the fact of creation but, as regards many things at least, the mode, and the order, in which the world was made.

In the six days of creation, we have a phrase which expresses a successive series of Divine works. The narrative unfolds, in accordance with the science of the age, when it was written, the origin and constitution of the various natures; and of that whole, which consists of all those natures. God's works themselves, when rightly investigated, form a commentary on the Word of God. Geology is a manifestation of the works of God, in the first formation of this earth of ours. Other natural sciences, which explain the natures and laws of corporeal things, can throw light also on the way in which the Author of Nature made these in the beginning. The greater our knowledge of natural sciences, the clearer will the Divine narrative become to us. It is the business of a commentary to make more clear the text which it explains; and not to give to the text an authority which it already possesses. This is especially true of the Divine text. The authority of it could not be greater than it is, since it rests on Divine inspiration. Whatever of real truth natural sciences contribute, is at our service, in order that our knowledge of those facts to which the Word of God testifies, may be more ample, and more clearly distinct. Since those things of which natural sciences take cognizance, are works of God, it is God Himself in the last resort who, through His own works, manifested to us, is interpreting His own Word.

Natural sciences contain the knowledge which man has of the works of God; while the word of God is an expression of Divine knowledge. God's knowledge ought not to be reduced to the norm of man's knowledge. It is man's knowledge which ought to be conformed to the norm of the Divine knowledge. One of the two must follow, or must be reduced to the norm of the other; since the two are bound to agree, and they exist in different orders. Man's knowledge is liable to error; the Divine knowledge is infallible. That which is liable to error ought to be reduced to the norm of the infallible. If it is not, there will be perversion of order; and a way will be opened to the greatest errors when, leaving an infallible leader, a leader is followed to whom it is possible to go astray.

A *norm* may be either a positive norm, or a negative norm. A *positive* norm is a norm which we must follow in our actions, lest we should go astray; and apart from which, if it is an adequate norm, we cannot be acting rightly. A *negative* norm is a norm which must not be contradicted, if one is to avoid error. There are some things with regard to the *mode*, and *order*, of the formation of the world, which we are taught by the word of God. As regards these, the word of God is a *positive* norm. It must be followed. There are many other things which God has passed over in silence, and has left to man's enquiry. Whatever the human mind may gather by investigation, and reasoning, we ought always to take care that the result is not in conflict with that to which the Divine word testifies. That which is opposed to Divine knowledge, and to Divine testimony, must necessarily be false.

We must, moreover, bear in mind that, in this matter, the object which is knowable is *contingent;* and *dependent* on the Divine will. There are many ways of effecting a thing, which are known to the Divine mind; while our knowledge with regard to the first constitution of natures is a merely *mediate* knowledge. We do not know, or certainly we are ignorant that we do know, all the adjuncts which may possibly have changed the condition of the earth. It may be that some things have, as matter of fact, taken place, of which there does not now exist one single trace. God, on the other hand, certainly knew what He willed to do; and the way in which He willed to do it. Human reason, therefore, cannot affirm anything which is contrary to that to which the author of a Divine work testifies; and we are, moreover, bound to hold as true that to which God gives testimony.

A man would be imprudent who should repudiate the aid of natural sciences, on the ground that God might, perhaps, have made use of miracles in His making of the world. In the first institution of nature, it became God to lay down natural laws, by which His creatures should be ruled, in their being and action; and there is no reason for gratuitously anticipating miracles. Miracles, moreover, themselves suppose the institution of a natural order, to which they are exceptions. We are to look, therefore, not for miracles, but for natural laws which, through natural sciences, can be more or less known to us.

There is no distinction of operations in God, except *in idea*, within our minds. Distinction of Divine operations is derived from the different *termini* which proceed from God, as He is operating. It is by reason of a *created* terminus, that the action of God is called *creation*. By reason of a terminus which is merely *formed*, the action of God is called *formation*.

Formation is an operation which, from already created matter, moulds different natures, fittingly compounds them, collects them into one synthesis furnishes them with their own proper forces, and ordains them towards an end.

In the Book of Genesis, Divine operation is described as twofold. First, there is creation of matter; and then there is the institution of various natures, from pre-existing matter. The terminus of the first operation was *substance*. The terminus of the second operation was the existence of *corporeal natures*.

That which is effected through creation—and is the subject of forms and qualities, and can be disposed in different ways—is *substance*. By the first Divine operation, all material substance was produced out of nothing. From this material substance, there were formed celestial and terrestrial bodies, both inorganic and organic. The *formation* of these does not demand the production of a new reality; but only some special mode of composition. In effecting these, therefore, substance is not, properly speaking, *produced;* but corporeal natures are, properly speaking, *made*. From different combinations of substances, are made the different principles of operations, and of phenomena, which are called the *principles of nature*. To the second Divine operation, there belongs the allocation of corporeal natures in certain parts of space, in order to the harmonious agreement of them. This *allocation* may, however, be reduced to the *formation* of corporeal natures, as a natural consequence of formation.

Although the work of formation is said to have taken place successively, during six days, there is no necessity for us to suppose that those were days of twenty four hours apiece. There is, however, an obvious reason why the seven periods of time, or epochs, should have been called by the name of *days*, rather than by another name. The series of epochs was a type of the week, which is a measure of our time; and the seventh day was a type of that day on which man was to rest from labour, and to give himself to the praise of God.

2.

The existence of the angels also is due to creation; for whatsoever is not God has been created by God. The existence of angels is a truth which has been divinely revealed. The general persuasion of the existence of angels has not sprung from the teaching of the pagan philosophers about their demons, genii, and inferior gods; whom they imagined as standing midway between God and men. Their opinion was a corruption of the tradition of primitive revelation, which was preserved among the Hebrews, as a people; and the public and religious doctrine of the Hebrews was more ancient than the pagan teaching, and was certainly independent of it.

A brief consideration of some truths with regard to the angels, our fellow creatures, will throw some light on the mind, and will, and power of His Divine Majesty, our common Creator and Lord.

The angels are *spirits* and, moreover, *pure spirits*, that is to say, spirits which are not *naturally* united to any material body, as is a human soul. A pure spirit is of itself a *complete nature;* and is not a *part* of any nature, as a human soul is a part of a human nature.

It is certain that the angels, since they are spirits, cannot be *in a place*, as commensurate therewith. The different parts of a material body, which lie outside each other, correspond with the different parts of the space in which that body is. This they do in the same way as a body, falling flat on wet clay, leaves the impress of the different parts of it on different portions of that clay. A spirit, unlike a material body, is *simple*, and has no parts. Angels are, however, *in a place*, in the sense that when they are in *this* place, they are not in *that* place. When they are *here*, they are not *there*. They must certainly be *somewhere;* and, as certainly, they cannot at one and the same moment be *everywhere*. Further, a created spirit, and therefore also an angel, can occupy an extended space; or such space as a material body would naturally occupy. This a spirit does, however, in a more perfect way. A spirit exists *as a whole* throughout the whole, and as a whole also in every part of the extended space which it occupies. Angels can also be moved by local motion; that is, by movement from place to place, or by passage from one terminus of departure in space, to another terminus of arrival in space; and that by passing through the intervening space.

The angelic intellect is more excellent than is the human intellect. This truth is expressed when it is said, that angelic nature is superior to human nature. The natural crowning point of both natures is intelligence. If in both natures there were equal force of understanding, there would be no reason why the angels should, in the order of nature, be superior to men. The angels, moreover, are not only spirits, but *pure spirits*. Man's soul is a spirit; but its knowledge is partly sensitive, and partly intellective. Through its sensitive knowledge, it is helped to its intellective knowledge. Man's soul is *naturally* united to a material body; and exists as a *part* in a compound nature. His soul's force of knowing is therefore divided, as it were, into *parts;* and its intelligence stands in need of the aid of sensation. In an angel, on the other hand, the force of knowing is reduced to oneness; and there is no need of sensation, in order to understanding. An angel is wholly mind. His intellect is, therefore, more akin to the Divine intellect; and more excellent than is the intellect in man. In the creation of the angels, God, by His Divine efficacy, moved their intellects to a naturally intuitive apprehension, both of their own substances, and of the substance of other existing things, both corporeal and spiritual. This determination, existing from the beginning, was sufficient in order to give form to the knowledge which belongs to angels, and which is natural to them. With this determinated knowledge, the angelic intellect, in virtue of its own energy, sees the essences and properties of things. Since this intuitive vision of theirs is always persevering, the successive phenomena which occur in material objects are seen by them. Among these phenomena are also new substances, which are made out of pre-existing matter.

The nature of the angelic intellect is such that it does not, as regards *all* the objects of its knowledge, proceed successively, from the already known, to the as yet unknown, by way of reasoning. This process is proper to the human intellect. Since the angelic intellect is *essentially* more perfect than is the human intellect, it demands to have an immediate knowledge of the *essences* of things, and of their *properties*. Such knowledge is not in contradiction with a finite intellect; and it is becoming in a nature which holds the highest grade, within the finite order of intelligences.

It is not impossible, however, for an angelic intellect to reason in some matters; so that there should be successive progress from something already known, to something as yet unknown. An angel's knowledge is finite, and it is capable of increase. An angel can come to know that which is virtually contained in something already known. Further, there are some things which only in this way an angel can know. As regards *natural* knowledge of God—that is to say, knowledge apart from revelation, or from supernatural intuitive vision—an angel does not naturally *see* God. He has only an *abstractive* knowledge of God; derived from things which are not God. This knowledge of God is determined by knowledge of those created objects; and it must be later than that knowledge, because it is distinct from it.

As regards knowledge of *free acts*, of which an angel is *naturally* ignorant, if he is naturally to know something of those acts, he must with more or less likelihood divine it by conjecture from signs and effects. In acquiring this knowledge there is a reasoning process; since many signs which present themselves successively to angelic vision have got to be put together. Different principles have also to be applied in the case of different matters; so that at last there should be obtained some sufficiently likely knowledge of a hidden cause, or of a free act.

By "cogitations of the heart" may be understood, in general, all immanent acts of the will and intellect, and of the internal senses, and sensitive appetite. Between these acts, however, there is some difference. Acts of will, and of intellect, are wholly independent of matter. Other acts are acts of an organic faculty. Acts which are *formally* free exist only in the will. Acts of other faculties participate in freedom ; as and in so far as they are subject to the bidding of a free will.

Knowledge can be had of *internal* acts, either with an immediate and certain knowledge, or with a knowledge which is mediate. This *mediate* knowledge may be either *probable*, from some more or less probable conjecture ; or it may be *certain*, from some extrinsic effect which itself is known, and which is necessarily bound up with a determinate cogitation. The question here is not whether an angel is capable of knowing the cogitations of one who wills his cogitations to be manifest to that angel ? or whether he is capable of knowing cogitations which God has revealed ? The question is, Can an angel of himself, and naturally, come to know the cogitations of another, independently both of that other's will, and of God's revelation ? We answer, that an angel cannot, of himself and naturally, have *immediate* and *certain* knowledge of immanent acts of the will, and intellect, of another, whether man or angel. It is a truth of Divine revelation, that certain and immediate knowledge of "cogitations of the heart," is a prerogative which is proper to God alone. Such knowledge is regarded in the Sacred Scriptures as a proof of Divinity, Jesus did not trust Himself to the Jews, "for that he knew all men, and because He needed not that any should give testimony of man, for He knew what was in man." On another occasion, Jesus, *seeing the thoughts* of the scribes, said, "Why do you think evil *in your hearts?*" Manifestation of the hidden things of the heart, is a certain proof that God is in him who manifests them; that is to say, that God alone could manifest these secrets of the soul, and that he who lays them open is speaking as from God. God is called, as by a name which is proper to Him, the Searcher of hearts, and the Discerner of the cogitations and intents of the heart.

The *heart* here signifies that faculty to which affections and volitions belong. These are said to be *of the heart*, because the heart is in common usage spoken of, as if it were the organ of the sensitive affections. Acts of the will, which are perceived by the intellect, and expressed by the judgment, are rightly called *cogitations*. Acts of the intellect, which are made at the bidding of the will, and so with some affection, are called *cogitations of the heart*. God alone can search the heart; and this prerogative belongs to God, inasmuch as He is the Creator of the heart.

Free events of the future are either immanent acts, whether elicited by the will, or commanded by the will; or they are external effects which depend on determination of will, whether the will of God, or the will of some other intelligent being. He who cannot *naturally* have knowledge of the immanent acts of another person, while these are in the present, can still less have knowledge of such acts, while they are yet in the future. Further, he who cannot *naturally* know future immanent *acts*, certainly cannot know future *effects* of these acts. Knowledge of a free event of the future includes, more or less, knowledge of the free act of the *cause*, from which the event proceeds. When this knowledge is not had, knowledge of the future event will not be had.

Those future events which, before they actually come to pass, have not been determined in the causes of them, cannot possibly be known, except *in themselves*. In order that they should be known in themselves, there is required an *infinite* intellect. This is God alone. Further, in order that anything whatsoever which is future should actually be, there is required the will of God, or the permission of God. Hence, when it is not known what God wills to do, or what He wills to permit, there cannot be certainty of any future event. God alone *naturally* knows what He wills to do, or wills to permit. Knowledge of the future is a proper sign of Divinity; and so it does not belong to angels. It is the prerogative of God. Hence the origin of the word *divination*, to express what is, or what is pretended to be, a foreknowing and foretelling of the future. The angels hear the prayers of the faithful, which are addressed to them; even if they are made by way of internal cogitation alone. The angels can also, if one may say so, hear the cogitations of other angels, who wish to communicate with them. If this *hearing* is mutual, there will be *speech* between them. This faculty is *natural* to the angels. It would be absurd that there should exist a multitude of intelligent beings, of the same order, who could not hold intercourse with each other; and this intercourse there could not be, without *speech*, or without the equivalent of speech. If men are able to mutually manifest their meaning, and in this *speech* consists; why not angels? since power of speech is certainly a perfection, and angels are so much more perfect than are men.

3.

Among the *visible* works in the realm of creation, God's most noble work is—man. This is evident, if we look to man's nature, and compare it with other *visible* natures. The Fathers give as a reason why, among so many natures, man's nature was the last to be produced, that man is the proximate end of all visible creatures, and so is, as it were, the visible king of God's visible creation.

Man is a microcosm. In man the spiritual and the material meet, and are wedded, in the unity of one personal being. Man is thus fitted, in virtue of his compound nature, as it comprehends in itself somewhat of all created natures, to be in a manner the Lord of creation, and its High Priest.

Man was made *immediately* in his own human species. We do not by the word *immediately* exclude the co-operation of some second cause, as for instance of an angel, in the *formation* of man's body. Neither do we exclude the pre-existence of some matter, which was of itself indifferent; and which was formed, by the action of a cause, into a body, into which was then infused a soul. That which we exclude is a *transformation of species*, as if human nature had first existed virtually in the nature of a brute animal, which was successively transformed, from one species to another species; until at last, by an evolution of this kind, it arrived at human nature. In that case, the formation of the human body would really have begun from the beginning, when the first brute animal was formed; and would have gone on gradually, until from some mere animal there emerged a body, which was adapted for human functions. The formation of man would not, in that case, have taken place *after* the existence of other natures.

God, in instituting the creation of the world, willed absolutely the existence of the human species; for the sake of which all other visible things have been created. If, therefore, God had instituted transformation of species, there must have been a law of nature—or of the Author of nature—that when at last there should be in existence a body which was fitted for human life, the existence of that body would, by force of the law of the institution of all natures, have demanded the infusion into it of a rational soul. The consequence would have been, that the pair of brute animals, of which such a body was immediately begotten, would have been truly the parents of Adam, regarded in his entirety as a man. For no other reason are those who beget us, although they beget only our bodies, said to be the parents and progenitors of the whole man; than because, in virtue of generation, they produce a body to which, by a law of nature, a rational soul is due. If Adam had parents, it was false to say that among the animals there was found no helpmate like unto him. If Adam sprang from the animals, so from them also could, and ought, the woman to have sprung. If the body of Adam was begotten of a brute, either his rational soul was infused by God into the embryo, conceived in the womb of that favoured mother ; or it was infused into the living body, of which that mother had been already delivered, and thereby displaced a brute soul. On the one hypothesis, the first man would have been born of a brute ; on the other, His Divine Majesty would have been like to the false gods of the pagan poets, who were said to transform brute animals into men.

It is a Divinely revealed truth that human nature consists of two elements, and of two only, a material body, and a rational soul. The synthesis of those two elements consists of substances which are so united as to constitute one subject, and one nature. They are, therefore, said to be *substantially* united. The formal principle of the life of the human body, is the spirit which is united with it. This spirit is, therefore, called the *soul* of that body. Of this principle of life, and of the body to which it gives life, there is made *one nature*.

The Sacred Scriptures attribute to man, as to *one subject*, things which are proper to the body, and things also which are proper to the spirit. The same being who is said to be born, to die, and to rise again, to see, to hear, to burn with desires of the flesh, and the like ; is said also to understand, to believe, to love, and to worship God. It is the same being who exercises all these attributes. Body and soul in man coalesce so as to constitute one principle, and therefore one nature. When finite beings coalesce, so as to constitute one principle, they mutually perfect each other, and there is constituted a new nature. When the human body returns to the dust, from which it was taken, the spirit returns to God who gave it; and this spirit which so returns is an immortal and intelligent spirit. While it was in the body, it gave life to the body, and was therefore called the *soul* of the body. Since this soul is itself a spirit, it is not only a *lifegiving* soul, it is a *rational* soul.

It was defined by the Council of Vienne that the rational soul is, *of itself* and *essentially*, the *form* of the human body; that is to say, the spirit is an *essential part* of man, and it is the *formal* part. It is the *soul*, or principle of life, to his body; and with his body constitutes one nature. The life of the body is dependent, therefore, on the spirit, as on its formal principle. There is in man no other soul, besides his intellective soul; and the body of man is not of itself a living body. The definition of Vienne was reiterated in the Fifth Lateran Council; and it has again been confirmed by Pius IX.

When a thing is called a *partial* substance, it is not thereby denied that it is *truly* a substance, and a substance *by itself*. It is called a partial substance because, since it is an incomplete nature, it is a part, along with another partial substance, of one nature. Human nature is *one substance*, but a *compound* substance, composed of two substances. Hence both truths are to be held—that the oneness of man is a *substantial* oneness—and that man consists of two *partial* substances, his body and his soul; each of which is truly by itself a substance.

It is a Divinely revealed truth that all men spring from one parent, created by God; so that both by origin, and by specific oneness of nature, all men belong to the same family, and share the same humanity.

Specific oneness of nature consists in this, that the several individuals who have the same essential notes, belong to the same species of nature. There could be specific oneness, without oneness of *origin;* but if there is oneness of origin, or origin of all from one, this carries with it specific oneness, or oneness of species.

It is certain that when Adam was created there was then no other man in existence, or, that he was the first of his race and species; and that no woman existed before the creation of Eve. Never and nowhere has there existed on the earth, after Adam, a man who was not descended from Adam.

The whole aggregate of human souls was not created at once in the beginning; nor is any one human soul derived from another human soul. Every single human soul is produced by creation, and is not created before the existence of its body. It is created then when its body is fitted to receive it. Since the soul is united to the body, as the form of the body, so that in the body it may exercise operations of life; the body will then be fit for reception of the soul, when it has become a fit instrument for some at least of the operations of life.

The human soul is of its own nature immortal. This was solemnly asserted by Leo X. in the Fifth Lateran Council, when he condemned the opinion of those who say that an intellective soul is mortal. The mortality of a soul would be possible cessation of its existence; and so the immortality of a soul is negation of cessation of its existence. It was therefore defined that a rational soul is to exist perpetually, and without end. Not only the *fact* of the soul's everlasting existence, but also the *law* of its immortal existence, was asserted by the Pontiff. That opinion was condemned which asserts that the nature of the rational soul is mortal, or in other words, that the rational soul is of its nature mortal; and so there was affirmed the natural exigence and necessity of the soul's perpetual duration. That this was really the scope of the conciliar definition, is manifest from the precept which was afterwards given to all public professors of philosophy, by which they were bound to teach, and to persuade their hearers, by every means in their power, of the Catholic truth of the immortality of the soul. If this Catholic truth had been a truth of *fact* alone, and not also a truth of *law*, philosophers might have been commanded not to say anything against the truth of the fact; but it could not have been prescribed to them that they should persuade men by *philosophical* argument. Philosophers could not prove the immortality of the soul, except by demonstration that the nature of the soul demands its immortality.

The immortality of a spiritual being is opposed to its annihilation. It consists in its always being, and in its always living. This immortality may be considered in three ways, as essential—as natural—or as gratuitous.

It might be *essential;* that is to say, it might necessarily flow forth from the *essence* of an immortal being, which has this *from itself*—that it should always be. Secondly, it might be *natural;* and in that case, there is an exigence of perpetual preservation in being; which proceeds from the *nature* of the being in question, inasmuch as in its nature there is no positive principle whereby it can cease to be, and it is furnished with properties, and is subject to laws, which are, in the nature of things, bound up with perpetuity of existence. Thirdly, the immortality of a spiritual being might be *gratuitous*, depending solely on the will of God, without any demand of nature.

Essential immortality is proper to God alone. Gratuitous immortality might be bestowed by God on any creature. It is *natural* immortality which belongs to the human soul.

Looking to that soul itself, the natural capacity of its intellect, and of its will, could not be fulfilled, if it were not immortal. Its intellect would have a natural propension, and the terminus of it would be impossible. It belongs to the capacity of the intellect, to be capable of knowledge of every being, of intimately understanding the natures of beings, and of unerringly apprehending the bonds between them, and the reasons of them. In like manner, the natural capacity of the will is for the attainment of perfect good, without admixture of any evil. Both capacities are *natural* to the soul of man, because both flow forth from the essence of that soul; and neither of them can possibly be fulfilled, if man's soul does not survive his body. That a capacity should have been divinely given, and that it should be incapable of fulfilment—that it should exist, and that it should exist in vain—involves contradiction.

Looking to the moral order, man has from nature an inextinguishable desire for happiness. Along with this, there is in man a natural and necessary law, which prescribes virtue, and prohibits sin, even at the cost of all worldly goods, and of life itself. Between the existence of those two—that desire, and this law—there would be contradiction, if the life of man's soul ends with its life on earth.

Looking to the social order, there would be universal error in the morally universal persuasion of mankind, that there is for the soul a future life. Apart from this persuasion, where would be observance of the rights of others, submission to authority, and self sacrifices for the common good?

Looking to the order of justice, it is evident that completeness of execution of the moral order must be within the power of God. He must not be wholly hindered by a creature's will, and must be able to reduce to subjection His rebel creature, on whom He would otherwise be dependent. Further, if the soul is not immortal, the virtuous will have had no adequate reward, and they will have been of all men most miserable.

The desire for happiness is natural and necessary to the human soul. It is the foundation, the root, and the reason of all other desires. Whatsoever we desire, we desire it, because we desire our happiness. This desire cannot be got rid of. Even when we will that which for us is evil, it is because it presents itself to us under some appearance of the good, in partial happiness. A happiness that is partial, and a happiness that is passing, will not avail to fulfil the capacity of a soul which, of its very nature, can be satisfied only with a happiness which is unmingled, absolute, and eternal.

The soul of man, in the natural immortality of its everlasting life, is a created image and mirror of the essential immortality of the ever-living God.

CHAPTER X.

GOD, AS THE AUTHOR OF THE SUPERNATURAL.

THERE are certain kinds of goods which, in the sum of them, are called by the Fathers *nature*—goods which belong to nature—goods which are in the power of nature—goods which cannot be lost, so long as the nature remains entire—goods which are necessarily bound up with creation—goods which do not exceed servile condition—goods which are only less properly called graces.

There are certain other goods, which are said by the Fathers to be *above nature*—to be graces, which are not in the power of nature—to be goods which are outside the substance of those on whom they are bestowed—goods which belong to the grace of justification—goods which have properly the name of *graces*—goods which can be lost, while the nature remains in its entirety—and goods by means of which man is raised to a certain *deification*, through assimilation to God, and union with God.

That which the Fathers teach, theologians explain. They make a clear distinction between a *natural* order, and a *supernatural* order. In the *natural* order they include whatsoever is necessarily bound up with the *essences* of things, and flows from them, and is exacted by them, and does not exceed the worth and condition of them.

By the name of *supernatural*, theologians designate that which exceeds the worthiness and condition, the force and faculty, of nature; and either constitutes friendship with God, Divine adoption, and beatific vision—or is in touch with these, either as an effect, or as a means.

There are, therefore, two distinct series of created goods. One series consists of those goods without which nature cannot exist—which nature exacts—which nature can attain to by its own forces—which are bound up with the worthiness and condition of nature—and which do not raise nature to a state which is higher than its own state.

The other series of goods consists of those goods without which nature can exist—goods which are not exacted by nature—which exceed the forces and faculties of nature—which are above and beyond the condition, and desert or worth, of nature—and which raise nature to a state which is higher than its own state.

In short, there are goods which are natural, and *due* to nature; and there are goods which are supernatural, *not due* to nature, and wholly gratuitous.

Setting aside other meanings of the words

nature and *natural*, we shall, for the purposes of our present consideration, use the word *nature*, as opposed to that which is *above nature*, as signifying a *substance*, and the *subject* of those things which are in it—and the word *natural*, as signifying those things which are *necessary consequences* of a nature.

The *natural* is distinct from the *nature*; and is that which is exacted by a nature, lest that nature, and the forces of that nature, should exist in vain ; or, lest that certain degree of perfection in which the nature, and the forces of it, are constituted, should be in vain.

To this may be reduced all things natural which are in any way distinct from a nature. Thus, the end, and the attainment of the end when the nature is rightly operating, is *natural*. Entireness of organs, necessary in order that the forces may exercise themselves, is *natural*. The concurrence of God, without which action is impossible, is *natural*. The operation of other causes, which are necessary in order that the forces may be able to act, is *natural*. The objects of the faculties, along with the attainment of these objects, are *natural*. The termini of activity, when activity is being exercised, are *natural*; or, that is *natural* which can be done through one's own proper and natural forces. Those subjects in which the nature can and ought to exercise its own forces, are *natural*. Co-existence, and association, with others of the same perfection, without whom certain forces, or a certain degree of the exercise of them, cannot be developed, is *natural*. Co-existence with superior beings is also *natural*; and, generally, it is *natural* to be subject to other causes, and to receive from them that of which one's own natural passivity is capable, and which those causes can effect, in accordance with their own forces; as for instance, it is *natural* for bodies to be moved by angels. Hence we observe that the sphere of the *natural* is wider, than is the sphere of the *essential*.

Certain things are *exacted* by a *nature*, lest that nature, and the forces of that nature, should exist in vain. These are exacted by reason of a perfection which they possess. The perfection belongs to the genus, or to the species, of the things. Since, however, a genus cannot exist except in a species, and species cannot exist except in individuals, the existence of an *individual* is exacted. There cannot again be individuals, except as existing in some determinate number. As regards a certain determinate number of species, or of individuals, the nature which exacts either of them is indifferent. It is, therefore, in the power of the Author of nature to make any number, great or small, of individuals. Animal nature exacts the existence of those things which form fitting food for it; but that there should exist a certain number of species of aliments, and a certain number of individual aliments, in each species, nature does not exact; nor does nature exact one particular determinate species of aliments, or any determinate individual aliment. Inasmuch, however, as some species in a genus, and some individuals in a species, are exacted by nature; all the species, and all the individuals, however many they may be, are *natural*. They are contained within that order of perfection, in which those things actually exist, which the *nature* exacts. An exuberant abundance, therefore, of things which contribute to the beauty and adornment of the universe, and to the greater wellbeing of other creatures, is an effect of the liberality of the Author of nature; but it is not something which is *above nature*.

Even if something is not exacted by one determinate individual in a nature, yet it may be exacted by the nature of that individual, regarded universally, or by a class, consisting of several individuals of that nature. If so, although the thing is not exacted by any determinate individual of that nature, there is, however, more or less, a proximate potentiality of its existence. It is, therefore, *natural*.

All the *natural* objects, which we have enumerated, may be reduced to the *active* power, and the *passive* power, of a nature. Whatever is exacted lest a nature, and the forces of that nature, should exist in vain, is exacted either as a terminus of the *activity* of the nature; or as a complement of the *capacity* of the nature. Capacity may be manifold. That is a natural capacity, the complement of which is exacted by the nature, lest it, and the forces of it, should be in vain—or the terminus of which other causes, which have an active power of completing that capacity, exact, lest those causes, and the forces of them, should exist in vain.

To complete the notion of those things which are *natural*, we must look to universal nature; for that which one nature can effect in another nature, is to be regarded as simply *natural*.

In this consideration, the *active* power of nature must be accurately distinguished from the *passive* power of nature. It is not to be supposed that everything which nature is capable of receiving from God is *natural*. If this were so, there would be no possibility of *supernatural* good.

The *natural*, regarded from the point of view of *universal nature*, or, of natures in general—is that which either *constitutes* a nature—or is a *necessary consequence* of a nature—or is *exacted* by a nature, lest it, and the powers of it, should exist in vain—or which can be *effected* by one nature *in another* nature—or which is *contained within* the order of those things which are exacted by nature.

2.

The *supernatural* is opposed to the *natural*, by way not of the *contradictory*, but of the *contrary*, and through its supereminence. Both the natural and the supernatural *suppose* the *nature*, in which they are—but the *natural* does not exceed the limits of the order of nature, since it is in accordance with the exigence of nature—while the *supernatural* exceeds the order of nature, since it is beyond and above the exigence of nature.

A thing may be called *supernatural*, in the first place, because the action by which it is made is supernatural; that is to say, it has its origin not from nature, but from the Author of nature, and from beyond the order of nature. It is supernatural, even if the terminus of the action is itself natural; as in the case of miraculous restoration of health. This is called being supernatural *in mode*, or in the way in which the work is done. This *mode* regards the *action*, and not the *effect*. It is called, and it is, supernatural, because it is not within the power of nature. A thing may also be called supernatural, as regards the thing itself; inasmuch as in its own *essence*, regarded

U

formally, it contains the idea of supernatural good.

Supernatural good may, in contrast with the opposite notion of *natural* good, be described as being a perfection which *neither constitutes* anything of the essence, or nature, of the thing in which it is—*nor is a necessary consequence* of that essence or nature, nor can be conceived to be its consequence—*nor is exacted* by any nature, lest that nature should be in vain—*nor is contained within* the order of those things which a nature demands, lest it should exist in vain—and which, therefore, is not contained in any *active* power of the nature, or in any *passive* power of the nature, so that other created forces should exact the possibility of their effecting it; lest they, or the forces of them, should exist in vain—and, finally, the supernatural is a perfection which is *greater than natural* perfection.

The supernatural is a *perfection;* and therefore sin, although it is not a necessary consequence of any nature, and is not exacted by any nature, is not *supernatural.* It is *contra-natural*, or against nature.

Supernatural goods may be compared with natural goods, as regards the genus to which they respectively belong; as the former are supernatural, while the latter are natural. From the point of view of this comparison, every supernatural good, whatsoever, is greater than is any natural good; since the order to which it belongs—and that is the idea to which we have regard in this comparison—is the higher order of the two. If, however, supernatural goods are compared with natural goods, as regards the species to which they respectively belong, as the one good is this determinate good, and the other good is that determinate good; it is not necessary that every supernatural good should be ontologically greater than is every natural good. It is sufficient that the supernatural good should be greater than is a parallel good in the natural order. Thus immortal life is greater than is a life which is at any time to end; although immortal life may not, perhaps, be greater than is some perfection of knowledge.

Those things, however, which are in the highest degree of the supernatural order, and which are called *simply supernatural*, must necessarily exceed in perfection all goods whatsoever, which are *naturally* due to creatures.

The *capacity*, and *force*, of a nature are *better* fulfilled through supernatural gifts; but they are, nevertheless, *wholly*, or completely, fulfilled through natural endowments. By subsistence in a human person is fulfilled, for instance, the whole capacity of a human nature for subsistence; so that a human nature could not receive another person at the same time. A Divine person, however, fulfils the capacity of a human nature for subsistence, in a more noble manner, and with greater advantage to the nature. It, nevertheless, does not more fulfil that nature's capacity for subsistence. This capacity would be completely fulfilled by subsistence in a human person. The same vessel is more nobly filled with a precious liquor, than it is with a worthless liquid, but the vessel is not more full.

Natural good may exist apart from supernatural good, but supernatural good cannot exist apart from natural good, or without the perfection of natural good. In supernatural acts there is the whole perfection of a vital act, and of a free act; and this perfection is from nature. In *supernatural* beatitude, there is the whole of the perfection of knowledge, and love, and possession, which would have had place in *natural* beatitude. That which is excluded by the existence of supernatural good, is the good having a merely natural character; such as an act which is *purely* natural, or beatitude which is *purely* natural. These natural goods are distinct from the supernatural goods which correspond to them; although the latter contain the perfection of them, and something more. The nature itself remains always the same; but has in addition the gratuitous gifts bestowed upon it.

When the exigence of a nature, lest it should exist in vain, can be satisfied in either of two ways, and these ways differ in perfection, the less perfect of the two is that which is *exacted*. By the more perfect mode of satisfaction the nature would be satisfied, not merely in order that it should not exist *in vain*, but in order that it should exist in a still *better* state. This satisfaction may be *becoming to* the nature, but it cannot be *exacted* by the nature. If, however, the more imperfect, but sufficient, mode of satisfaction is not forthcoming, then the nature *exacts* another and equivalent mode, even if that mode should be more perfect.

This is the general norm for discerning, among goods which complete the *capacity* of a nature, that which is natural, from that which is supernatural.

What we have said with regard to natural good comes to this, that there should be an exigence of the nature for it; and this is what is signified, when something is said to be *due to nature*. It is no question of debt in the moral order. The debt is in the ontological order. That is *due*, or *owing* to a nature, which, given that nature, ought to exist; either as necessarily bound up with the nature, or in order that the nature itself should not exist in vain.

In considering a good as *due to nature*, the nature is not to be taken, as it exists in this or in that individual—under these, or under those, determinate contingent conditions—but simply as it is a nature. The goods must also be regarded relatively to the nature. The nature is presupposed, and the existence of it is supposed, when real goods are spoken of in connection with it.

As a natural good is said to be a good which is *due* to nature; so a supernatural good is a good which is *not due* to nature. The *not due*, and the *gratuitous*, are one and the same.

We have again to observe that the *terminus* with which the goods, which are said to be *not due*, are compared, is the nature *simply;* and not the nature as already furnished with some gratuitous good, on account of which the nature, so supplied, can *exact* other and greater goods.

Nature itself, and the *natural*, may, in a certain sense, be said to be *not due*, or to be *gratuitous*. It was of His simple benignity, that God freely created nature, and the natural. There was no exigence of their nature on the part of creatures. To them it was gratuitous. The institution of nature at the first was gratuitous; and so was the bestowal of all those things which are consequences of created nature.

In quite another way are supernatural goods said to be *not due*. All supernatural goods are said to be *not due*, because the subject of them, although he is in existence, does not have *right to them*—while all natural things were *not due*, because there was no subject to exact them. Supernatural goods, therefore, are not due, *positively*, since there exists a real subject to whom they are not due—while natural goods were not due, *negatively*, since there was no subject to whom they could be due.

Although certain natural goods are not due *positively*, yet they are not *simply* not due; because the perfection which they bestow, whether regarded generically, or regarded specifically, is of itself due. It is not as regarded *formally*, but as regarded *materially*, that those natural goods are *not due*. The perfection of supernatural goods is *of itself* not due. As regarded *formally*, therefore, supernatural goods are *not due*.

To be called *not due*, and *gratuitous*, belongs *properly*, therefore, to supernatural goods, and not to natural goods; for a thing is *properly* called that which it is positively, and of itself, or formally, and not merely negatively and materially.

3.

The division of goods into the *supernatural*, and the *natural*, is an adequate division, since it is made by way of contraries, between which there is no mean; for every good is either exacted by nature, or it is not exacted—it is either in the power of nature, or it is not in the power of nature—it is either due to nature, or it is gratuitous.

The *supernatural* may, however, be subdivided. A good may be not due to the nature on which it is bestowed, and it may not be exacted by universal nature, and it may not be in the power of any natural cause to effect it; and, nevertheless, that good is a good which does not of itself exceed the limits of the whole realm of nature. We have an example in the immortality of body, and in the freedom from concupiscence, which were bestowed on human nature, as it existed in the first man. These goods are contained within the order of universal nature; since they are natural to certain natures, namely, to pure spirits.

A good which is *not due* to nature, in such wise that neither the nature on which it is bestowed, nor any other created nature, can either achieve it, or exact it, and which bestows a perfection which is outside the order of the whole of created nature, such as is the beatific vision, is called *simply supernatural.* This species of supernatural goods is so called, because it participates more perfectly in the idea of its genus—the supernatural.

The other species of goods, which are *above nature*, but are, nevertheless, contained *within the limits* of nature; in order that it may have its own name to distinguish it, and to signify that it is *less above* the natural, than is the simply supernatural, is called—the *preternatural.*

The preternatural stands midway between the supernatural and the natural. It is above the natural, and it is beneath the supernatural. Everything which is intermediate participates in somewhat of both extremes; and so the *preternatural*, as *not due* to nature, may be reckoned among supernatural goods. As *not exceeding* the order of the whole of nature, it may be numbered among natural goods.

4.

The greatest and most precious supernatural gifts, such as are faith, hope, charity, and sanctifying grace; through which, to borrow the language of inspiration, we are "made partakers of the Divine nature," come to this, that we are called and are—sons of God. A son may be regarded in two states of sonship—as not having yet attained to the inheritance of his father—or as having already entered on that inheritance. In the first state, a son has the power of attaining to it, and he has right to it, inasmuch as he is a son, and he will certainly one day attain to it; unless for his demerits in the interval, he deserves to be excluded from his inheritance. In this state that son is in a manner as yet on the way. In the other state of sonship, the son, having secured possession of his inheritance, has nothing more that he can desire; and yet he does not cease to be a son, if during the lifetime of his father he is admitted to enjoyment of the inheritance. His condition as a son is, on the contrary, perfected and completed, when he is conjoined with his father, by an indissoluble bond, and perfect communion of goods.

Through sanctifying grace, with which the theological virtues of faith, hope, and charity are bound up, justified men are adopted as sons by God; and destined to beatific vision of God, and enjoyment of God, as their inheritance.

There is no need for us first to prove that the vision of God is supernatural; and then to prove that the grace, by which we are constituted sons of God, and made fit for that vision, is supernatural. The two are not to be divided. If the supernatural character of the heavenly kingdom is proved, there is proved also the supernatural character of the adoption of sons; through which we obtain power and right thereto. Adoptive sonship, on the one hand, and possession of the end in Fatherland, on the other hand, are not things of a different order. This sonship has not merely the idea of a *means*, in order to beatific vision. A means, which is *merely* a means, ceases when the *end* is obtained. Adoptive sonship is in such wise a means, towards possession of the heavenly kingdom, as the *beginning* of a thing is a necessary means to the *consummation* of that thing. Adoptive sonship does not, therefore, cease, but is fulfilled, completed, and crowned, in possession of the end. Divine sonship, in the case of creatures, is an *adoptive* sonship. Those are sons of God, and born of God, who have faith and charity. They are sons of God by adoption, and the dignity of sonship, and the communication of those goods by which sonship is constituted, are, both of them, supernatural. Adoptive sonship, of itself, implies two things—participation of rights and goods which are proper to the Father, and are due to His Son by nature—and participation of rights and goods made to a stranger who, of himself, has no claim to those goods and rights which are communicated to him.

On account of the infinite distance between God and His creature, Divine adoptive sonship can be only an *analogous* participation of goods and rights which are proper to God. The analogy properly consists in the mode in which the goods are participated. In order to there being truly adoptive sonship, goods and rights which are naturally proper to God, must be truly participated, although not all of them. They will, however, be participated in such wise that there will be an essential difference, as regards the *mode* of participation ; and therefore also as regards *fulness* of participation.

Men who, through adoption, are called to Divine sonship, are *strangers;* that is to say, they have not *of themselves* any right to those goods, which they acquire through adoption. Those goods are, therefore, *not due* to them. Adoption is a gratuitous benefit, which cannot be merited by any work of nature ; and so cannot be *due* to nature itself. It is not merely by reason of sin, that Divine sonship is not due to us since the fall of man. Divine sonship was never natural to men, or due to men. If it were only on account of sin that Divine adoption is not due to human nature, it would have been due before sin. A son to whom a crime is forgiven by his father, and to whom the rights of sonship are restored, is not said to be *adopted;* nor is the restoration of those rights *adoption*, since he is a son already, and by nature. There is only restoration to favour, and the son who is restored is a son by nature, and not by adoption.

Divine adoptive sonship is *simply supernatural;* for not to any creature, who by nature is a *slave,* is there due, by nature, participation of those goods, by means of which a man is constituted an adoptive son of God. The notion of a *slave,* properly so called, includes four elements. A slave is, in the first place, bound to do the will of his master, in any work which his master gives him to do. Secondly, the work of the slave ought to be done for the profit of his master; and as a service which is due to him. Thirdly, although a slave can demand from his master those things which are necessary for support of life, and for the service of God; or may even demand some wage for his work; yet this is entirely apart from and outside all family obligation, and friendship. The slave has no right to the inheritance of his master. Further, and fourthly, those three elements rest, as on a foundation, on this, that the slave is reckoned as the *property* of his master, through lawful possession. A slave is one in whom another has a right of property, and who is bound to do that other's will, and to direct all his works to his master's profit and service, and who has no right to family privileges, or to his master's friendship, or to inheritance of his master's fortune.

A son, on the other hand, who proceeds from his father, through natural generation, has right to family privileges, to his father's friendship, and to his father's inheritance. Although a son ought to work for his father's advantage, and contribute to his father's honour, he is, nevertheless, working at the same time for his own profit; since the good of his father is his good, and his father himself has in view the good of his son, since he loves him with a love of friendship. The father rules his son indeed, but for his son's own good, and he does not treat him, or use him merely, as if he were no more than a slave.

It is most certain that God has the fullest right of property in his rational creature; and that He has this right by the title of creation. God, nevertheless, wills the good of His rational creature, and loves him with the love of benevolence. With the same love of benevolence, is the rational creature destined by nature to love his Maker. There exists, therefore, even in the natural order, a certain friendship between God and His rational creature. This friendship is founded in communion of goods, and in reciprocal love. The rational creature obeys God, as one who is not merely using him, but who is ruling him for his good; and thereby loving him. The rational creature, nevertheless, has not by nature any right to those goods which are by nature the property of the Divine nature. He is destitute of this right, because he is not a son *by nature*, but is a *creature;* that is to say, because he is not *begotten*, or does not proceed by an immanent operation, but has been *caused* and *made*. The stable dignity, or worthiness, through which such a right is participated, and through which he who receives it is assimilated to the Son of God *by nature*, is what is called *adoptive sonship*. The creature, as a creature, is destitute of the right to share with God's Son by nature in the family privileges, and in the friendship, and property, of the Father. The creature is said to be a *slave by nature* in contradistinction from the *Son by nature*. There cannot be any greater distance than is that which exists between being a slave by nature, and having right to reign. Divine adoptive sonship gives right to reign as heir, and coheir, with Christ in His heavenly kingdom. That sonship, and this right, must necessarily wholly exceed all exigence of the creature, and be entirely supernatural. The idea involves contradiction, that to the creature there should belong, by reason of its created nature, any right to the Divine inheritance.

By Divine adoptive sonship we are, says St. Peter, made partakers of the Divine nature. Thus, as St. Augustine, St. Basil, St. Cyril, and other Fathers say, are we *deified*. This *deification* is none other than a participation of those goods which are *above nature;* a state of existence, and a mode of existence, which is wholly supernatural. Whatever those goods of a man, which are due to human nature, and which are contained within its limits, might amount to, the man remains no more than man. In order that the man should be *deified*, and be worthy of being called "god, and son of the Most High," he must perforce participate in those goods which are proper to God; and these most certainly cannot be conceived as *natural* to any creature. They are, therefore, *simply supernatural.*

The intuitive vision of God, regarded in itself, which is the inheritance of the sons of God, who have right and power to attain thereto; and also that knowledge whereby we are prepared therefor, are, on the testimony of the Word of God—supernatural. Christ said "No one knoweth the Son, but the Father; neither doth any one know the Father, but the Son, and he to whom it shall please the Son to reveal Him." Christ is here speaking of knowledge of God, under the distinct conception of the Father, the Son, and the Holy Ghost. In the intuitive vision of God there is seen the Father, the Son, and the Holy Ghost. This knowledge, which is attributed by the words of Christ to the Divine persons, in such wise that others besides them can have capacity and power to enjoy that knowledge, only in so far as God wills to communicate it. The words "to whom it shall please Him" signify that it is free to God to communicate that knowledge to one, or to many, or to no one. Others who are excluded from knowledge of the Father and the Son, and who are signified by "no one," are intelligent creatures. It follows that, if knowledge of the Father and the Son *were due* to intelligent nature; or if intelligent nature could *demand* that knowledge, the words of Christ would be false. His words deny not only the *fact*, but the *power*, and every power which has not origin from the free will of God. They exclude any power which is inborn in intelligent nature. They exclude it, not only in human nature, but in angelic nature. Further, it is most clear that if this power, to attain to supernatural knowledge, does not belong to any intelligent creature, it certainly cannot belong to any created nature whatsoever.

If created intelligent nature exacted this knowledge, it would no longer be free to God, when that nature was in actual existence, to reveal to "no one" the Father and the Son; for to those, at least, who by their merits had prepared themselves for this knowledge, it would be *due* as a reward, and end.

The same truth was declared by St. Paul, when

v

he wrote to the Corinthians—"We speak wisdom among the perfect; yet not the wisdom of this world, neither of the princes of this world, that come to nought; but we speak the wisdom of God in a mystery, a wisdom which is hidden, which God ordained before the world, unto our glory; which none of the princes of this world knew; for if they had known it, they would never have crucified the Lord of glory. But, as it is written, That eye hath not seen, nor ear heard, neither hath it entered into the heart of man, what things God hath prepared for them that love Him. But to us God hath revealed them by His Spirit. For the Spirit searcheth all things, yea the deep things of God. For what man knoweth the things of a man, but the spirit of a man that is in him? So the things also that are of God no man knoweth, but the Spirit of God." The *wisdom* of which St. Paul is speaking is the doctrine of the Faith, of which the consummation is the intuitive vision of the Trinity; and it is wholly supernatural. It is the wisdom *in a mystery*, the *hidden* wisdom, hidden from the princes of this world; and these are either the wiser of this world, or demons. When the Apostle says that eye hath not seen, or ear heard, and that it hath not entered into the heart of man to conceive the things which God has prepared for those who love Him; he signifies that those goods are unknown to men, at least in this life. He denies, not only the *fact* of their being known, but also the *possibility* of their being known, at least in this life. Further, he teaches that the Christian doctrine, on the one hand, and heavenly beatitude, on the other hand, are both of them of the same order. Again, and principally, he teaches that men gain this wisdom, through the Spirit of God. He gives as a reason why it is the Spirit of God, and no other, who communicates this wisdom to men, that the Spirit is the Searcher of all things, even the deep things of God, which cannot be known by any other. The wisdom, which is proper to the Spirit of God, cannot be in the power of any creature, nor can it be exacted by any creature. Such goods are not only above all *merits* of men, but above men's *nature*. They are above nature, because nature is in the condition of a slave—and man is born a slave, because man is a *creature*.

It is not a supernatural *end* only, but the *means* also towards that end, that is not due to any created nature; for means which are necessary, in order to an end which is *due*, cannot be *not due*.

Divine adoptive sonship is in itself a perfection, which is not merely a moral perfection, but is an *ontological* perfection. Participation of the Divine nature, which Divine adoptive sonship carries with it, is something ontological. It is, in other words, real. It actually exists. It is not an imagination, or mere figment of the mind. The terminus of it, which is the vision and possession of God, is an ontological good. The life which we are now leading on earth, the life of faith, hope and charity, which is in proportion with that terminus or end, has ontological perfection, or real existence, as has all and every life. As we are born to natural life, so are we born again to the life that is supernatural.

5.

An *innate* appetite is called an *appetite*, from the analogy of an *elicited* appetite. An elicited appetite is a *vital act*, which follows apprehension. An *innate* appetite is antecedent to any act. It is not distinct from the *nature*, of which it is an appetite. It is attributed to every nature, whether rational or irrational. Speaking generally, this appetite is an ordination of nature towards some good; or, it is the nature itself, as it has been ordained towards some good. This order may be either an order of *capacity*, or an order of *exigence*. Hence, when we speak of an innate appetite we may be referring either to the one order, or to the other order. Sometimes an innate appetite is defined to be simply a *power* which is susceptive of a good, or a *capacity* for a good which is becoming to the nature in question.

Sometimes, again, an innate appetite is defined to be ordination towards a necessary good, without which good the nature would exist in vain; and so it is an *exigence* of that good, or an *essential* ordination towards that good. A *capacity*, however, as well as an exigence, is something essential. There is said to be an *essential* order of a thing towards some other thing, when this other thing is exacted from it, by reason of its *essence*. If the essence of a thing is indifferent towards some particular good, then the order is to something which can be absent, without damage to the thing in question. This is called an *accidental* order, to distinguish it from an *essential* order. The name of *appetite* more properly belongs to that which is an *essential* order; since we do not *desire* a thing, simply because we are *capable* of it.

An *elicited* appetite is an act of appetite, which follows apprehension. An *innate* appetite is not an act; and it does not follow apprehension. An elicited appetite may be manifold. An innate appetite is one. An elicited appetite can be borne towards that which is not becoming to the subject of it, or even to that which is impossible; if it is apprehended as becoming, and possible, or if it is something which is hypothetically desired. An *innate* appetite is not borne except to that which is becoming, and possible; and, if it is an appetite of exigence, it is not borne to that which is not, at least at some time, contained within the order of the real.

There does not exist in any created nature, an *innate* appetite, which is an exigence, for *supernatural* goods.

An *elicited* appetite, since it follows apprehension, can be borne towards every thing which is apprehended *as good*. The good which is apprehended may be either a *necessary* good of nature, and so a good which corresponds to the *innate* appetite of *exigence;* or it may be only a *possible* good of nature, which therefore corresponds to the *capacity* of the nature; or it may be even a good which is not possible to the nature. In this latter case, if the impossibility is adverted to, the desire of the thing will really be *conditional*, and expressed by—I would, if this were possible. The good which is apprehended may be some good which is not becoming to the nature—or it may be an evil which presents itself under the appearance of good, and is apprehended under the idea of the good.

The appetite is called *efficacious*, when the nature can attain to that which it desires. The appetite is *inefficacious*, when the nature cannot attain to that which it desires. Hence appetite or desire of the vision of God, which is efficacious in us, because we can attain to it through grace; would be inefficacious, if it existed in a nature which was not destined to the vision of God. Since the appetite can be borne towards every good to be attained, the appetite is not only for that which is due to nature; and so from appetite it cannot be gathered that the thing which is desired is *due to* the nature of him who desires it. If a man has the desire to fly, it does not follow that there is due to him the faculty of flying.

6.

Through bestowal of supernatural gifts, nature is raised by God to an order of being, which is *above* it, and which is *not due* to it. To this raising, on the part of God, there corresponds, in the subject raised, a power; in accordance with which, the nature is capable of receiving those goods which are bestowed upon it. There is in every creature twofold passive power. There is a passive power as regards the *natural* agent, and there is a passive power as regards the *primal* agent; who is able to reduce every creature to an act, which is higher than is the act to which it is reduced by the natural agent. This power in the creature is called its *obediential* power. It is a *passive* power, because it is a power of receiving from God that which no natural cause can bestow, and which it cannot bestow upon itself. This power is in all creatures, for in every one of them there is passive power, that of it may be made that which God may command.

Since every created nature is partly passive and partly active; that is to say, can receive and bear, on the one hand, and on the other hand, can bestow and act, each of these powers is a subject which can be raised by God. To each of these powers, therefore, there belongs an *obediential* power. When the active faculty is thus raised, it is raised, through an aid which is not due to it, to produce something which of itself it could not produce. As it is raised, the faculty is passive; receiving, as it does, something which of itself it does not possess. This passivity, or the power to bear and receive what is bestowed upon it, is its obediential power. Obediential power has place, therefore, in both of those natural powers, the active and the passive.

This obediential power is distinct in idea, but not in reality, from the *natural* passive power, by which the nature is capable of receiving. This natural power implies an *innate* appetite. Obediential power does not imply an innate appetite. Nature can acquire natural goods for itself, or through other causes, which are acting naturally; but nature cannot by itself, or through other naturally acting causes, acquire supernatural goods. It can acquire these only by means of an aid of God, which is not due to nature.

There is, therefore, a distinction between the two passivities. The first is called a *natural* power, because a nature demands an object towards which it is borne; and because the power can be fulfilled through the forces of nature. The other passive power is called *obediential* power, because it cannot be fulfilled without an aid of God which is not due to it; and because the nature is not of itself borne towards the supernatural good, but can be borne towards it by the Supreme, to whom every nature is subject. That it is not through something superadded, but as it is a nature, that a created nature is capable of receiving those supernatural gifts from God, or is adapted for being raised by God to the supernatural order, proves only that obediential power is distinct in idea alone, and not in reality, from the nature, or the faculty, in which it exists. There cannot be conceived any means, by which the nature should be made capable of receiving the gratuitous gifts; for if the means were itself something gratuitous, there would again be required for the reception of the gratuitous means, another means, and so on without end. Nature is therefore of itself capable of elevation; and it receives immediately in itself supernatural goods. The ultimate subject of supernatural goods is necessarily the nature. Some capacity is certainly required in a nature, in order that supernatural goods may be bestowed upon it; for it is not on every nature, that every gift can be bestowed.

Since, however, a power is known in accordance with its terminus or act, and since there always remains a difference between the passive power of a nature for *natural goods*, and the passive power of the same nature for *supernatural goods*, and this difference is a real difference; it cannot be said simply that *obediential* power is *natural*. Hence the one power is called a *natural passive* power, to signify the passive power of a nature for the goods which that nature exacts, and which it is naturally able to acquire. The other power is called an *obediential* power, to signify the passive power of a nature for goods which it in no way exacts, and which it cannot attain to, without an aid of God, and this an aid which is not due to it.

As it is certain, that obediential power is not something other than nature; so is it also certain, that obediential power is not something other than an active faculty of the nature in which that power is. The *intellect* and the *will* are those faculties which have obediential power for supernatural acts; that is, power to elicit supernatural acts, supposing gratuitous movement by God, and gratuitous aid from God. It is not as if there were merely, in the faculties, obediential power to *receive* something which would *itself* elicit the supernatural acts. If this were the case, there would not really be obediential power for *acting*, but only obediential power for receiving. There would not be power for an *act*, but only power for that which should be the *cause* of an act.

Since the supernatural act, for which there is obediential power, is a *vital act*, it cannot be elicited except by a living principle, such as are the faculties of a spirit. The obediential power in the spiritual faculties, for supernatural acts, is such that, given the gratuitous aid of God, it is those faculties themselves which, under the movement of God, elicit the whole of the supernatural act. The *subject* of obediential power, therefore, is a created *nature*, or the *faculties* of that nature. The *act* of the obediential power is supernatural. The *agent*, who reduces the power to an act of it, is God.

7.

There is in man *appetite* or desire, which tends towards that good which is an object of the senses. The *formal object* of this appetite is a good which is pleasurable to the senses. The appetite can, therefore, be borne towards all those things which share in this *formal idea* of the *pleasurable;* while it can recoil from the opposite which is displeasing.

Among the goods which are objects of the

senses, and which are naturally desired by the natural appetite in man, there are many goods which, as regards either themselves, or the mode of them, it is not right for a man to will. The goods which it is right for man to will, are those the deliberate desire of which is becoming to man in accordance with reason. Besides these, there are many objects of the senses, the pursuit of which is not in accordance with reason. Hence, many movements of the sensitive appetite are said to be contrary to reason; because they of themselves tend towards an object which it is unlawful for the will of man freely to will. Since these movements of the sensitive appetite are acts of one and the same subject, who is rational, as well as animal, and since these movements anticipate exercise of reason; they allure the will towards willing that pleasurable thing, which pleases the senses otherwise than as reason demands. These movements, which anticipate exercise of free will, or which follow, while the will is either not willing them, or is positively forbidding them, are *indeliberate* acts. It is in these indeliberate acts of desire that *concupiscence* consists; that is to say, the concupiscence which we are now considering, and which we are regarding as it is distinct from the free will, and from acts of free will.

On account of those movements of the sensitive appetite, which tend towards some good which is unlawful, as contrary to some dictate of the reason, there exists a *warfare* or struggle between reason and appetite. We mean here by *reason*, not an *act* of the rational part of man, which might be consenting to the appetite; but the *exigence* or demand of the reason, that is to say, those principles which the reason perceives with certainty, as norms or standards of its rational operations.

Appetite, as it is presupposed to acts, is a faculty of tending towards a pleasurable good, which is apprehended by the senses. Between this appetitive faculty and the reason, there exists a struggle; inasmuch as the object of the faculty is pleasurable to the senses, and towards that object the appetite can be borne before exercise and deliberation of the reason, and can allure to it the reason itself, to will that which is pleasing to the appetite. When this power exists unhindered in the appetite, it may easily happen that the will should be drawn, although, indeed, freely drawn, either to loving that object of the senses, which is not lawful, or to loving it for this reason alone that it is pleasing to the senses. This is a motive of love which is not in accordance with reason. In this way there arises, in the faculty of appetite, rebellion against the reason. The name of *concupiscence* is given, both to inordinate acts or movements of the appetite; or to the faculty itself, as it may be rebellious against the reason. It is not the appetite itself, but a *mode* of the appetite, that is to say *inordination* of the appetite, which is called the *fomes*, or fuel of sin.

Concupiscence, as it is an *act*, is called *actual* concupiscence; as it is a *proneness*, it is called *habitual* concupiscence.

Besides spontaneous movements of the *sensitive* appetite, of which we are now speaking under the name of *concupiscence;* there are found in man certain other indeliberate affections, which are proper to the *rational* part of man, by which his will is affected towards that which is not in accordance with the ordinance of reason. Among these are indeliberate movements of pride, envy, and the like; which are improperly called *passions*. These movements are possible to nature, before any free inordination whatsoever. By nature, the mind is so constructed as to love itself; and it is only by the use of accurate reflection that the mind apprehends, with clearness and certainty, the order which it ought to observe. In the absence, therefore, of reflection, either habitual or actual, and at a time when the good of due order does not allure the will, or only slightly allures it, the mind is borne spontaneously towards that which it apprehends as being good for itself apart. In the same way, the mind spontaneously recoils from that which it apprehends as being bad for itself apart, although this is not in conformity with the order of reason. Such indeliberate acts, and the habitual power of which they are acts, may indeed be comprehended under the common name of *concupiscence*, in the same way as they are also not seldom called *passions*. That, however, of which we are treating, is the *sensitive* concupiscence; and sensitive concupiscence is always to be understood as meant, when concupiscence is spoken of without any qualification.

Freedom from concupiscence is not absence of sensitive appetite. It is absence of *inordination* of that appetite; or of the *rebellion*, as it is called, of the flesh against the spirit.

In man's present state, a movement of the sensitive appetite towards a pleasurable good, follows immediately on apprehension by the senses—anticipates an act of the reason and the will—and allures the will to the unlawful. Thereafter may follow a movement of the appetite, at the bidding of the reason; and it may be ordained by the reason towards that which is in accordance with reason. The will can refuse assent to the movements of the sensitive appetite, and can resist them. Through continued exercise of resistance, a man can arrive at a condition in which the inclination of his appetite is so modified that, if not always, at least more frequently, there should not be excited in his appetite indeliberate movements towards an unlawful good; and that there should rather be excited an oppositive movement, in conformity with the inclination of the will. The same object can be considered under different ideas, according as it presents itself, by means of the imagination, as a thing which is pleasurable, or as a thing which is to be abhorred; and it is in the power of the reason to set forth one and the same object under different ideas, as for instance, an eatable, either as pleasurable, or as deadly. The reason can thus move the appetite in different directions. Moreover, through exercise of virtue there can, more or less, be hindered that commotion of spirits, by which the imagination and the appetite are disturbed.

That which can be obtained incompletely through virtue, is obtained completely through that gift which is called *immunity* or freedom *from concupiscence*. Immunity from concupiscence comes to this, that the sensitive appetite is wholly subdued to the reason, so that the movements of the sensitive appetite, which are excited by apprehension through the senses, are never borne towards that which is contrary to reason—and so never allure the will towards that which is not lawful to it—but are always in conformity with the inclination of the reason—and the reason can always and easily ordain movements of the appetite towards that which is becoming.

A thing may either be absolutely evil, or it may be only relatively evil. The *relatively* evil is that which, although in itself good, is nevertheless not becoming to a man, as depriving him of the due order, wherewith he, and all his actions, ought to be regulated. What is *simply becoming* to man is that which is becoming to him in accordance with reason.

Man consists of two substances, flesh and spirit, and those two, when conjoined, constitute one complete nature. Since man is both rational and sentient, and to each of his forces—the force of understanding and the force of feeling—there belongs its own inclination towards the good which is becoming to it; man experiences in himself two inclinations which tend in different directions. Hence the struggle of inclination in man, which is proper to man; since human nature alone contains within itself a twofold life, the intellective life, and the sensitive life. If, therefore, the movements of the sensitive appetite, whatever they may be, are compared with the *nature* of man, as that nature is *sensitive*, those movements are a *perfection* of it, and a *physical* perfection. To the physical perfection of a nature, there belongs the exercise of its own

w

proper faculty. If, however, the movements of the appetite, which are called concupiscences, are compared with the *nature* of man, as that nature is *rational*, those movements, although physically a perfection, bring *imperfection* to the subject of them; inasmuch as they are movements of a *rational* subject. They introduce imperfection, not only because it is, in general, an imperfection to be lacking in some perfection—and it would certainly be a perfection in a rational being not to be liable to those movements—but also specially, because, although it is not undue, it is less becoming, to a rational being to be liable to movements towards that which such a being cannot will, in accordance with the order of reason.

Such movements, as regards the effect which they are capable of begetting, and do beget, are an *evil* to man. This they are because, anticipating exercise of reason—striving against its government—and alluring the will to pursuit of pleasurable good, they both render the exercise of virtue difficult, and frequently draw the will towards freely willing forbidden good, and so to sin, which is, of all evils, the greatest evil that can befal a man.

The movements of concupiscence are, therefore, unbecoming to man, as man is rational; and in this sense those movements are said to be *evils* to man. The evil which is found in these movements belongs to the *moral* order; for they are evil to man inasmuch, and so far as, they provoke him towards sin. Moral evil does not, however, exist in them *formally*, because they are not *free acts*. Morality begins there and then, where and when there begins to be freedom of mastery. The evil is in the movements of concupiscence by way of *cause*, or rather by way of *occasion*. Evil is not in them with perfection of causality, for the *cause* of sin is the *will;* but with that *incomplete* causality, which deserves to be called rather an *occasion* than a *cause*.

The foundation of this causal evil, in the movements of concupiscence, is a *physical* imperfection. It amounts to an imperfection of the nature, which is lacking in force to repress inordinate movements, and in force for always bending the appetite towards those physical objects which are becoming to the reason.

The power of sinning, which is proper to all created freedom, is not a perfection, but is an imperfection, of that freedom, and a *physical* imperfection. It reaches, however, also to the *moral* order; inasmuch as it is a *condition* which may lead to sinning. Similarly, the evil of movements of concupiscence reaches to the moral order; inasmuch as the movements form a motive, which does not determine indeed, but which does allure the will towards sin.

Concupiscence is a privation of a good which, in virtue of the Divine institution, ought to exist in human nature; for God made man upright, and free from concupiscence, and He willed that this prerogative should be propagated, along with sanctifying grace, to all men. Concupiscence is, therefore, an absence of what, supposing this primeval Divine institution, would be a due perfection, and so it is *privation* of a good. It is, therefore, *formally* an evil; since evil is formally privation of good. Under this aspect, concupiscence is not a moral evil, but a *physical* evil, since it is defect of that force by which the physical movements of the sensitive appetite were perfectly contained within their own order, under the reason.

That certainly is not a good, as regards man, which cannot be loved by man, and which he ought to resist, in order that he may be good, and may safeguard his moral perfection.

As the movements of concupiscence are in this way evils, so may also the principle of them be called an evil. The principle of them is, not simply the sensitive appetite, but an inordinate appetite, or an unhindered power in the appetite for an act of tending towards goods which are unbecoming to the reason, which anticipate exercise of the reason, and which allure towards evil. This is what is called *habitual* concupiscence.

This power is *evil*, for the same reason for which an act of it is evil, and in the same sense; and in this sense it may be called *sin*, or *vice*, or the *origin* of sin.

Freedom from concupiscence was not exacted by even innocent human nature, and—looking simply to the nature of things, and apart from any free institution of God—it was not in itself *due* to human nature, but was *gratuitous* on the part of God. Human nature could have been made without it; without any injury being thereby done by God to man.

It is *natural* to man to consist of intellect and senses. Sensitive appetite is therefore *natural* to man. It is *natural* to man that, in the exercise of his faculties, *sense* should anticipate *intellect*. It is *natural* for the sensitive appetite to be borne towards a pleasurable good which is an object of the senses, and as that good is pleasurable. It is *natural*, therefore, for the sensitive appetite in man to be borne towards every object which is represented to it by the senses as pleasurable. It is *natural* to man, by reason of the oneness of the subject of those two faculties, that what is pleasing to the sensitive appetite should also allure the will, which has power of willing whatsoever comes before it clothed with the appearance of the good. It is therefore *natural* to man, that there should exist in man movements towards a pleasurable good which are not becoming to the reason; and that those movements should anticipate exercise of reason, and allure the will. Since, on the other hand, the reason is *of itself* borne towards good which is becoming to the reason, it is *natural* that there should exist in man a warfare, or struggle of inclinations; and that the exercise of virtue should be difficult. It is to be carefully observed that we have been, and are here considering that which is of itself *due* to nature; or that which God *owes* to human nature, simply as He is the *Maker* of that nature, and not as He is in any way Rewarder.

If human nature, as God made it at the first, had not been free from concupiscence, there would have been in human nature some defect, but this is no more than that which is common to all created natures. Since every defect is in a way a *misery*, there would have been this misery in human nature. This misery, however, would not have been *privation* of a good which was *due to* human nature. Absence, therefore, of this good would not have been inconsistent with the Divine justice in God, as He is the *Maker* of human nature.

Since the evil in concupiscence does not belong

formally to the ethical order, but to the physical order, a man is not constituted through concupiscence *ethically evil*, but only *physically imperfect*, and this without any necessity of contracting ethical evil.

Those who say that God would be the author of sin, if He were to make an innocent man with liability to concupiscence, are supposing that God ought to make nature with all its faculties in *actual* exercise. If man were made with sensitive appetite, and habitual concupiscence, there would not in any way be sin, or vice, properly so called, or such as springs from the will. There would be only habitual natural inordination, inasmuch as the appetite, left to its own nature, would not be subordinate in all things to the reason.

Those men are supposing also that the act of concupiscence is formally sin. This is false. With regard to this there cannot be controversy amongst Catholics. The Council of Trent has denied that concupiscence is truly and properly sin, and has declared that concupiscence is called *sin*, because it has proceeded from sin, and inclines towards sin.

They are supposing again that by the movements of concupiscence the soul is necessarily drawn towards sin, if man is left to the forces of his nature. This is false. In many matters the will could easily resist, and does resist. In other matters the will would indeed experience difficulty, but never true impossibility of acting rightly. Finally, they are supposing that the difficulty which is begotten of concupiscence cannot be lessened by God, except through *supernatural* aids. This again is false. Divine aids of the natural order could be given. Such aids would have been supplied in the state of *pure* or mere nature, if that state had ever existed. Who shall say that God could not, by means of Divine aids, have assisted and perfected nature in order to its own *natural* end? This He could have done by enlightening the understanding, by exciting the will, and by removing perils of evil, and furnishing fitting occasions of good. These Divine aids would not be *supernatural*; not on the ground that they were *not due*, but because, in order to the supernatural character of Divine aids, it is required that they should raise the nature, on which they are bestowed, to a higher order; while these aids would only be perfecting the nature within its own order. The attainment of his end must be morally possible to man, and it is not to be believed that man would be regarded by God as worthy of eternal punishment, if he failed to do that which was for him morally impossible. Those Divine aids would belong to the *completeness* of the state of pure or mere nature.

Freedom from concupiscence is, therefore, a gift which is *not due* to human nature. It is a *preternatural* gift. That is certainly preternatural which, although it is outside the *exigence* of any created nature on which it is bestowed, either belongs to another nature, or completes something which already actually exists in a nature. In a nature which is purely spiritual, freedom from concupiscence is found in a more perfect manner; and some beginning of the freedom, more or less perfect, is capable of attainment, by human nature, with the help of virtue.

8.

It is proper to human nature that the intellect should be determinated towards an act through sensation—and that the intellect should acquire knowledge of various matters by *reasoning*; that is, should gradually proceed, from a knowledge of the known, to a knowledge of the previously unknown, by way of analysis and synthesis. This is what it is to be *rational;* and it excludes necessary demand of any *infused* habit of knowledge.

An infused habit of knowledge of the natural law is not exacted, in order that man may act rightly, as he is bound to do, as soon as the use of reason is fully developed. For this there suffices a knowledge of certain principles, and of those consequences which are most manifestly derived from them. This knowledge man can acquire for himself, and if he acts in accordance with those principles, and the consequences of them, which are known to him, and if he does not culpably neglect to get to know what he ought to know, he will always be *formally*, at any rate, acting well. That which of itself is demanded, in order to the rightness of an act, is *formal* goodness, and not material goodness.

Ignorance, therefore, or error, if they exist without fault, will not be imputed as evil, nor will they cause acts which are determinated by them to be morally evil. Ignorance on many points, and even with regard to the natural law, and error which has crept in without one's will, are *physical* defects. They are not moral defects. They are defects, the possibility of which is a necessary consequence of the condition of rational nature. When, therefore, they actually take place, they are *natural* defects. Hence, also, it is a *natural* defect that a man does actions which are *materially* evil, from invincible ignorance or error; for that is bound up with his nature which is capable of error, and of ignorance, with regard to many matters. No being demands exemption from those defects which are *natural* to it. It follows that an *infused habit* of knowledge, a means of knowledge which is not in accordance with that mode of *acquiring* knowledge which is *natural* to man, and which would remove the natural defect of ignorance, or possible error—is *not due* to human nature.

That which is *due* to human nature is power to acquire knowledge of the law of nature. In this power two degrees can be distinguished. There is required a power which is proximately unhindered, as regards the principal precepts of the law. With regard to the ultimate and more recondite consequences of the natural law, there is due indeed a *physical* power, but there is nothing to hinder there being at the same time a *moral* powerlessness, or great difficulty. This difficulty the mode of acquiring knowledge which is proper to human nature carries with it; and many natural adjuncts in which man finds himself increase the difficulty.

A human nature created without an infused habit of knowledge is created with a *defect*, which is ignorance. It is at the same time, however, created with a power of gradually divesting itself of that defect. The nature is not created with error, or with the *necessity* of erring, but only with the *possibility* of erring, and even with a certain proneness towards erring, in many matters; although with an antecedent power in the nature of always avoiding error. These defects are an absence of a good which is *not due* to the nature when it is created. The nature can be called *miserable*, in so far as it is not so happy as it might be. The nature cannot be called miserable in the sense that it is destitute and deprived of a good which is *due* to it.

Immunity or freedom from *ignorance*, through an *infused* habit of *knowledge*, is a *preternatural* gift. This mode of knowing does not lie outside the order of the whole of created nature. Witness the case of the angels. Some beginning of it also and even progress, is already contained in human nature which, both by acts and by a habit acquired through acts, arrives at knowledge.

9.

There are two kinds of *immortality*—the not being able to die—and the being able not to die. A *remote* possibility of not dying belongs to all living creatures. A *proximate* possibility of not dying comes to this, that in a living creature there should be—whether intrinsically only, or also extrinsically, through means of which it can avail itself—a sufficient reason to prevent death.

Possibility of not dying may be either absolute or conditional. It is *absolute*, if it is not bound to any condition which can fail of fulfilment; and from failure of which the immortality can cease. The possibility of not dying is *conditional*, if it is bound to a condition; so as to cease if that condition fails of its fulfilment. *Absolute* immortality is proper to the Blessed. *Conditional* immortality was bestowed on human nature in its creation; and it is a gift which is *not due* to human nature.

A subject which consists of a spirit, in union with a *naturally* corruptible body, is *naturally* mortal. When that body is corrupted, and so becomes unfit for the operations of life, the union of the spirit with it necessarily ceases, and thus death occurs. That a human body is *naturally* corruptible is manifest, not only because it consists of parts, but also because it is *naturally* subject to the corrupting action of physical causes. These through the proper force of their own nature, can gradually alter the elements of which the body consists, and render it unfit for organic functions; or they may even violently dissolve the bond between the various parts of the body in a moment of time. There is not intrinsically in the human body a force so great as to be able always to sustain itself against the continual action of the vehement pressure of all extrinsic causes.

Further, there does not exist in man an exigence of the *incorruptibility* of his body. Such an exigence has no foundation in the human body itself. This body cannot exact that which is at variance with all the physical laws to which it, like similar bodies, is subject. Neither has exigence of incorruptibility of the body any foundation in the human soul, which is a spirit, and immortal; and for the good of which the body exists. The soul could only exact the incorruptibility of the body, in so far as its perennial union with the body was necessary, in order that the soul should attain its end. Inasmuch as the human soul is an immortal spirit, perpetual union with its body is not necessary to it, for the attainment of its end.

Mortality is, therefore, a *natural defect* of man; as it is natural to man to have an organic body, which is naturally subject to physical laws. Immortality is *not due* to human nature. When it was bestowed on human nature, it was a *preternatural* gift.

10.

By *physical evils* we mean all those troubles and annoyances to which man is liable, both in body and in soul. He is subject to them in his body, which in itself is infirm, and liable to suffer from extrinsic agents, whether necessary agents or free agents. Man is subject to physical evils also in his soul, which can suffer from privation of goods which are becoming to it, as from stupidity, ignorance, loss of honour, hatred, falling away of friends, and the like, and which can experience sadness, fear, and other afflictions. Even man in a state of innocence would *natur-*

ally be liable to those evils. Immunity or freedom from them is not exacted by human nature.

Physical evils are not absolutely evils to man. They do not deprive him of good which is proper to him; and which consists in his attainment of his end, and in the right ordination of himself towards his end, through exercise of his faculties. Physical evils may, on the contrary, contribute towards the good of man, and they frequently contribute towards his good, more than do their opposites. Besides that, by means of physical evils, we are more easily withdrawn from love of the things of sense, and warned to seek after the end which is due to us, they provide occasion for the exercise of very many and most splendid virtues, which could not be exercised except in adversity. If we had no physical evils, we should not have the opportunity of proving our love of God through patience and fortitude.

There is a difference between being *simply* evil, and being *absolutely* evil. Those things are *simply* evil, which deprive of some good. This physical evils do, and so they are simply evil, They are not *absolutely* evil, because, although they deprive us of some *physical* good, they nevertheless contribute towards our *ethical* good; and so towards our attainment of our end. Those two goods are the chiefest goods of man.

Under this aspect, physical evils can most truly

be called goods; that is, means which are useful towards attainment of our end.

11.

Pure or mere *nature* is a nature which has *all* and *only* that which is due to it *as a nature*. There is in the idea of pure nature exclusion of all those things which do not belong to the *constitution* of it as a nature—and of those things which are not *exacted* by it, lest as a nature it should exist in vain—and of such sin as does not spring from one's own will, and with which fallen man finds himself defiled as soon as he exists. Among the things which are excluded by the idea of *mere* nature, are sanctifying grace, and destination to the state of grace, a supreme end consisting in the vision of God, charity and other infused virtues, the aid of actual grace, freedom from concupiscence, immortality of body, and immunity from physical evils.

Along with exclusion of these gifts, there is contained in the idea of *mere* nature, existence of all the properties and faculties of a rational soul, as well as all that is necessary in order that those faculties should be exercised; such as an end in proportion with the nature—the Divine concurrence which is absolutely necessary at every moment in order to the preservation and continuance of created being—and the like.

A man with such a nature would be in a state of *pure* or mere *nature*. Such a state, as matter of fact, never existed among men; but the possibility of the existence of such a state, if God had willed to establish it, is theologically certain.

CHAPTER XI.

The Paradise of God's creation.

WHEN God created man in the Paradise of pleasure, which He had prepared for him on this earth of ours, He endowed him with the gift of freedom from concupiscence. In unfallen Adam there was no concupiscence, either habitual, or actual.

Through this gift, man enjoyed what theologians call *integrity of nature*.

This integrity is a special perfection. It consists in perfect subjection of the sensitive appetite to the rational will. There is no movement of appetite against the will; nor does appetite anticipate exercise of reason.

Human nature, regarded simply as it is a nature, is, as it were, divided into parts. It has affections which may tend in different directions. It is thus, in a manner, crippled for walking uprightly, and steadily, and straight in the moral path. Hence, if there is given to human nature internal peace and concord between possibly antagonistic faculties, it is said to be *integrated*, or made whole and entire. It is thus enabled to walk, as becomes it, in the moral way.

This integrity of his nature was bestowed by God on the first man, in his creation.

Adam was also constituted by God, in his creation, in the state of habitual and sanctifying grace. His possession of this grace sanctified him, or made him holy. It raised his nature above its level. It placed him in the supernatural order. It gave him right to actual graces in time of need. It was to him a pledge, and an earnest, of everlasting glory. Possessing grace on earth, he held the title deeds of Heaven. He was the friend of God. He was more, he was a son of God.

For a time, he was to be on probation in the Paradise of pleasure. When he had been proved, and found faithful, he was to be translated alive, from the paradise of earth, beneath the stars, to the paradise of Heaven, beyond the stars.

During the period of his probation he was to become a father of sons and daughters, conceived immaculate, and born in holiness. Begetting them into the world, he was to beget them also unto God. His destiny was to be theirs; and with him, as heir of Heaven, they were to be co-heirs.

We read in the Book of Ecclesiasticus, that God created man of the earth, and made him after His own image, and gave him power over all things that are upon the earth. He put the fear of him upon all flesh, and he had dominion over beasts and fowls. He created of him a helpmate like unto himself. He gave them counsel, and a tongue, and eyes, and ears, and a heart to devise, and He filled them with the knowledge of understanding. He created in them the science of the spirit, He filled their heart with wisdom, and shewed them both good and evil. He set His eye upon their hearts to shew them the greatness of his works, that they might praise the Name which He hath sanctified, and glory in His wondrous acts, that they might declare the glorious things of His works. Moreover, He gave them instructions, and the law of life for an inheritance. He made an everlasting covenant with them, and He shewed them His justice and judgments, and their eye saw the majesty of His glory, and their ears heard His glorious voice, and He said to them, Beware of all iniquity. And He gave to every one of them commandments concerning his neighbour.

The eminence of knowledge which is here described, was possessed by our first parents, not potentially merely, but actually, and by way of habit.

We find certain indications of this knowledge, in the Book of Genesis. We read that the Lord

God brought to Adam all the beasts of the earth, and all the fowls of the air, to see what he would call them; and Adam called all the beasts by their names, and all the fowls of the air, that is to say, he gave to every kind of them a name, which was appropriate to it, and which expressed its nature, or its properties. Adam was therefore endowed with a knowledge wherewith he knew the nature, and the properties, of all species of animals; and this knowledge was such as no man of his posterity has ever attained to in its perfection. Since this knowledge was given to him, it cannot be doubted that he was furnished also with other matters of natural knowledge, and especially with those which are necessarily connected with this knowledge. When Adam received Eve, created and given to him by God for his wife, he had already a perfect knowledge of the nature of matrimony, and understood that he would have in the future a posterity. This knowledge belonged to the natural law; and it supposed many other matters of knowledge. Adam, therefore, had knowledge of the law of nature.

A knowledge such as this is, Adam did not acquire by his own exertions; but received it from God by way of infusion. It was *infused*, or poured into his mind, in the creation of his soul.

A reason for God's bestowal of knowledge in

this way on our first parents, is to be found in the office in which He had placed them. Those two were not to exist for themselves alone. They were to be the principle and origin of all other human beings. They were to be the parents of the whole human family. They were to be parents, not only through generation of a posterity, but through the government, and instruction, of those who should spring from them. It was a condition which was natural to human nature, that men should constitute a society, that this society should have its government, and that men should be taught by one who had authority to teach, so that all might easily arrive at necessary knowledge. In order that both of our first parents, and especially the first man, might rightly fulfil this function, of which the principal part belonged to him, his intellect was not left to its own exercise of itself, but had knowledge communicated to it by God. It would have taken too long a time for those two to have acquired their knowledge by experience; and it was immediately necessary for them to possess knowledge, since it was lawful for them at once to lay the foundations of their parental office.

Left to themselves, the knowledge acquired by our first parents would have been liable to many errors. These errors, existing from the beginning, and in the head of the whole human family, would have entailed irreparable damage. There was, therefore, communicated to them a knowledge of those things which were necessary to be known by the heads of a human society, in order not only to its existence, but also to its well being.

Since this human society was raised, in the first man, to the *supernatural* order and state, the first man had a supernatural knowledge of *faith*, which was given to him by God.

Man's knowledge was communicated to him by God in the act of his creation. It could not have been communicated to him by way of teaching; since teaching supposes some ideas already existing in the mind of the taught, which have been otherwise acquired. It was necessary, therefore, that knowledge should be bestowed on Adam by way of *infusion*; that is to say, through an infused habit of knowledge. By means of this habit, when it was extrinsically determinated to an act of knowledge, his exercise of intellect would most easily issue in a distinct and adequate knowledge of the object, to which it had been led by way of the senses. This habit of *infused* knowledge was of the same character as is that habit of ours which we *acquire* by means of a series of acts. Adam's habit of natural knowledge was, therefore, *supernatural* as regards the *mode* in which he obtained it; but it was at the same time *natural* in itself. It was the same as the habitual knowledge which he might have arrived at for himself by means of study, in the process of years.

2.

Besides these gifts—of unerring knowledge, and of integrity of nature—there was given also to our first parents a gift of *immortality* of body. By reason of this gift, they were freed from the physical necessity of dying. They would never have died, however long they had remained upon this earth, if they had fulfilled the Divine condition which was Divinely attached to the continuance of this preternatural gift.

Along with immortality of body, there was bestowed on them a gift of freedom from all those sufferings and infirmities which are the harbingers of death, and from all sorrows. This freedom constituted a preternatural gift of *happiness*. It was gratuitously bestowed upon them by God in their creation.

3.

Although this threefold freedom—from concupiscence—from death—and from suffering and sorrow, is not, of its own nature, necessarily bound up with the sanctifying grace which makes the possessors of it holy—and that *supernatural* gift of grace is not necessarily bound up with those *preternatural* gifts—yet, in virtue of the institution of the Divine Creator, the retention of those gifts was made dependent on the continuance of this grace.

Those things are not, of their own nature, necessarily bound up together, the essences of which have their own proper notes; so that the one is not an element of the essence of the other, or its essential terminus. The idea of sanctifying grace is one thing, and the idea of every one of those preternatural immunities is another thing. The order of sanctifying grace is distinct and separate from the order in which those immunities are contained. The one order is simply *supernatural;* while the other order is only *preternatural.*

In virtue of the Divine institution, however, there existed a *bond* between the supernatural gift, on the one side, and the preternatural gifts, on the other side; so that if grace should be lost, the threefold immunity would be also lost. The grace, with which those gifts were thus bound up, was the grace which was bestowed in man's creation. God did not bind up His preternatural gifts with His gift of grace in such wise as that wherever there should be sanctifying grace, those gifts should accompany it. On the contrary, if the supernatural gift of grace bestowed on our first parents should be lost by them, those preternatural gifts would not accompany that grace, in the event of the restoration of it.

That which is true of human nature is true also of angelic nature in its creation. It was raised by God to the supernatural order of Divine adoptive sonship, and of destination to eternal beatitude.

Such were God's intelligent creatures in their creation, when God brought them, by an act of His omnipotent will, from previous nothingness into actual being. He realised in them His eternal conception of them. He made them in precise accordance with the *idea* of them, which was from eternity in the Divine mind. He made them mirrors in which He beheld Himself reflected. They mirrored also to themselves the perfections of their Maker. Studying themselves, and studying their fellow creatures, they were studying their common Maker. The study of creatures belongs, therefore, to the study of the Creator. There is no study of any creature which has not place, and its own place, in that all-embracing study which is Theology. All other studies are of their nature handmaids of the Queen of Sciences; and the noblest of them must say to her, what the Queen of handmaids said to the Divine Majesty her Master—Be it done to me according to Thy word.

CHAPTER XII.

THE INNER LIFE OF GOD.

FROM contemplation of God in creatures—as His Divine Majesty is Creator and Lord of all and of every one of them—we return to contemplation of God *in Himself.*

We shall henceforth consider Him, not directly as He is the God in Whom we live and move and are, but in what we may call His own inner life—the life of God, as He is a Spirit—and the vital processes of His infinite, necessary, and self-existent life.

That one supreme essence, which is God, has the idea at once of the *absolute*, and of the *relative*.

Since, in that imperfect mode of knowing which alone is possible to men on earth, we are powerless to embrace in one conception the whole plenitude of being, we must, if we are to have some more distinct understanding of God, endeavour to obtain it, as it were, *by parts.* These parts will be various inadequate conceptions of essence—intellect—will—wisdom—goodness—and other perfections. To all of these conceptions there corresponds the essence of one infinite Being. This Being is both intellect, and will, and every other perfection. Perfections are not in God distinct realities. They are in Him one infinite *being*. This being is equivalent to all these perfections, which are considered by us as if they were so many diverse faculties and functions. That, for instance, which we conceive under the idea of infinite wisdom, is in reality not only IN God, but it IS God Himself. The same objective reality, which corresponds to our inadequate conception of infinite wisdom, *is itself* the Divine essence—the Divine goodness—the Divine omnipotence—the Divine justice—and every other conceivable Divine perfection. It is all these, inasmuch as it is the *plenitude of absolute being*.

Whatever we explicitly conceive, under the ideas of wisdom, goodness, omnipotence, and other attributes, we call *formal objective ideas*. The result of the operation of our mind, in thus conceiving, is a *subjective* distinction of idea. These formal ideas are not, in that reality which corresponds to them in God, distinct one from the other. They are, one and all of them, that one most simple Being, which is apprehended by us under distinct or different and inadequate conceptions of those various perfections.

The infinity of Divine perfection, which is equivalent in its supereminence to all those perfections, as thus conceived, is the foundation for the *objective* truth which really underlies our conception of the Divine *Being*, under these different formal ideas. This is what we mean by —distinction in idea *with foundation* in reality.

From the same principle of the infinity, and so of the simplicity, of the Divine Being, we understand that, as in the case of God's absolute attributes, there is no real distinction of them from the Divine being itself; so also there is no real distinction between the Divine being, under the formal idea of the *absolute*, and the same Divine being under the formal idea of the *relative*. The same being is at once absolute and relative, and has the functions both of the absolute and of the relative. Under the formal idea of the absolute, there is the one Divine essence; while under the formal idea of the relative, there is *real distinction*, since relations in God are *substantial* relations. Every one of them is itself a substance, while no one of them superadds anything of reality to the one infinite essence.

2.

Real relation in creatures is an accident in the subject of relation; that is to say, in the person or thing that is related. In virtue of this accident that subject is ordained towards a terminus which is different from itself, and which is also real. That relation is not distinct from the terminus towards which it relates the subject, nor from the accident in the subject, which is the foundation of its relation.

Relation *in God* is not an *accident*, which inheres in, or cleaves to, a subject. The relation is itself the Divine *substance*, formally as that substance is *relative*.

As in creatures a relation is not merely an accident, but is an accident through which the subject of it is *related* towards a real terminus, so in God relation is a *substance*, formally as it is intrinsically related to a real terminus.

In creatures, however, inasmuch as the relation is an *accident*, the mutually related termini are distinct from each other, as they are *separate* substances. In God, on the other hand, and because the relation is not an accident, but a substance, the relation is itself the terminus. Since in God the *absolute* is wholly one, the termini are distinct one·from the other solely under the formal idea of them as they are *substantial* relations.

The Divine intellect is not a *faculty* which is superadded to the Divine essence. It is the Divine essence. It is not an intellect in potentiality, or in habit towards acts of it, but is itself, of its own inmost nature, a *pure act*. It is infinite, substantial, actual understanding.

The *object* of this understanding is God Himself

—or the Divine essence, with which the Divine understanding is identified, and in the Divine essence all the *true*.

Hence Divine understanding is not *perfected* or perfectible, as in creatures, by a multiplicity of elicited acts. It is itself one *substantial act* which comprehends *itself* the infinite true, and *in itself* all the true. So far we have been able to have knowledge by the light of nature, and through reason.

The infinite substantial Divine intellect, by understanding itself, produces its *Word*. Of this we have knowledge by Revelation alone.

A created spirit—which is an image of the infinite Spirit who is God—by understanding itself, produces in itself a *word*, or intellectual expression of itself. This word, or conception of the mind, is, even in a created spirit, a likeness of that which is understood. When a spirit understands itself, the word or intellectual expression of itself is, as it were, the spirit as understood, in the spirit who is then understanding. The more perfect will this *word* be, the more fully and adequately it expresses that which is understood—the more it approaches to identity with that which is understood—and the more perfect that is which is understood, and which is expressed by the word.

In us a word always falls short of fulness of perfection because, in the first place, the more perfect things are in themselves, the less can we express them by means of a word, in the whole of their idea and intelligibility. Secondly, those things which we more perfectly express, by means of a mental word, are in themselves imperfect. Thirdly, the word in our minds is an *accident* only, and a *likeness*, and not a *substance*. It is also not the thing itself, which has been understood. When a created mind expresses itself by a word, that word fails of perfection in all those three ways.

As God's understanding is infinitely perfect, so is the word which is expressed by infinite understanding, infinitely perfect. God is understanding Himself, and so that which is understood is infinite. He understands and comprehends Himself, in the whole of His infinite intelligibility. By this understanding of Himself, He produces not that kind of image of Himself which is an *accident*, but an *immanent substantial* word, or idea of Himself. The Divine substance, which is thus understanding itself, with a substantial understanding which is expressive of the Word, does not multiply, but communicates or, to use a phrase of St. Basil's, *radiates* the same substance as that substance is *understood*.

Hence the substantial understanding, which

through understanding produces the substantial Word, and the immanent Word thus produced, are one in essence. The substantial understanding, which expresses itself in the substantial Word, and the Word thus expressed, are nevertheless two in number. They are relative to each other, by a relation of *origin* of one from the other, since there is a real proceeding of one of them from the other.

As the infinite *true* is in God the infinite *good*, so understanding of Himself, as He is the infinite True, is at the same time necessarily love of Himself, as of the infinite Good.

Further, as God's understanding of Himself, of its own inmost idea and fecundity, expresses His Word as an immanent terminus, in the way which we have described; so God's loving of Himself is an act which produces Love, as its own internal terminus.

The Divine essence has both the formal idea of understanding, and the formal idea of loving; or rather, the Divine essence is itself both understanding and loving. Divine understanding is, therefore, really and identically Divine loving. There is nevertheless, however, one function under the formal idea of understanding, and another function under the formal idea of loving, in these internal productions. The Word proceeds under the formal idea not of loving, but of understanding, and the Love, who is the Holy Ghost, proceeds through the formal idea of loving, and not through the formal idea of understanding. There is, therefore, between Divine understanding and Divine loving, a *virtual* distinction. The functions are distinct, in the order of their relation towards two *really* distinct immanent termini; and this, as if the understanding and the loving were themselves really distinct, the one from the other.

It is not understanding which presupposes loving, but it is loving which necessarily presupposes understanding. This it does, not in order of time, but in the inborn idea of formal ideas. Of the internal formal ideas of understanding and of loving, the *good* is being loved inasmuch as it is *known*, while it is not being known in virtue of its being *loved*. As there cannot be loving without understanding, so there cannot be perfect understanding of an infinite good without loving. The difference is, that loving, of its own proper formal idea, exacts previous understanding; while to perfect understanding of infinite good there necessarily follows loving, and this by reason of the nature of good which is comprehended by understanding.

Of the inmost necessary nature of the case, therefore, God, who is an infinite Spirit, through understanding Himself, loves Himself; while He does not, in the inverse order, understand Himself through loving Himself.

The formal idea of His loving is founded in the formal idea of His understanding; and loving presupposes, in a necessary order, an act of understanding.

In an infinite spirit this understanding has, in accordance with a necessary exigence of its nature, the Word eternally produced, as an immanent terminus. The formal idea, therefore, of an act of loving, of which the terminus produced is the Love which is the Holy Ghost, presupposes the formal idea of an act of understanding, with its terminus produced, which is the Word. Without this word, understanding in action which—by a necessary exigence of its perfection, is eternally productive of the Word—could neither be, nor be conceived as being.

Since there are expressed and communicated to the Word all the ideas of the producer of the Word, with the sole exception of that formal productive idea by which the Word itself is produced, there is also communicated to the Word the loving which is productive of Love. Since this loving demands previous understanding, in the act which produces the Word, the loving which is productive of Love, and so the proceeding of this love, cannot be conceived unless as simultaneously from the producer of the Word, and from the Word.

As regards substantiality, and the real distinction of the love produced, from the principle which produces it, that which is loved is the infinite substantial goodness; that is to say, the Divine essence in the whole idea of its infinite goodness. The *act* also which loves is the same Divine essence. This act is therefore not an *accident* of a substance, but is itself a *substantial* act, or an act which is a *substance*. Hence the terminus produced, which is immanent to the substantial act of loving, is substantial Love; or a love which is itself a substance, and that substance the Divine substance. In like manner, to this terminus—or to the Love produced by the act whereby the infinite substantial Divine goodness is loved in the whole idea of its loveableness—there is communicated, and there is in it, the whole infinite substantial goodness of the numerically one Divine essence.

As God *understood* is in God Who is *understanding* Himself, so in God Who is *loving* Himself, there is God Who is *loved*. There are not three Gods, because the absolute essence is numerically one. There is one, however, who by understanding *produces* or "says" His immanent Word—another, who is this Word, as produced by understanding—and another, the Love which is produced by the one common loving of Him Who produces His Word, and of the Word Who is produced. There are, therefore, three who are really distinct one from the other, since one proceeds from another, as from a principle by a real, although an immanent procession; and the three are relative one to the other. There are three who are substantial, because these three, who are every one of them distinct from the others, are, nevertheless, all of them at the same time the Divine intellectual essence, which is a substance, and a substance in the truest sense of the term.

He who, being distinct from others, is an intellectual substance, or subsists distinct in an intellectual nature, is a *person*. There are, therefore, three Divine Persons of one Divine Essence. The three would not be distinct one from the other, unless every one of them were relative to the others, through real proceeding of one from another. They would not be every one of them a Divine person, unless they were the Divine substance or essence. The foundation of personality is *intellectual substantiality*. The formal idea by which the persons are distinct is *relation*.

3.

A person is commonly defined as being—an individual substance, of a rational nature. This definition, rightly understood, is accurate and adequate.

A definition consists of two parts, the genus,

and the differentia. In the definition of a person the genus is "individual substance," and this genus is itself the definition of an *hypostasis*. The only difference between an hypostasis and a person is, that a person is necessarily "of a rational or intelligent nature," while an hypostasis is not necessarily so. The one term is wider than is the other. Every person is an hypostasis, but not every hypostasis is a person. Those hypostases alone are persons, which are of a rational nature. An hypostasis is a being which is in itself, and is not IN another, or OF another.

There are two orders of being, the *real* and the *ideal*. The *ideal* depends from, and is the offspring of the mind which conceives it. The *real* exists independently, and apart from all consideration of the mind. An hypostasis is a being of the *real*, and not of the *ideal* order. It is a real entity, and not a mere figment of the mind. Again, all real beings belong to one or other of two classes—they are either substances or accidents; substance and accident being an exhaustive distribution, or complete division of real being.

It is most certain that an hypostasis is not an accident. The definition of an accident is—a being which not only inheres in, or cleaves to another being, but which also connaturally, although not necessarily, requires another being in which it may inhere, or to which it may cleave. In other words, an accident supposes a substance as its subject of inhesion—and it requires such a subject of inhesion, in order to its connatural mode of existence; although at the same time there is nothing philosophically contradictory in an accident existing apart from any subject of inhesion. Such separate existence is merely not its connatural mode of existence. It does not, however, follow that by such separate existence, apart from any subject of inhesion, an accident thereby becomes a substance. Although restrained from actual inhesion, an accident will still retain its connatural inhesiveness.

Substance, on the contrary—the other term of this exhaustive distribution, or complete division of real being—is distinguished from accident by being, and is therefore defined as being—a real being which stands by itself, and does not need another being in which to inhere, or to which it may cleave.

That a substance can *stand by itself* does not of course deny its dependence for existence from another Being, who is the Creator and Cause of all being. It denies merely that substance has need of any other created being, as a subject of inhesion. Instead of needing this, substance is itself the subject of inhesion to all real beings which are not substances. These, to distinguish them from substances, are called accidents. In this sense, substance is said to be, in a manner, more really a *being* than accident is. Scholastic philosophers speak of accidents as "beings which belong to being," when comparing them with substance. To substance, by reason of its independence, they specially appropriate the name of *being*.

This metaphysical imperfection of being, which belongs to accidents, necessitates the exclusion of them from our conception of God. God is the sum of metaphysical perfection, and so in God there are not, and cannot be conceived to be—any accidents. The word "substance" etymologically supposes accidents, of which it is the substratum or support—that which stands under them. This is, however, a mere description, and not a definition. As a description, moreover, it is taken from the creature, and the connatural modes of the creature's existence. The idea of *substance*, which is expressed in the definition which we have given of it, applies to God, as He is a substance, in the very highest sense. "That which stands by itself," affirms His independence of any cause for existence; and not merely, as in the case of the creature, independence of any subject for inhesion. The only constituent of our notion of substance which does not apply to God is the supposition of accident. Although

He is in all things by essence, by presence, and by power, and although in Him all things live and move and are, yet He is not their subject of inhesion. They do not inhere in, or cleave to God, nor does God support them in their being as a created substance supports its accidents. It is impossible to conceive God as being a subject of inhesion, since even the Divine essence is not the subject of inhesion to the Divine perfections. These perfections do not inhere in, or cleave to, but are identified with and ARE that essence.

This necessary denial of accidents in God confirms what otherwise also we know—that an hypostasis is a substance, and not an accident. Substance forms the genus in the definition of an hypostasis.

Further, every substance is either singular or universal. This, again, is an exhaustive distribution, or complete division. Every substance, therefore, which is not the one must necessarily be the other. It will be either a singular substance, or an universal substance.

Universal substance cannot, from the very idea of it, be an hypostasis; but, on the contrary, contains under it hypostases. Signified in the concrete, it is predicated of many who are hypostases, as *man* is predicated of Peter and John. Signified in the abstract, substance is conceived as being in, or as possibly being in, that concrete; as, for instance, humanity in man, either actual or possible. The word *man*, therefore, taken by itself, and without any prefix or addition to determinate it—such as *this* man—expresses a concrete universal. The word *humanity* expresses an abstract universal.

Now it is clear that neither an abstract universal nor a concrete universal can be an hypostasis. We cannot say that *humanity* is an hypostasis, nor can we say that *man* is an hypostasis. It follows that an hypostasis must be *singular*—the distribution of substance into universal and singular being exhaustive, and the division complete. This supplies, then, the second member of our definition, or its first differentia. With regard to the genus, we found an hypostasis to be a *substance*. We add our first differentia, and say that an hypostasis is a *singular* substance.

But further, there is a variety of difference among the modes of the existence of singular substances. A singular substance may either be part of an entire substance, whether as an *integral part*—pertaining to the integrity or entirety, and completeness, of the whole, as in the case of the several members of an organic body, whose existence as such is required in order to the entireness or completeness of the organism, as one structural whole—or as an *essential constituent*—as in the case of the human body and the human soul, both of which are essential constituents, and necessary component parts, of a human being, as a human being—or again, a singular substance may be itself an *entire substance*, one complete substantial whole.

Now, a *part*, so long as it retains the idea of a part, is not an hypostasis. It is either IN an hypostasis, or OF an hypostasis. A part is, of the very idea and nature of it, something which is imperfect, which requires to be perfected by another, and which attains to its perfection through union with that other, and in the whole which is the result of the union of its several parts. A part does not stand by itself, but is IN another, and belongs to another, namely, to that whole of which it forms a part. A part does not, as does a perfect thing, *possess* others which are in it. It is itself *possessed* by the perfect whole. Finally the part is not *that which* acts. A part can, at the most, be that *by which*, or *through which* the whole, of which it is a part, acts.

Aristotle, for instance, speaking of the human soul as an essential constituent, and so as a *part* of the human whole which is "this man," or a particular individual man, affirms that it is more correct to say, The man thinks or learns by his soul, than to say, The soul thinks or learns. If this be true of the human soul, that it is not an hypostasis, it is still more manifestly true of the human body. It is true of both of them, by reason of this that neither of the two is in itself a whole. Each of them is a part, which has its perfection through union with the other part, and existence in the individual man, that perfect whole which is the result of the union of those two constituent parts.

By an *hypostasis*, therefore, we mean something which is *perfect as a substance*, so that it stands BY itself and IN itself, and is neither IN another or OF another—which *possesses* all things which are IN it, and is not itself *possessed* by any other thing —and which is the agent, or *principle* of action, or *that which* acts.

Thus we arrive at the third member, and second differentia, of our definition of an hypostasis, which is—*entire*. The genus was *substance* —the first differentia was *singular*—the second differentia we find to be *entire*—and summing up we say that an hypostasis is a *singular, entire substance*.

With this definition of an hypostasis we might rest content, if there were no other hypostases in existence besides created hypostases, and if there were no other modes of subsistence possible to created natures, besides those modes which are connatural to them. Inasmuch, however, as we know with a certainty which is higher than metaphysical certainty that, as matter of fact, there do exist uncreated hypostases, as well as created hypostases, and that those uncreated hypostases. who themselves created all things from nothingness, are the archetypes of the created hypostases which they created and create—any definition of hypostasis which does not apply to uncreated as well as to created hypostases, and which does not include all hypostases, is an inadequate definition, and scientifically imperfect. It is a mere empirical description, and not a scientific definition. Science contemplates effects in the full light of their cause. Empiricism groping in the twilight, feels after the cause by means of the effects.

Had we no other light than the light of reason, we might rest satisfied with our definition of an hypostasis, that it is a *singular, entire substance*. We know, however, by means of God's revelation of Himself to man, that although the Divine Essence is a *singular, entire substance*, that Essence as such is nevertheless *not an hypostasis*. We know, moreover, and from the same source in Divine revelation, that the Sacred Humanity of the Incarnate Word of God is a *singular, entire substance*, and that nevertheless that Humanity is *not an hypostasis*. It follows that our definition of hypostasis is partial, inadequate and incomplete. It does not include ALL hypostases. It applies to only *derived* hypostases. It does not apply to the underived hypostases whence these are derived.

It contents itself with the shadow, and ignores the archetype. Furthermore, even with regard to created natures, it extends only to connatural modes, and leaves out of view possible modes of their subsistence.

Two more members, therefore, are required to complete the definition of an hypostasis. The first is this—an hypostasis must be in itself a whole which does not subsist in, and is not possessed by another hypostasis.

This third differentia seems at first sight to be superfluous and redundant, as already sufficiently covered by, and included in the second differentia. It would be so, if the connatural mode of the subsistence of a created nature in a created hypostasis were the only possible mode of a nature's subsistence. We know, however, and with absolute certainty, that there is a created nature which subsists apart from any created hypostasis, and which is possessed by an uncreated and Divine hypostasis. We know that this created nature, so subsisting and so possessed, is not a PART which forms, along with another part, one entire substance. We further know that the nature with which it is united was before that union an *entire substance*, perfect and complete in itself, selfsufficing to its own perfection, and in no need of union with any other nature. We cannot call the Sacred Humanity a PART, since affirmation of one part is in reality affirmation of the other part or parts which constitute the whole. We cannot possibly conceive a part *as a part* without supposing the existence of another part, as a part—both imperfect with the imperfection of parts—both tending towards union, in order to their perfection—and finding that perfection through existence in the whole. Were, therefore, the Sacred Humanity a *part*, the Divine nature would be equally a *part*. This our reason tells us that we may not say. To affirm of anything that it is a *part*, is to affirm, in so far, the imperfection of it. All that we can say is this, that the Sacred Humanity is a *quasi-part*, that it exists after the manner of a part, subsisting in, and possessed by the Divine Person who is the Eternal Word. This existence *after the manner of a part* suffices to negative the hypostatic character of the Sacred Humanity, and to shew that it is not an hypostasis, but is IN and belongs to an hypostasis. This hypostasis is—a *whole in itself.*

There remains only one other constituent of an hypostasis, and that is—its *incommunicability.* This note of incommunicability gives the difference between an *hypostasis* and a *nature.* A nature is common to many subjects which are hypostatically or individually distinct the one from the other. A nature may be communicated and derived from one subject to another—from the father to the son—but personality cannot be communicated. Personality cannot be derived, and cannot be shared.

Among human persons their human nature, although *specifically* one, is *numerically* as manifold as are the persons who share it. The Divine *nature* of the Divine Persons is not *specifically* one. It is *numerically one*. It is not a nature of the *same species* which subsists in the three Divine Persons. It is numerically the self same nature which is in the Father, which is also in the Son, and which is also in the Holy Ghost. That *nature* is communicated from the Father to the Son, and from the Father and the Son together, as from one principle, to the Holy Ghost.

The *personality* of the Father is not communicated, nor is the *personality* of the Son, for personality is *incommunicable*. It is through this *incommunicability* of the hypostatic, that the three Divine Persons are constituted in their ineffable distinction, the one from the other. Without this note of incommunicability, therefore, the definition of an hypostasis would be partial and incomplete. It is required in order that our conception of the *hypostatic* should be absolute, universal, and adequate.

If we add to these constituents of the *hypos-*

tatic the farther constituent of the *rational* or *intelligent*, we have the conception of the *personal*.

The personal has dignities of its own, which do not belong to the merely hypostatic. A person, or rational hypostasis, alone is conscious to himself of his own hypostatic existence, his own oneness, and his distinction from all others. A person alone can reflect upon himself, and say *Ego*.

A *person* alone can, by his own intrinsic forces and faculties, freely determine himself to his own acts.

Persons, or rational hypostases, alone are and can be *ends*, to which other hypostases are ordained as means. The good which accrues to irrational hypostases is not for themselves, nor is it properly good to them. It contributes to the good of rational hypostases, or persons. Irrational hypostases cannot be said to *use*. They are themselves *used* by the rational hypostasis, for his personal good. Finally, irrational hypostases cannot suffer any injury, since they have not any rights. *Persons* alone are the subjects of *right*, and therefore to persons alone can *wrong* be done. This, however, by the way.

To return to the idea of the personal as it concerns God, Theology tells us that the *will* follows the *nature*, and not the *person*. Were it otherwise, there would be three wills in God, since in God there are three Persons; or there would be but one person in God, since there is only one will in God. So likewise, if the *will* followed the *person*, and not the *nature*, there would be two persons in the Incarnate Word, in Whom there are two wills; or, since there is but one person, there would be only one will.

4.

Having now considered at some length the notion of an *hypostasis*, and of a *person*, as a person is a rational or intelligent hypostasis, we can speak more freely with regard to the real distinction of the three Divine Persons, one from the other.

Deity—or the absolute Divine essence—is indeed an essential individual substance; in the sense that, of its own absolute perfection, it is not only distinct, but infinitely diverse from all other substances, either actual or possible. This absolute Divine essence, however, which is numerically *one*, is at the same time three Persons, who are distinct one from the other, and who are the Father, the Son, and the Holy Ghost. Those three, as we know with certainty from Divine revelation, are *one God*. Deity, therefore—or the absolute Divine essence—is really common to the three Persons who, both singly and all together, are one God; for the one

God is one infinite essence which cannot be multiplied.

This absolute essence, under the formal idea of the *absolute*, is not an "individual substance," in the sense in which an hypostasis is conceived as an *individual substance;* since it is *not incommunicable*. The *absolute* Divine essence is, on the contrary, the nature of God the Father, in such wise that it is at the same time the nature of God the Son, who is other than God the Father; and the nature also of God the Holy Ghost, who again is other than the Father and the Son.

The self same Divine essence, under the formal idea of the *relative*, is an "individual substance" in the sense of its being *incommunicable*. This incommunicability is the formal reason why the Divine essence is said to *subsist in itself*, or to be an hypostasis.

Among creatures the case is manifest. Humanity, for instance, as common or communicable to many, is not an hypostasis, but a common nature. The hypostasis is the individual man, who is distinct from all others of the same nature, that is, from all who have specifically the same humanity.

In our inadequate mode of conceiving, by way of composition, we conceive a Divine *Person*, as it were, *informed* by the Divine essence—or the Divine *essence*, as it were, *affected* by the *relation* which constitutes the person. From the infinity of the Divine essence, however, and the simplicity of a Divine Person, it is evident that this *relation* is not a distinct reality which is *superadded* to the Divine essence. It is also evident, and for the same reason, that the Divine essence is not properly a *form*, or really distinct from the relation which constitutes a Divine *Person*. What there really is, is one most simple *being*, which we apprehend under the two virtually distinct formal ideas of the *absolute* and the *relative;* and to both of these there truly corresponds one and the same reality. This twofold idea we, in accordance with previous notions derived from creatures, conjoin by way of composition, in forming our conception of a Divine Person.

The Divine Essence, under the formal idea of a substantial relation, that is, a relation which is itself a substance, is a Divine Person. Under the idea of one determinate substantial relation, the Divine Essence is one Divine Person—and under the idea of another determinate substantial relation, the Divine Essence is another Divine Person.

There are not two realities, or two ideas, which are distinct one from the other with objective precision—the absolute and the relative—which concur to compose one reality. There is one supreme reality which we conceive under the idea of a Divine *relation*, such as *paternity* in the abstract, or *father*, in the concrete; and this is in reality at the same time the absolute Divine Essence. The very same thing, on the other hand, when it is conceived under the idea of the Divine Essence, is at the same time the three substantial relations, and every one of them; and these, not under the idea of essence, but under the idea of the relative, are distinct one from the other.

Our conception of the *relative*, which is derived from creatures, does not at the same time express the *absolute;* as the conception of the *absolute* does not at the same time express the *relative*. That twofold idea, therefore, which belongs to the Divine essence, in accordance with the functions, both of the absolute and of the relative, is conceived by us under a twofold inadequate notion. As, however, that which we apprehend under the notion of an attribute, as for instance, the Divine Wisdom, is in reality absolute, infinite being itself, in every line of its perfection, and is therefore the true God—so that which we apprehend by an inadequate notion under the idea of a *relation*, as for instance, *paternity*, is in reality, and at the same time, both *paternity* and *absolute being*, and is true God subsisting in an absolute nature.

Eternal generation, and paternity—nativity, or

eternal procession through generation, and sonship—and eternal procession through spiration, and being breathed forth from the Father and the Son—are all of them in reality the same, without any distinction, and so without any priority. There is not first in idea the Father, as an already constituted person, and then the Father, as generating. The Father is constituted, and constituted *as a person*, by the eternal necessary relative act of generation—or, this necessary substantial act, the substantial understanding which, of its own intrinsic nature, is eternally producing, and having its immanent word produced, is itself the Father. So also on the other hand, *generation* is not prior to *paternity*, for the Father Himself, under the formal idea as He is the Father, and this one determinate person, generates; and through this eternal, necessary, relative act of generation, He is a distinct and determinate Person, namely God the Father. There cannot possibly be first an indeterminate person, who is later on, through an act of generation, constituted the Father, and this one determinate person. *Paternity* and *generation* are, in the full and explicit conception of them simultaneous, so that neither of them can be understood as prior in idea to the other. The same is true of sonship and nativity, in the Son of God; and of active and passive spiration or procession, in God the Holy Ghost.

The understanding which produces the Divine Word is not an *elicited* act of a person, as is understanding in creatures. Divine understanding is a pure substantial act which formally as, of its own intrinsic necessary perfection, it is *relative* to the Word eternally produced, is—God the Father. Hence this relative act is not, as it were, inhering in any presupposed person; but is itself—this one determinate Divine Person, who is distinct from the Word, and from the Holy Ghost.

Active generation in God is a relative act which, of intrinsic necessity, is always complete, as always having for its intrinsic terminus the Word eternally produced. Hence that complete act of generation is not first in idea, so that from it paternity should follow; but that relative act is *itself paternity*.

It can be said—The Father is, because He generates—and it can also be said—He generates, because He is the Father. This is not as if paternity and generation were either of them to be conceived as prior to the other. It is because the one conception includes the other as its own formal idea; as that which is defined includes the definition, and the definition includes that which is defined.

We may, nevertheless, follow the analogy of creatures, in our contemplation of the Divine

Persons, and their relations and notional acts, and conceive one person as if he were prior to another. The first Divine person, or the Unbegotten, can be confusedly conceived by us without an explicit conception of paternity, and then afterwards as generating. In this way, a confused notion of the person comes first in our idea, and the notional act comes later. We might also regard paternity merely as a *relation*, prescinding from this that a *Divine* relation is itself the Divine *substance*, and is therefore a Divine *person*. Hence, since among creatures the relation of paternity follows generation, we can, in accordance with this analogy, conceive in God generation, as the foundation of the relation; and so as prior in idea to paternity, as thus inadequately regarded. This analogous mode of conceiving is imperfect, and needs correction, lest we should form a judgment that there is in reality first a Person, Who is afterwards constituted the Father, by an act of generation. Keeping this, however, in view, it is a way of expressing the process of our minds which is not uncommon, and it has its convenience.

There are in God three *subsistences*, under the formal idea of *relatives*; and there is not in God any *absolute subsistence*, which is common to the three Divine Persons. One who is said to be *subsisting*, is one who is *incommunicably* existing in himself, and is therefore distinct from all others, even of the same essence or nature. A *subsistence* is in fact the same as an hypostasis, in the sense in which we have defined *hypostasis.*

Given revelation of the existence of three Divine Persons, the word "God" has no other signification than simply that of the one Divine *Nature* which cannot be multiplied—with adsignification of *subsistence,* either indeterminately and confusedly, or of a trine subsistence, or determinately of one subsistence of the Three. In whichever of those ways *subsistence* is adsignified, it has always the formal idea of the *relative.* The only difference is somewhat of a difference in our mode of conceiving. In the second and third of those modes of our conception, we *expressly* conceive subsistence as *relative.* In the first mode, we can conceive subsistence confusedly, without the *express* notion of the *relative.* Even then, however, Divine subsistence cannot be conceived with *exclusion* of the relative, and under the *express* idea of the *absolute;* since objectively and in reality it has no existence except under the formal idea of the *relative.*

The Divine *essence* does not give subsistence to the Divine *relations;* nor do the Divine relations give *subsistence* to the Divine essence— for neither are the relations really distinct from the essence, nor is *subsistence* a reality which is *superadded*, either to the essence, or to the relations.

The most simple and infinite Divine essence is, in reality, of itself and of its own internal exigence, the subsisting Father, Son, and Holy Ghost. As regards relations, on the other hand, *paternity* is of itself God the Father—*sonship*, is God the Son—and *passive spiration* is God the Holy Ghost. More properly, therefore, will the one most simple essence be said to have the formal idea at once of the *absolute*, and of the *relative*; so that under the idea of the *absolute* it should be understood as the *Essence*, which is common to the three distinct Persons—while, under the idea of the *relative*, it is the Father distinct from the Son, the Son distinct from the Father, and the Holy Ghost distinct from both—and therefore incommunicably subsisting, as the Father, as the Son, and as the Holy Ghost.

Nevertheless, since essence and relations are distinct *in idea*, and there is one function under the formal idea of *essence*, and another function under the formal idea of the *relative;* we can, in accordance with our inadequate mode of conceiving, say that the Divine *essence* gives to the Divine *relations* that they should be *substantial*—and this idea of *substance* is a necessary foundation for the idea of *subsistence;* while the Divine *relations* give to the Divine *essence* the *incom-*

municableness which is the formal idea of *subsistence*, properly so called.

5.

Since the Divine substantial relations, as they are really distinct one from the other, and are, therefore, *subsisting*, are Divine persons, or formally constitute the Divine persons; it is evident that there are as many really distinct constituent relations as there are Divine persons. There is one, the formal idea of the Father; a second, the formal idea of the Son; and a third, the formal idea of the Holy Ghost; or, there is paternity—sonship—and procession.

Since internal relations in God are relations *of origin*, there is necessarily in every Divine procession a twofold relation of opposition. Through opposition there is distinction of relation. There is the relation between a principle, and that which is proceeding from its principle.

Since, therefore, there are in God two distinct processions—the procession of the Son by generation from the Father, and the procession of the Holy Ghost by spiration from the Father and the Son—there must be in God four relations. As the Father is the correlative of the Son, so is the Spirator the correlative of the Spirit who is breathed forth. In other words, as the Divine Fatherhood is the correlative of the Divine Sonship, so is active spiration the correlative of passive spiration. These are opposed, as is a principle with relation to that which proceeds from it, as from a principle.

Besides these four Divine relations, *to be unbegotten*, or *unbegetableness*, is a notion which is proper to one Divine Person only. It is not common to the other two Divine Persons.

Being unbegotten does not constitute a person, any more than does *active spiration* constitute a person. *Spiration* is distinct *in idea* only, and not in reality, from *paternity* in the Father, and from *sonship* in the Son. It is included in a *full conception* of the Divine Fatherhood and Sonship. In like manner to be *unbegotten*, as a notion which belongs to the first Divine Person, is included in a *full conception* of the Divine Paternity.

Active spiration supposes, in accordance with our imperfect mode of intellectual conception, the two Persons, the Father and the Son, already constituted; and to them a common act is conceived as supervening. This *act* of active spiration does not *really proceed* from the Father and the Son; and so there is no opposition between the act, and the two persons whose act it is. It is not therefore really distinct from them. Through this act of spiration, however, there does really proceed the Divine Spirit, or God the Holy Ghost, from the Father and the

Son. Through this their common act, and in accordance with the formal idea of the Divine Spirator, the Father and the Son are related to the Holy Ghost as is a principle to that which proceeds from it, as from a principle. They are thus really distinct from Him.

The Divine Spirator does not denote a person, distinct from the Father and the Son. It signifies one spirative force, or one act and one relation of spiration, which is common to two persons. Confusedly also it adsignifies the persons to whom the spirative force belongs. It does so very much in the same way as the word *Creator* signifies the one Divine Essence under the formal idea of a creating act, and confusedly adsignifies the persons whose essence it is.

Since active spiration, however, is in the Father really identified with paternity, and the same active spiration is in the Son really identified with sonship, and is only *in idea* distinguished from paternity and sonship; the conception whereby spiration is—in accordance with our imperfect mode of understanding, by way of composition—conceived as supervening to persons who are already constituted as persons. This conception can be improved on, so as somewhat better to correspond with the Divine simplicity; as we have seen is the case with our imperfect conception of the constitution of a person through relation and essence.

In order that the two relations of paternity, on the one hand, and active spiration, on the other hand, which are not opposed to each other, may be understood as being one person—and, in like manner, in order that the relation of sonship, along with the same active spiration, which is not opposed to it, may be understood as being one person, the following consideration may be of service.

The Divine essence or nature, under the formal idea of *understanding, which is expressing the Word*, is God the Father. The same Divine essence or nature, under the formal idea of *understanding expressed*—or, as the immanent produced terminus of the paternal understanding is—the Word or Son of God. Divine understanding, both as it *expresses* the Divine Word, and as it is the Word *expressed*, is at the same time Divine love which is producing, as breathing forth, its own immanent terminus, which is—the Holy Ghost. Paternal understanding has at the same time the formal idea of love which is breathing forth. Under one idea, therefore, it is related to the Divine Word, while under another idea, it is related to the Divine Spirit who is breathed forth.

Since, however, in every spirit, and even in an infinite Spirit, loving presupposes understanding, while understanding does not presuppose loving—and because the Divine Understanding which expresses the Divine Word, of the inmost nature of the case, communicates the Divine Essence to the Divine Word under all its formal ideas—with the one exception of the formal idea of expression of the Word, of which the Word is the really distinct terminus—the Word is therefore expressed by communicating the Divine essence under the formal idea also of love which is breathing forth. Hence Paternal understanding has not the formal idea of the love which is breathing forth, except as supposing (in order of origin) *expression* of the Word; and the Word is *expressed* as having the same formal idea of love which is breathing forth. The Father "fecund of the Holy Ghost" expresses by generation His Word, as "fecund" of the same Holy Ghost.

Hence as *essence* and *paternity*—the formal idea of the intellect which is expressing its word—are not two which are really distinct, but are one supreme essence, under the twofold formal idea of the *absolute* and the *relative;* so *paternity* and *active spiration* are not two relations, but are one essence under a twofold formal idea; and this essence is relative to a twofold really distinct terminus. Since those two formal ideas have not opposition one to the other, so between them there is not real distinction, and that which in them is relative is one. Since, however, that one has an order of relation, under the formal ideas of begetting, and of breathing forth, to two really distinct termini—the Son and the Holy Ghost—*paternity* and *active spiration* are two relations which are distinct *in idea*, and the distinction in idea has a *foundation in reality*.

The relations are two in number, not by reason of mutual opposition, for between them there is no opposition, but by reason of the termini to which there is relation. If these two relations were really distinct one from the other through mutual opposition, they would be two persons. Since they are distinct in idea only, they are one person. Relations which are opposed, says St. Thomas, are persons, and there are two persons if there are two relations; but relations, which in the same person are not opposed, are two relations, indeed, or two properties, but not two persons, one only.

The same is to be said of the distinction *in idea*, and real *identity*, of *active spiration*, as it is communicated to the Son, as regards His relation of sonship. The Son, from the very mode of His procession from the Father through understanding, is begotten as being with the Father one principle, which is fecund of the Holy Ghost.

The Divine Paternity and the Divine Sonship,

if apprehended with fullness of conception, include Divine spiration, so that without it, they would not be fully conceived. Active spiration is a relation which does not constitute a person, but it is a relation which does distinguish the first and second Divine Persons from the third Divine person, God the Holy Ghost.

6.

Besides the four Divine *relations*, there is a *notion* which is proper to one Divine Person alone, namely, to God the Father, and that is—*unbegetableness*. By a notion we here mean a formal idea, or character, by which a person is known to us as distinct from other persons.

Being *unbegotten*, or *unbegetableness*, does not merely signify *uncreatedness*, for that is an *absolute* attribute of the Divine essence, and is therefore *common* to the three Divine Persons. Further, the word *unbegotten*, as applied to the Father, is not used simply in opposition to being *begotten*. If it were, it would apply also to the Holy Ghost, who is said, in the Athanasian Creed, to be "not begotten." This He is there said to be, in comparison with the Son Who is the Begotten of the Father.

In a more strict sense the term *unbegotten* is opposed, not merely to a *mode* of procession through *generation*, but to all procession whatsoever, or all *origin* from a principle. In this sense to be *unbegotten* is proper to the Father alone.

Since the term "unbegotten" designates not a nature but a hypostasis, it signifies in God not the *absolute*, but the *relative*. "Unbegotten" is a negative word indeed, but when God is concerned, negation cannot be negation of any perfection. It is only our imperfect mode of conceiving that which in God is *positive*, and a perfection. In the order of the absolute, negation sets forth an absolute perfection by excluding imperfection; or, what comes to the same thing, by negation of any perfection which is limited, by the lack of farther perfection, as is every created perfection. It is a negation of a negation, and so it is an affirmation of an absolute perfection which is inadequately and confusedly conceived by us; through comparison of it with perfections which are limited, as in the case of the negative attributes, *infinite*, *uncreated*, and the like.

An absolute attribute cannot be denied to be, at the same time, the other absolute attributes, because these attributes are not really distinct one from the other. Hence, it would be false to say that in God Justice is not Mercy, although the conception of justice is one thing, and the conception of mercy is another. We may say, and we ought to say, that—the conception of the Divine Justice is not the conception of the Divine Mercy.

Relatives in God, as contrasted with *absolutes* in God, are, on the other hand, under the formal idea of the *relative*, really distinct one from the other. The Father is one, and the Son is another, and the Holy Ghost is yet another. Hence, of these relatives in God it is to be denied that they are each other. The Father is not the Son, and is not the Holy Ghost. The Son, again, is not the Father, and is not the Holy Ghost. The Holy Ghost is not the Father, and is not the Son.

A negation so conceived does not, however, set forth any notion, and formal idea, of a person, other than an affirmation that there is one Father; that is to say, that this one, under the formal idea of Father, is related to the Son, and distinct from the Son; and under the formal idea of Spirator, which is included in the Divine Paternity, is related to the Holy Ghost, and distinct from the Holy Ghost. The same is to be said of the relation of the Son to the Father, and the relation of the Holy Ghost to the Father and the Son.

In the Son, and in the Holy Ghost, there is, besides these, no other notion which is distinct in idea, by which either person is opposed to other persons through negation.

In the *first* Divine Person, on the other hand, negation of procession from another, whereby He is said to be *unbegotten*, in opposition to the

Begotten Son, and the proceeding Holy Ghost—gives another formal idea which is, in consideration of the mind, distinct from *paternity*, and distinct from *active spiration*.

Procession from a principle is certainly not an imperfection in the Son, and in the Holy Ghost; but procession from a principle would be an imperfection in the first Divine Person. It would be a negation and destruction of that Person.

Hence negation of the relation of being *begotten* and of *proceeding* is, in the Father, *affirmation* of a relative or personal perfection.

As God is essentially *unbegotten Being*, in the sense that God is essentially *selfexistent* Being, so the first Person of the Trinity is, of an intrinsic necessity of nature, a *selfexistent* Person. This hypostatic or personal perfection of His, we conceive and explain by way of negation of *origin*.

The first Person of the Trinity, Who is therefore a selfexistent Divine Person, is, of the intrinsic nature of the case, the *principle* of the other Divine Persons, that is, of the Son, and, with the Son, of the Holy Ghost.

7.

The reason why there are only two Divine processions is to be found in the *infinity* of God's perfection. It is not by many acts, but by one simple and infinite act, that the Divine intellect comprehends the Divine essence, and in that essence all the true, in all the ideas of its intelligibleness. It is still more accurately true to say that the Divine intellect *is itself* that one infinite act of comprehension. As infinite, and, therefore, as incapable of multiplication, it expresses, as its intrinsic terminus, an *adequate*, and consequently an infinite Word. A plurality of infinite Words would as much involve contradiction as would a plurality of Gods. As the Word of God is an adequate and infinite expression of the Divine intellect, it embraces every possible expression of all the true. Whatever is understood by the Divine intellect is expressed by the one Divine Word. The only other expression which is possible is an external adumbration of that infinite internal expression. The necessary oneness of infinite *Being* not only does not exclude, but includes the possibility of beings which, as external adumbrations of it, are *beings* analogically. An infinite word, in like manner, does not exclude, but includes the possibility of external adumbrations and imitations of that Word. The Divine Intellect is "fecund" of one Word alone. This singleness of the Divine Word follows from, and manifests, the *infinite* fecundity of the Intellect which through it expresses itself.

There is the same reason for the singleness of the one Divine Spirit, God the Holy Ghost.

The Divine love is adequate to the Divine goodness, and that love is therefore *infinite*. The immanent terminus of that love must be single. It is incapable of multiplication. If anything were wanting to the Divine act of understanding and of loving, that act would not be infinitely perfect.

Divine understanding, which produces a Divine Word, is not an action which emerges from a potentiality. It is an eternal, necessary, pure act, which has its eternal, necessary, intrinsic terminus—the Divine Word. To *produce*, therefore, is in God the same as having from eternity, in an act which is *complete*, a necessary intrinsic terminus. It is an eternal substantial relation, or, an eternal relation which is itself a substance. This cannot be, and cannot be truly conceived as being, without its own eternal correlative terminus. So also *to be produced* is to be *actually* produced from eternity; and this is as necessary as Divine understanding is eternal and necessary. There is no *priority*, except in the idea of the order of *origin*, among the Divine Persons. There is, if we may say so, a perfect simultaneity. One Divine Person cannot be, and cannot even in idea be conceived as being, without the other Divine Persons. The Father, for instance, cannot be conceived as ever being without His Word, nor can the Word or Son of God be conceived as ever being without His Father.

The Divine loving, through which the Holy Ghost proceeds, is the loving of the Divine essence, with all its attributes, which are identified with it.

This loving, as it is in God the Father, is the loving of Himself, and His loving of His Son. As this loving is in God the Son, it is His loving of Himself, and His loving of His Father. Hence the Fathers speak of the Holy Ghost as produced by the *mutual loving* of the Father and the Son. It is not as if there were a twofold loving, or, as if the two, as it were, *conspired* to produce the personal Love as one terminus. The two Divine Persons love with a *substantial* loving, or a loving which is itself a *substance*, and this loving is in these two numerically one. It is so, inasmuch as it is the loving of the Divine essence, as it is in itself, and the loving of that essence in all the ideas of its loveableness. The Divine essence is every absolute perfection, and is at the same time the three Divine Persons. One and the same loving embraces reflexly, as it were, itself as loving, and its intrinsic terminus, God the Holy Ghost, who is eternally proceeding from it.

Any difficulty which this may present to our minds arises from our imperfect mode of understanding, by which there is conceived the love producing, as *prior* to the love produced.

God the Father is not *formally* wise through His Word, as if He were constituted as wise through that Word. The Father and the Son are also not *formally* loving, through the Holy Ghost. No Divine Person can be formally wise, or formally loving, through another Divine Person who is really distinct from Him. The Father is formally wise, and the Father and the Son are formally loving, through the *absolute Divine essence*, which is the *absolute* Divine Wisdom, and the *absolute* Divine Love. God the Father is, therefore, *wise* through God the Word, not *formally*, but as that Word is the necessary, immanent, terminus of His fecund Wisdom, a terminus without which there would not be Divine Wisdom. In the same way, the Father and the Son are *loving*, through the Holy Ghost, as He is the necessary, intrinsic, terminus of their loving, a terminus without which there would not be Divine Love.

8

The difference in the procession of the second and third Divine Persons is—no less than procession itself, and the distinctness of the Divine Persons—revealed in the Sacred Scriptures, which are the Written Word of God. This difference is declared through the names which are proper to the Divine Persons respectively.

Between the first and second Persons there is, as we are Divinely taught, the relation of a principle, to that which is produced by this principle. Besides this indeterminate fact, we are also taught what is the determinate relation between those two. It is the relation of father and son. The Incarnate Word said to the Jews that God was *His Father*. St. Paul wrote to the Romans that God spared not even *His own Son*. St. John says that the *Son of God* is come, and that He has given us understanding, that we may know the true God, and may be in *His true Son*. He also speaks of the *Only-begotten* of the Father, whom He identifies with the Word Who was in the beginning with God, and Who was God, and Who in the fulness of time was made flesh, and dwelled among men. Of Him he declares, that God so loved the world as to give *His Only-begotten Son*, and that the man will be judged who believes not in the name of *the Only-begotten Son of God*.

The idea of *Father* is so proper to the first Divine Person, and the idea of *Son* is so proper to the second Divine Person, that through this idea alone they are really distinct one from the other. By the same idea they are distinguished from the third Divine Person. When the Holy Ghost is spoken of, whether by Himself, or along with the other Divine Persons, He is designated as *proceeding*, but not as proceeding as God the Son proceeds, and therefore as proceeding by a mode of procession which is distinct from *generation*. The Incarnate Son prescribed Baptism to be given in the name of the Father, and of the Son, and of the Holy Ghost. At His own Baptism, when the Spirit of God descended as a dove, and came upon Him, the Voice from Heaven said, This is My Beloved Son. Before the departure of Jesus from this earth He said, I will send you from the Father the Spirit of truth, Who *proceedeth from the Father.* St. Paul wrote to the Galatians—God hath sent the *Spirit of His Son* into your hearts. To the Romans he wrote of the *Spirit of God* dwelling in them, and leading them, and of the Spirit of God giving testimony, and of the fruits of the Holy Ghost, and of the Spirit helping their infirmity, and of the Spirit Himself asking for them. St. Luke also speaks of the Spirit of Jesus; and St. Peter, of the Spirit of Christ.

As the second Divine Person is alone the terminus of *generation*, that is, as He alone is the *Son*, so generation is, in the Sacred Scriptures, predicated of Him alone. He is expressly declared to be God's own Son, through an eternal generation, which was never at any time in process, but was always and from eternity complete. St. Paul wrote to the Hebrews—"God in these last days hath spoken to us *by His Son*, Whom He hath appointed *Heir* of all things, by Whom also He made the world, Who, being the Brightness of His Glory, and the Figure of His Substance, sitteth on the right hand of the Majesty on high, being made so much better than the Angels; for to which of the Angels hath He said at any time, 'Thou art *My Son*, to-day have *I begotten Thee?*' and again, 'I will be *to Him a Father*, and He shall be *to Me a Son.*' But to the Son He saith, 'Thy throne, O God, is for ever and ever. Thou, in the beginning, O Lord, didst found the earth, and the works of Thy hands are the heavens.'"

When God says to His Divine Son, "To-day have I begotten Thee," the word *to-day* expresses, not a beginning of generation, but the changeless *now* of the eternity which is outside time; an eternity in which the Son neither was, nor will be, but is ever being begotten, and His generation is ever, as an act, complete.

That which is revealed in the words *generation* and *son*, is in God entirely free from all the imperfection which the ideas, expressed by those words, have in creatures. Hence, supposing revelation that there are two processions in God, and both of them by a communication of the

Divine nature, but this in such a way that the one procession is properly *generation*, while the other procession is not generation, we can arrive at some understanding of the difference between the two processions.

The proper idea of *generation*, by which it is distinguished from all other processions, is manifest to us in creatures. That procession which among creatures is called, and is, *generation*, corresponds with generation in God, not as identical in idea, but analogously, by way of likeness and imitation. The word *generation* signifies more properly and more perfectly generation as it is in God, than it signifies generation as it is in creatures. In created beings there is only an adumbration or shadow of generation.

All the imperfections which cleave to generation in creatures, but which do not belong to the proper idea of generation in itself, have to be set aside. This revelation itself instructs us to do, not only in its general teaching on the *infinite* perfection of God, but also by specially declaring Divine generation to be *intellectual*.

The *Son* of the Father is the *Word* of the Father. Both names of the second Divine Person designate one and the same idea, but under a different analogy.

Son signifies an hypostasis, and an hypostasis who proceeds from another by that special communication of nature which is generation. Among created spirits there cannot be *generation*, and consequently there cannot be a *son*. Generation, and sons, are possible to corporeal beings alone among creatures. Among these, however, generation is not through communication of the *whole* substance which is in the generative principle, but by a vital separation from the substance of the generater. Hence, oneness of nature between father and son is only a specific oneness, or oneness of species. It is not a numerical oneness. A created father also, as he is a hypostasis, is prior to his son. Further, the hypostasis of a created father, and the hypostasis of his son, are not only distinct, but separate, in numerically different natures, along with other differences which follow from distinctness of nature. Hence it is also that the likeness between father and son, among creatures, cannot be an *absolute* likeness. It is only in a nature which is numerically one that likeness can be absolute.

All these imperfections, which attach to finite and corporeal creatures, involve contradiction in God, Who is an infinite Spirit.

The idea of *intellectual* generation—the only generation which is possible to a pure or mere spirit—Divine revelation directly expresses by the name of The Word. A created spirit, by its understanding of itself, produces a *word* of itself, that is to say, a *mental* word, or idea, such as is expressed by an *uttered* word. An internal word is a conception of the mind, which is manifested and communicated by means of the word of the lips. This mental word is immanent. It *remains* in the mind of him who conceives it. It is not transient, as is a vocal word. When that is uttered, it is gone. The mental word abides.

A mental word, or idea, in the mind of a created spirit, falls short of perfection, since it is not a *substance*. He, therefore, who produces it, and the word produced by him, are not both of them hypostases. It follows that we cannot say that there is, in a proper sense, intellectual *generation* among created spirits.

These two analogies are to be conjoined, so that the one should correct and complete the other, by supplying that which is defective in it.

Among corporeal emanations, it is not every production, even of the living—and even amongst those productions which are from the *substance* of the principle which produces them—that is properly *generation*, or is entitled to that name. Generation has its own special and proper characteristics.

Among spiritual perfections, those perfections alone are *substantial*, or are a substance, which are in God Who is an infinite Spirit.

Hence it is that the procession of the Word of

God is properly *generation*. The generation of the Divine Word, and His name of The Word, is not metaphorical. His generation is as real as is His name of *Son*, or as is generation among creatures.

The *essence* of generation, properly so called, includes three notes. Generation must be a proceeding of *the living from the living*. Among inanimate creatures, the production of one of them through the force and operation of another, is only colloquially called *generation*, as when fire is said to *generate* heat. It is essentially different from generation of the living from the living. Generation is also more noble, the more noble the nature is, and the life of both the generater and the generated. Generation, in creatures which are living with an animal life, is more noble than is generation in creatures which are living with a merely vegetative life. The two are the same in genus, but they differ in their species. Generation is more noble still in men, who are living with a rational life, than it is in brute animals. Since, however, power of propagation and efficacy of generation is, even in rational animals, not from the nature, formally as it is rational, but from the nature, formally as it is animal, the difference is more in the nobleness or less nobleness of the nature which is propagated, and in the relations which spring from generation, than it is in the generation itself. Hence we rightly speak of *generation* both in brute animals and in men, but it is amongst men that there is most properly *father* and *son*.

Generation amongst pure spirits, who have no animal life, and who are living with a solely intellectual life, would be more noble still. Among finite spirits, however, that which is produced by an intellectual act is not produced by propagation, or communication of their nature from one to another. It is therefore not a substance. Among pure spirits, such as are angels and devils, *generation* has consequently no place.

In God, Who is an infinite Spirit, and a pure act, Who is essentially Life, and selfexistent Life, there is produced by an intellectual act a substantial *word*, or a word which is a *substance*. Under this idea generation, as it is procession of *the living from the living*, is in God infinitely perfect. It is as infinitely perfect as is the Life of God. Christ is the Son of the Living God, and He said "As the Father hath Life in Himself, so has He given to the Son also to have Life in Himself."

Secondly, it is contained in the idea of *generation*, that there should be production *from the substance of the generater*.

Thirdly, it is required that the production should not only be from the substance and nature of the producer, but that the nature of the producer should be propagated, or communicated to the produced, through an *intrinsic principle which is ordained for propagation*, or communication of nature, and which may be called the *principle of fecundity*.

Both of these ideas are to be found in every generation, properly so called, even amongst creatures. They are essential. If either of them is absent, there is not *generation*, but production of another kind. In creatures, however, both ideas are, as we have seen, imperfect; and there is in creatures only an adumbration of the infinitely perfect generation which is in God.

Generation among creatures is, moreover, not complete, except by separation of the produced from the producer. It is not, therefore, an immanent or abiding, but a transient or passing action.

Further, the intrinsic principle of fecundity in creatures passes from the potential to the actual. In them, therefore, generation is not necessary from the fact that there is in them an intrinsic principle of fecundity, nor is generation in them always actual.

Finally, that which is the foundation and origin of all these imperfections is, that the generation of creatures is annexed to the material and the corporeal, and is perfected through acts of the animal life. It belongs, therefore, to an inferior and essentially imperfect order.

In communication of the Divine nature, on the other hand, all these imperfections are excluded by the infinite perfection which is opposed to them. Generation in God is *intellectual*, and through a most pure and absolute act of substantial understanding, or of understanding which is itself a substance. There is therefore no passing from the potential to the actual; but an eternal, necessary, complete act, with its own immanent terminus eternally produced. This terminus is The Word. This Divine act is itself the intrinsic principle of fecundity, and of its own intrinsic perfection it is ever complete.

The Divine essence is itself substantial understanding, and as it is understanding of itself which produces the Divine Word, or is relative to the immanent Word, it is an essence which is identified with the Person Who produces. There is therefore procession of the *whole* essence or substance of Him Who produces. This truth is also otherwise evident, since the most simple Divine substance has no parts. The Son is so of the substance of the Father, as to be consubstantial with the Father.

The more perfect the life is, in generation—the more perfect the production from the substance of the producer—the more perfect the communication, and the oneness, of nature in both—the more intrinsic, and essential, and entirely actual, the principle of fecundity is—the more fully and perfectly will there be that which is signified by the name of *generation*.

In generations among creatures—from which we derive our first knowledge of what this special kind of production is, and from which first comes the name of *generation*—we find all these constituent ideas of generation, but in an imperfect manner. All these constituent elements are in God, and that in the most perfect of all ways.

As regards that which is signified by the name of *generation*, it is first in God, and in God it is in its infinite perfection. It is in creatures only analogously, through a participation and adumbration of it derived from their Creator; as is the case with other created shadows of uncreated perfections.

The last essential note of *generation*, in the proper idea of it, is in the intrinsic character of the producing act; namely that this act should be of its own nature directed towards expressing a substantial likeness of the producer. This last note is distinct and separable from the other notes. There can, therefore, be production in accordance with those notes, without its being an expression of an image and likeness, and hence without its being *generation*. We should not have known, apart from revelation, that as matter of fact there is such a procession in God, since we find no such procession amongst creatures.

There is this evident difference between the expression of a mental *word* through understanding, and the procession of love through volition, that the intellect, by the very nature of an act of it, produces by understanding an express likeness of the thing understood; while the will by willing does not, of the nature of an act of it, produce a likeness of the thing loved. It produces only an inclination towards the thing loved, and a complacence in it.

In this we have the reason why the *procession* of the third Divine Person is not generation.

9.

That which we call an *absolute attribute* in God is in reality none other than the most simple Divine *essence*, conceived by us under the formal idea of this or of that perfection, such as wisdom, justice, or the like. One attribute has no real origin from another attribute, nor from the Divine essence. If it had, it would not be an *absolute* attribute. This it is, as absolved from relation. By proceeding, the attribute would be *relative* to its principle of procession. In that case there would be as many Divine persons, as there are Divine attributes.

It is not only because the Divine attributes are really the Divine essence, but it is also because those attributes have no real origin, either from that essence or from one another, and so no relations of opposition to one another; that, as with the Divine essence by itself, so also with the same essence, regarded under the formal ideas of the various absolute attributes—the essence is one, and incapable of multiplication.

Hence, if any absolute attribute were conceived as in one Person, for instance, in God the Father, and denied to be in another Person; the most simple Divine *essence*, or Divinity, would be denied to that Person.

If an attribute were only specifically the same, and numerically distinct, in distinct Persons, there would thereby be distinct *essences*, and consequently many Gods.

On the other hand, although the formal ideas of the Father, and of the Son, and of the Holy Ghost, are really the Divine essence itself, and therefore do not proceed from that *essence* by real origin, and are not really distinct from that essence; yet the real relations, by which the Persons are constituted, and so the Persons themselves, are really distinct one from the other, as is a principle from that which it produces, so that the Father of the Son is not the Son, and the Son of the Father is not the Father.

It is in no way against the oneness of the Divine essence and attributes, in the three distinct Divine Persons, that the Divine essence in the Father is not communicated to Him, and is communicable and communicated by Him—that in the Son, there is the Divine essence communicated to Him from the Father—and that in the Holy Ghost, there is the Divine essence communicated to Him from the Father and the Son. The Divine essence might thus seem at first sight to be different in one Person, from what it is in another. There is, however, merely a diversity of *mode;* and this diversity of mode does not affect the essence regarded *absolutely*, or the absolute Divine *Being* which is wholly one, and in no way distinct. These *modes* are in reality the *relations* of paternity, of sonship, and of procession, respectively. The *absolute* Divine essence is at the same time *relative;* and it is under the formal idea of the relative, and under that alone, that there is distinctness, and it is a real distinctness.

In the same way that the nature of the three Divine Persons, with all its absolute perfections, is one, and in no way distinct, as are the Persons, every external operation of Theirs is also one, and in no way distinct from that of the other Persons.

External operation in God is none other than the Divine *essence* itself, under the formal idea of *absolute* intellect, and *absolute* omnipotent will, with connotation of an extrinsic terminus which is to be effected; that is to say, of a work to be done by God outside Himself, and in the sphere of His creation.

The Divine essence, under whatever *absolute* formal idea it is regarded, in our manner of distinguishing perfections—and so also under the formal idea of absolute understanding, and absolute volition—is numerically one, and the same, in all the three Persons.

Besides the internal relations, by which the Divine Persons are constituted in their real distinctness, all else that can be conceived in God is *absolute*. Divine external operation is therefore as one in the three Persons, as the three Persons are themselves one God.

The Divine Persons operate externally, not formally as They are distinct Persons, but as They are one God. The principle, or rather the subject, *which* operates in an operation, is an *hypostasis*, indeed, but the principle *whereby* the operation is effected is the *nature*. There are three Divine Persons who are *creating*, but there is one *Creator*.

10.

Although this is so, yet in the Sacred Scriptures, and in other documents of the faith, we find certain attributes, and certain operations, appropriated to one out of the three Divine Persons. *Power* is, for instance, appropriated to the Father, *Wisdom* to the Son, and *Goodness* to the Holy Ghost.

In order to *appropriation* it does not suffice that what is *absolute* should be explicitly set down to any one Person. There is then only appropriation, in the strict sense of the word, when the absolute is set down to one Person, *in comparison with* other Persons. Again, there is not appropriation, strictly speaking, when a name, which of itself signifies an absolute attribute which has affinity with a personal *property* or characteristic, is applied in a sense which is relative to the Person to be designated; as when The Word is called The begotten Wisdom, or The subsisting Wisdom, or when the Holy Ghost is called the proceeding or subsisting Love or Will. These names are not *appropriated*. They are *proper*. By these names there is not specially ascribed to one Person a common *attribute*. A personal or relative *property* is expressed. There is *appropriation*, in the strict sense, when attributes, or external operations, which are common to the three Divine Persons, are specially predicated of one Divine Person; so that, from such an attribute or operation, we are led to some understanding of that Person's *personal property* or characteristic. This is the scope of appropriation.

The law or foundation of appropriation is an analogy or likeness between certain absolute attributes and the hypostatic property of one Divine Person, in comparison with the other Divine Persons. Unless there were some peculiar affinity between this property and these attributes, as they are conceived by us; the special ascription of them to one Person would not help, but would rather hinder, our understanding of the personal and proper characteristics of that Person.

Since, however, these personal characteristics can be considered under several different ideas, in accordance with which it is that we see the correspondence; several attributes can be appropriated to one Person, while again one attribute can be appropriated, not to one Person only, but, from a different point of view, to other Persons also.

In the Sacred Scriptures, when two of the Divine Persons, or when all the three Persons, are connumerated, they are frequently distinguished by absolute attributes; not as if these attributes were proper to the Persons to whom they are ascribed, and not common, as they are to all the three Persons, but in order to designate a personal, and therefore proper, characteristic of one of them.

There belongs also to *appropriation* the very frequent attribution of external operations, by words which indicate the *relation of origin* between the Persons, who are operating with one operation. The Father, for instance, is said to operate *through* the Son, *in* the Holy Ghost —or, all things are said to have been created *by* the Father, *through* the Son, *in* the Holy Ghost —or again, *from* Whom are all things, *through* Whom are all things, *in* Whom are all things. In creation, likewise, *counsel* or *command* is appropriated to the Father, *execution* to the Son, and *perfection* to the Holy Ghost—or again, God *made* all things *through* His Word, and *through* His Holy Spirit He *animated* them. In the Creeds, the Father is represented as the Almighty, the Creator; the Son as the Lord; and the Holy Ghost as the Lifegiver, Who spoke by the prophets.

Christ Himself in His Sacred Humanity explicitly directed both His satisfactions for us, and His prayers, to God the Father, although all these refer to the Triune God. In her Sacred Liturgy the Church most frequently makes petition to the Almighty Father, the Eternal God, through Jesus Christ His Son, our Lord, Who with Him reigns in the unity of the Holy Ghost.

These and other examples tend to express the oneness of God, in the distinctness of the Divine Persons, along with the order of the internal processions in God.

11.

By reason of the numerical oneness of *nature* in the three distinct Divine Persons, there is a necessary mutual immanence, or abiding, or inexistence, of those Persons, one in the other. This truth Christ Himself declared, and expressed in so many words, when He said, " I and the Father are one. That you may know and believe that the Father is in Me, and I am in the Father. He who seeth Me, seeth the Father also. You do not believe that I am in the Father, and the Father in Me." To His Father He prayed for His apostles and disciples, "that they all may be one, as Thou, Father, art in Me, and I in Thee, that they also may be one in Us. The glory which Thou hast given Me, I have given them, that they may be one, even as We are one."

That this is true also of the Holy Ghost, we have the explicit testimony of St. Paul, who wrote to his converts at Corinth—"To us God has revealed through His Spirit. What man knoweth the things of a man, but the spirit of a man *that is in him?* So the things also that are of God no man knoweth, but the *Spirit of God.*"

In these passages there is declared the distinctness of the Divine Persons, formally as they are *persons*; and at the same time the oneness of their *nature* or *essence*.

The fact of the *inexistence* of the three Persons, one in the other, is not only a necessary consequence of these truths, but consideration of it sets these truths in still clearer light. If the Three who are distinct, one from the other, are one God, without any distinction in *essence*, the Father who is God through the Divine essence, and who is identified with the Divine essence, cannot be, and cannot be conceived as being, without His having in Himself the Son and the Holy Ghost, who are both of them identified with the selfsame essence, which is numerically one. For the same reason the Son, who is the same one God through the Divine *essence*, cannot be, and cannot be conceived as being, without His having in His essence the Father and the Holy Ghost, who are identified therewith. The same is equally, and in the same way, true of God the Holy Ghost.

This, however, does not by itself satisfy or exhaust the idea of *inexistence*. It does not amount to inexistence. Inexistence means more than this. We have hitherto only been conceiving—after our manner of understanding, in accordance with analogies drawn from creatures—a person as the *subject*, and in that person his nature, as if it were a metaphysical *form*. There is, as matter of fact, a real identity of *person* and *nature* in God. The selfsame most simple *essence*, under one idea of it, and as it is *absolute*, is called, and is, the Divine *nature*—while under another idea of the Divine essence, and as it is *relative*, it is called, and is, a Divine *person*. Where there is no real distinctness between several, there is not, and there cannot be, one of them *inexisting* in another. Here, however, we have person *really distinct* from person, and all the three persons identified with one nature. By reason of this distinctness, one of the *persons* can rightly be said to *inexist* in another.

Looking to the *mode* also of the procession of Person from Person in God, there must be mutual inexistence of one Person in another Person. The Word or Son, *immanent* in the Father Who produces that Person, and the Father immanent in the Word or Son produced by Him, must mutually inexist—the Father in the Son, and the Son in the Father—the Father in the Word produced by Him, and the Word in Him Who produces His immanent Word.

The mutual immanence of the Divine Persons, one in the other, is a necessary consequence of the *mode* of Divine procession; inasmuch as procession is through communication of a nature.

which is not specifically but numerically one. Of the three Divine Persons it may be said, that "God is *in* God, because God is *from* God."

This mutual inexistence of the Divine Persons is a compendious confutation of heresies with regard to the Trinity. Rightly understood, it excludes nearly all of them.

12.

It is explicitly revealed that, besides what is known of God through things that are made, there are also "deep things of God," which are above all human power of understanding, which the Spirit of God alone searches, and reveals to us.

To the number of those deep things of God there belong, in the first place, the internal processions in God, and the Trinity of Divine Persons. The doctrine of the Trinity is a *mystery*, properly so called. It is a truth which, apart from revelation, cannot possibly be known to man by the light of reason. Moreover, even supposing revelation of this truth, it cannot be demonstrated from principles of mere reason.

It is not enough to say that the idea of a person, and consequently of a trinity of persons, in God, is beyond our conception; so that, whether before or after revelation, we cannot apprehend the idea by a proper, but only by an analogical, notion.

Although this is most true, yet it is equally true of the Divine essence, and of all the Divine attributes; and nevertheless the existence of God, His omnipotence, His wisdom, and similar attributes, are not *mysteries* strictly so called. A mystery, in the strict sense, includes two constituent ideas. Neither the existence of the mysterious truth can be understood by the light of reason alone; nor can the intrinsic idea of it, even supposing faith, be apprehended by us with a proper conception, as distinguished from an analogical conception.

It does not, however, belong to the idea of a *mystery* that, supposing revelation of it, we should have absolutely no understanding of it, *what it is*. Unless we were in some way, and at least through analogical notions, to apprehend what that is which is revealed and set forth to be believed, explicit faith in a mysterious doctrine could not have place. It is not words, but the truths signified by words, which are the material object of faith. Our idea of a mystery, and *what it is*, is in the same position with regard to understanding of it, as is our knowledge of the absolute attributes of God.

Although the difference is chiefly in the judgment which we form of the mystery *that it is*—a judgment which in the case of the Trinity is wholly above reason, while in the case of God's existence, and attributes, it is not above reason—there, nevertheless, remains a great difference also in our apprehension of the mystery.

We arrive at an analogical conception of the attributes of God, by the light of reason, from the adumbrations or shadows of them, which we find in creatures, by way of affirmation, negation, and supereminence (see page 42), and so we ascend to a conception of the archetype. By means of this mental operation we arrive, not only at an analogous notion of *what the truth is*, but also, at the same time, at a judgment *that it is*.

We should never, on the other hand, apprehend the notion of persons who are *constituted by relations*, and who, under the formal idea of persons, are *really distinct* one from the other, while they are at the same time numerically *one in essence*—apart from previous positive teaching and revelation.

With revelation before us, we look for analogies in creatures, in order to form some conception. Although here human reason does somewhat, in virtue of its own proper natural light, yet the reason is always resting on positive revelation. From that which revelation supplies, the reason, as it were, descends to investigating the adumbrations or shadows of the Divine in creatures. This it does, not for demonstration of the existence of the truth, which rests on faith alone, but for the formation of some analogous conception of the truth to be believed.

The foundation and root of this difference is in this, that God the Creator and First Cause, Who by understanding, and willing, and in accordance with His absolute attributes, operates *externally*, exhibits those attributes, "His eternal power and divinity," to be "clearly seen, being understood by the things that are made." The Divine Persons, on the other hand—who are related, one to the other, and really distinct one from the other—are *immanent* relations; and neither Divine generation, nor Divine procession are *externally* related. The Divine Persons operate externally, as they are the one God, and not as they are related, the one to the other, and distinct one from the other, by their mutual relations. Hence God, as regards His absolute attributes, is knowable from His works, as a cause is knowable from its effects. He is in this way knowable *that He is;* and analogically *what He is*. It is not under the formal idea of the *internal* Divine *relations*, that God is the Cause of His external works; and so He is not in this way knowable, as a cause is knowable from its effects, —either *that He is*, or *what He is*.

After those Divine processions, and distinct Divine Persons, have been revealed, we can indeed find in creatures, and most of all in a created spirit, certain analogies, to aid us in the formation of some conception of the Divine processions, and of the Divine Persons—*what they are.* This is possible, because a created spirit, as it is an image of God, exhibits *immediately* an analogy of Divine understanding, and of Divine willing or loving. Hence, after we have knowledge from revelation of the fact, that there are processions in God by way of understanding and loving; we can *mediately*, through our conception of understanding and loving, arrive at forming some conception of the Divine processions.

Briefly, we analogically apprehend God's absolute attributes *immediately* from creatures; and, supposing revelation, from those absolute attributes, and so from creatures *mediately*, we analogically apprehend the Divine processions, and internal relations.

There are certain supernatural truths, a knowledge of which is necesssary for men, and which are, nevertheless, above man's reason. These truths cannot possibly be known, except through faith during this present life, and through *supernatural* vision in the life to come. That this is so, is contained in revelation itself. It is the subject of the second chapter of St. Paul's first epistle to the Christians of Corinth.

There are two kinds of *objective* wisdom; that

is to say, there are two distinct series of facts and truths to be known by us. The first is the wisdom which the Apostle spoke, as he says, "among the perfect"—the wisdom which "none of the princes of this world" had known—the "wisdom of God hidden in a mystery." To that wisdom is opposed the "wisdom of this world"—the wisdom which the Greeks sought after. To those two kinds of *objective* wisdom, there correspond two kinds of formal or *subjective* wisdom. These differ widely one from the other. One is the "mind of Christ," and through it men are "spiritual." Through the other subjective wisdom a man is wise indeed, but wise "according to the flesh"—a "scribe" or sciolist—a "disputer of this world"—a man who with this wisdom still remains "animal." The two wisdoms differ, therefore, in their efficient principle, or immediate source. Of the wisdom which is such as the Greeks sought after, the proximate principle is human reason, or God through the light of reason, on the one hand, and the works of creation, on the other. The principle of the other and higher wisdom is the Holy Ghost, in a far higher manner, and that in two ways. The Holy Ghost internally affects the rational soul, and renders men "spiritual," who were previously "animal." This may be done, and is done, in order even to a knowledge of those truths which are knowable by the light of reason. It is so done that the mode of the knowledge of these truths should be not "animal" or merely rational, but "spiritual" or supernatural. The Apostle is here, however, treating of truths which are utterly unknowable by the light of reason. He teaches that there is a twofold necessary operation of the Holy Ghost, in order to a twofold effect. The effect is, first, that a mystery, which in itself is wholly hidden and inaccessible to the natural human reason, should be rendered knowable. This is done by revelation, either internal or external. The second effect is, that the mystery should be known as it ought to be known, by rendering man "spiritual" by means of an internal grace. It is with the first effect that we are at present concerned.

The Apostle says that the wisdom which he spoke among the perfect, that is, the *objective* wisdom, truth, and doctrine—the matter which is the object of *subjective* wisdom—is wisdom in a mystery, and that from eternity.

From eternity God predestined a contingent fact to be verified in time, and to be supernaturally revealed. St. Paul has in view the incarnation, and the whole economy of redemption. Hence this wisdom none of the princes of this world knew. The "princes of this world" are those who are preeminent among men through prerogatives of this world, their natural gifts. That this wisdom was hidden in a mystery, and unknown to these princes, St. Paul declares by quoting the words of Isaias, that "eye hath not seen, nor ear heard, nor hath it entered into the heart of man, what God hath prepared (or predestined) for those who love Him." This includes the mysteries of redemption, and the foundation of them, which is Christ the Lord of Glory, the Incarnate Word, and in these mysteries, as the end and complement of redemption, the blessedness of Heaven. "Entering (or ascending) into the heart of man" is in biblical language the same as coming into the mind or intellect of man. St. Paul is speaking of universal human nature, and he declares that there is a wisdom which is beyond the range of all human intelligence. He enunciates not only the fact of man's ignorance of this wisdom, but also the fact that, of the nature of the case, from the nature of the wisdom to be known, and from the nature of man's mind, man must necessarily be ignorant of that wisdom.

The only principle of knowledge of a mystery is revelation by God, through the Holy Ghost. "To us God hath revealed through His Spirit." Hence the "animal" man, inasmuch as this supernatural principle of knowledge is wanting to him, does "not perceive those things which are of the Spirit of God, for it is foolishness to him, and he cannot understand," or form a true judgment. This there cannot be except through that supernatural principle. Through it a mystery is "spiritually examined.". Such utter ignorance of a mystery is not merely an, as it were, accidental occurrence, but a necessity, of the nature of the case; from the disproportion between the natural intellect, and the supereminence of this order of truths. Those truths belong to the number of the "deep things of God, a knowledge of which is natural to God alone. Like the power of creating, a knowledge of the deep things of God, is an attribute and note of His divinity. "What man knoweth the things of a man, but the spirit of a man that is in him? So the things also that are of God, no man knoweth but the Spirit of God."

Mysteries are therefore said to be not only above *human* reason, but also to be absolutely above the natural knowledge of every created intelligence whatsoever, nay, of every *possible* creature.

13.

Among creatures, actual understanding and volition are, it is true, necessarily produced by a spirit that has understanding and will. From this, however, we cannot gather, by the light of reason alone, and still less can we demonstrate that there are produced in God a Word and a

Love, with a real distinction of Three Persons who are one God.

That among creatures understanding and volition are *produced* by a spirit, follows from limitation of perfection. The substance of a created spirit is not *itself intellect*, and is not *itself love*. A created spirit has *potentiality* for an act, and the act is not itself the *substance* of the spirit, but a modification which perfects that substance.

Where, however, there is an infinite essence, and, by reason of its infinity, an essence which is entirely *simple*, and that essence is itself understanding, and is itself volition, without any real distinction of *act* and *essence*; there we cannot by the light of reason understand that the Word and the Love are in reality the Essence, and that they are at the same time—under the formal idea as they are *termini* of understanding and loving —the Word begotten, and the Love proceeding by a real procession; so as that there should be a real distinction between Him who begets, Him who is begotten, and Him who proceeds.

The whole order of the created universe, from our contemplation of which we ascend to an analogical understanding of the Divine perfections, supplies no foundation, and no analogy, for the formation of the conception of one absolute substance which subsists in three substantial relations; or in three relations each of which is itself a substance, so that there should be Three who are distinct one from the other, while at the same time the *absolute* essence, or the substance or nature which is common to the Three, is numerically one. Not only, therefore, is the existence and objective truth of this fact incapable of demonstration by the natural reason, but that reason is also unable to form a conception of the fact as even *possible*.

Hence there is a vast difference between the mode in which we conceive the Divine absolute attributes, and the mode in which, even supposing revelation, we conceive the Divine Persons.

We are able to conceive God as wise, and as good, and the like, by analogical notions derived from our previous knowledge of those perfections in creatures. In the mode of our conception there is imperfection, indeed, and, as it were, composition of the Divine essence with the attribute which affects that essence. The imperfection, however, which cleaves to our conception, we easily correct, by means of a judgment from principles which are certain, and which are known to us by the light of reason.

When, on the other hand, we endeavour to form a conception of a Divine *Person*, by the light of reason alone, from our previous knowledge of created perfections, the conception will always be that of an *absolute* person, and so of *only one* person, who is as necessarily one as is the Divine essence.

There does not, moreover, exist any principle of mere reason, by which our conception can be corrected, by means of a judgment made by the light of reason.

When, on the contrary, we know from revelation that there are three really distinct persons of one *absolute* essence, and that these persons are distinct one from the other, through relations alone, and not by anything which is *absolute*, we conceive a related person not under a single notion, but under the twofold notion of the *absolute* and the *relative*.

This imperfect mode of conceiving certainly needs correction through a judgment, by which we come to the conclusion that the *absolute* is at the same time *relative;* that is to say, that the Divine essence is in reality the Father, the Son, and the Holy Ghost. As, however, we have the notion of a substantially related person from revelation, and from revelation alone, so this judgment of ours does not spring from principles of mere reason, but is a *judgment of faith*, and springs from truths which are known to us by revelation alone.

From all this it follows and is clear that the doctrine of the Trinity, as it has been revealed by God, is *above reason*, both as regards the truth of its existence *that it is*, and as regards also our analogical conception of it, *what it is.*

In order that we may believe with an *explicit* faith those things which God has revealed to us, there is not required a *proper* notion of the things to be believed, as they are *in themselves.* It is, nevertheless, absolutely necessary—or rather it is contained in the act itself of explicitly believing—that we should conceive at least some analogous notion of the thing believed. This may be arrived at in one or other of three ways. We might obtain it by a supernatural light alone, through ideas and understandings which have been infused or shed into our souls by God. We might obtain it in another way—through prophetic vision, by a setting forth of the signs of the things—whether real or verbal signs, presented either extrinsically to the senses, or intrinsically to the imagination alone—from which the intellect, under the Divine enlightenment, is led to the forming of conceptions of the things signified, and to the forming of a judgment as regards the objective truth or fact of their existence. A third way in which it is possible for us to obtain, and by which we do obtain, our analogous notion, is through the Incarnate Word of God Who, existing in the Bosom of the Father, gives testimony to that which He sees; or at least through men who are legates or ambassadors of God, and who are furnished with credentials of their Divine mission and authority. Through their word and teaching the truths to be believed are extrinsically propounded, while grace intrinsically enlightens, prompts, and raises man to a conception of supernatural faith. It is with this third mode of revelation that we are now concerned. It is that which is in accordance with the present *ordinary* providence of God.

In this mode of revelation the internal light of grace does not itself infuse conceptions into the mind. It supposes an extrinsic propounding of the truths to be believed, which is in accordance with the character of the human mind. "Faith cometh *by hearing*, and hearing by the Word of Christ." The word, however, is not heard by us, nor is the doctrine intelligible to us, nor from the doctrine, when it is propounded, can we conceive any ideas of the truth set forth. Much less can we give to it an explicit consent, unless the revelation is in some way connected with notions in our mind which have been already conceived, and with truths which are already known to us.

When truths to be believed are propounded by the Word of God, the words of God are signs of ideas of which we have already some analogous notions, originally derived from our contemplation of creatures. Were it otherwise, the words would not be to us *signs*, in order to the conceiving of the ideas signified by them. The words would be mere sounds. When we are taught the doctrine of the Father, the Son, and the Holy Ghost, one God, one Deity, and three in number who are distinct one from the other, and who singly and as three are at the same time one God, there are presupposed in our minds manifold notions, and at least confused notions, without which God cannot be conceived. Among these are the notions of essence, person, generation or origin from another, identity, distinction, and the like. Without these previous notions the mind could not, and with these the mind can, form an at least confused conception of the truth which is propounded for belief.

The difference between rational and superrational conceptions of God is not in this, therefore, that we cannot in any way conceive superrational truths; and that we conceive rational truths in their own proper ideas, and superrational truths by analogical ideas. The difference is in this, that in rational truths concerning God we proceed to conceptions by way of *causality*, whereby we understand *that God is*, and by way of *negation* and *supereminence*, whereby we conceive a little more distinctly *what God is*, although only analogically, and not properly, as God is in Himself.

In superrational truths, on the other hand, there is no place for conclusion from effects to the cause of them. In place, therefore, of the way of *causality*, a positive revelation through the Word of God is necessary. Without it we should never arrive at those conceptions.

Since, however, revelation does not alter that mode of knowing which is connatural to men, it exhibits the superrational perfections, and internal relations, of God in accordance with analogy, and from the analogy of rational notions which we have already conceived, through our contemplation of creatures. Hence, if we here suppose a positive revelation, as occupying the place which, as regards rational truths, is held by the argument from *causality;* we can use, and we necessarily use, the way of *negation* and *supereminence*, in order to some more distinct analogous conception of the superrational truth, or revealed object, *what it is*.

The difference as concerns truths about God is chiefly with regard to the judgment *that they are*. This judgment, in the case of knowledge of God through reason, springs from the perceived connection between effects and the supreme cause of them; while, in the case of superrational revealed truths, the judgment rests solely on the authority of God revealing them.

As regards rational notions of God, however,

the mode of analogically conceiving *what they are*, is not by abstracting from the existence of God's perfections, but by regarding those perfections formally as understood in *necessary existence*. In the superrational objects of faith, the mode of conceiving them is as the existence of them is certain through faith. Hence endeavour to conceive the truths more distinctly from analogies, tends to an understanding of the facts, not as *possible*, but as *actually existing*. It tends also, and consequently, towards some understanding of the intrinsic idea of their *necessary existence*. Hence the principle of the Fathers—" Unless you believe, you will not understand." " Faith seeks understanding," to quote St. Anselm, which stands midway between itself and vision; of which the root and seeds are already contained in the mode of revelation, and in faith itself.

These are the principles on which the whole of sound speculative theology, and the cultivation of it, rests. It is the enquiry of the intellect from faith. " A Christian," to borrow from St. Anselm once more, "ought through faith to proceed to understanding, and not through understanding to come to faith; and he is not, if he is unable to understand, to withdraw from faith. I do not seek to understand in order that I may believe, but I believe in order that I may understand."

The analogies under which, in the Sacred

Scriptures and, later on, in the universal preaching of the Church, the mystery of the Trinity is exhibited to be believed by us, are chiefly three in number. When we are divinely taught that God the Father, God the Son, and God the Holy Ghost, Who is the Spirit of the Father and the Son, as proceeding from the Father and—since all things which are the Father's are also the Son's, His personal paternity and unbegetableness alone excepted—receiving from the Son, there is included in this revealed fact a fundamental analogy. Without this analogy we could not form any conception, while under this analogy —in accordance with notions which we have derived from our contemplation of creatures—we conceive three distinct persons, along with a oneness of nature. We then conceive the origin of the second Divine Person from the first Divine Person, and the mode of that origin through generation; or procession with similitude of nature, or a communication of the Divine Nature from an intrinsic vital principle, so that the second Person, thence existing in virtue of that mode of procession, is the substantial Image of the first Person. This we understand as expressed by the words or names, Father, Son, generation, image, figure of the substance of the Father, under which the mystery is revealed to us.

In like manner, we conceive the procession of

a third, distinct, Divine Person; inasmuch as these two have all things in common, or inasmuch as these two are *one principle*. We also understand, *negatively* at least, that the mode of this procession differs from *generation*, for the third Person is not the Son of God. Further, the notion of oneness of nature, and distinctness of persons, as we preconceive it from our contemplation of creatures, we learn to correct from another revealed doctrine; namely, that the three persons are one God, and not three distinct Gods. Hence also we understand that the oneness of nature, and of all and every absolute perfection, is not a merely *specific* oneness, such as we find among creatures, but a *numerical* oneness. From the same source we understand that the distinctness of the Divine Persons, is not distinctness in *absolute* substance, but distinctness in the formal *relative* ideas which are expressed by the names of Father, Son, and Spirit of God.

God is a Spirit, and so all imperfections which cleave to notions, derived from creatures, of father, son, and generation are to be denied; and the mode of *positively* conceiving these truths is exhibited in another analogy, which is taken from the spiritual and intellectual order.

He Who is the Son of God is the *Word* of God. When this analogy is conjoined with the former analogy, they mutually perfect each other.

What is wanting in the one is supplied by the other. In the former analogy there is more distinctly exhibited both the substantiality, and the real distinctness of the Persons, one from the other. In this analogy there is more clearly conceived both the mode of intellectual generation, which is immanent, necessary and eternal, and the oneness of essence and the mutual immanence of the Divine Persons in each other.

A third analogy stands in a manner midway between the two former analogies. It is taken from material proceeding of splendour from light, or of light from light. This is itself an image of intellectual procession, and it presents itself to the senses. Between this analogy and the other analogies there is a great difference. In the soul of man there is an *image* of God, while in material things there is only a far distant adumbration or *trace* of God. The names, therefore, Father, Son, Word, and Holy Spirit, which have analogy in a spirit, which has intelligence and will, are used in the proper sense of them, with regard to God; if the perfection which is signified by them is that which is being regarded. The words *light*, *splendour*, and the like, which are derived from material things, can never be *properly*, but only *metaphorically*, applied to God. Hence, in this last analogy there is only a comparison and metaphor to aid our intellect, through the ministry of our senses.

14.

The mystery of the Trinity, although it is *above* reason, is nevertheless not *contrary* to reason. A truth of reason, objectively and in itself, cannot ever be in contradiction with a revealed truth. Were it otherwise, the same thing would be at once true and false. It is impossible, therefore, that the reason should understand anything as an evident truth, and as at the same time evidently opposed to revelation, as understood in the genuine sense of it. Were it otherwise, the reason would be understanding, as an evident truth, that which is false. In that case, the light of reason, which of its own nature was made for the truth, would be inclining towards the false, and therefore God Himself, the Author of reason, would be inducing men to judge that to be true which is false.

In this, therefore, that through infallible faith we are certain of the truth of this mystery, we are no less certain that what is said to be contradictory of it, either is not the truth, or is not in contradiction with the mystery, or is in contradiction only with a representation of it, such as has never been revealed, and is moreover not true.

As Divine doctrine is founded on the light of

faith, so is philosophy, properly so called, founded on the natural light of reason. Both are from God. Hence it is impossible that those things which belong to sound philosophy, should be contrary to those things which belong to faith. They only fall short of the truths of faith. They contain, moreover, certain similitudes of the truths of faith, and certain preambles towards those truths, in the same way as nature is a preamble to grace.

We use Philosophy in Theology in three ways, to demonstrate those natural truths of reason which are preambles of faith—to make known, by means of similitudes, truths which are of faith—and to refute statements which are contrary to faith, either by shewing them to be false, or by shewing that they are not necessary conclusions.

In support of this assertion, there suffices a general comparison of the Divine eminence, and infinite perfections, with the imperfection and limitations of our intellect. From this it is evident that there may be many things in an *infinite* essence, which cannot be understood by the light of finite and limited reason. On account of the *infinity* of the Divine essence there are certain statements with regard to God which are not self-contradictory, which, if made of creatures, would involve evident contradiction. To assert the contrary would betray both arrogance and ignorance.

In Theology, however, in which "faith seeks

understanding," we ought to make an endeavour to render a reason why, for instance, the Trinity of Divine Persons is the one and only true God There cannot be demonstrated an evident contradiction in this, that in God, an Infinite Spirit, there really proceeds, through understanding, or is from eternity truly produced, an immanent Word. Contradiction is not evident from the nature of understanding in general, or regarded universally. It would, on the contrary, be more difficult to conceive understanding in act without an immanent word, than it is to conceive understanding with a word, as the immanent terminus of it. The contradiction is not evident in an understanding, which is Divine and infinite. All that is evident is this, that the Divine Word cannot be an *accident*, but must necessarily be substantial, because Divine understanding, or understanding by God, is itself a *substance*. There is not evident contradiction from the oneness of the Divine essence, which is incapable of multiplication. All that is evident therefrom is that the principle which produces the Word by understanding, and the Word, as the immanent terminus of this understanding, is the one *absolute* Divine essence. There would indeed be contradiction in production of the Divine *essence*; for this would be multiplication of that essence, and creation of it from nothingness.

It cannot, on the other hand, be shewn that there is evident contradiction in this, that from the intrinsic perfection of the Divine Intellect there is demanded an eternal and necessary procession of an immanent Word, personally distinct from His producing principle, under the formal idea of the *relative*—while, at the same time, the idea of Deity and *absolute* Essence is one and common in Him Who begets, and in Him Who is begotten.

This truth of the production of the Divine Word is undoubtedly *above reason*, because it cannot be understood and demonstrated. It is not, however, *contrary to reason*, since there is not, and there cannot be, a notion of reason which is evidently true, and evidently in contradiction with Divinely revealed doctrine.

When the Spirit of God, Who "searches the deep things of God," has revealed to us, and the "Only begotten Who is in the Bosom of the Father," has Himself narrated this mystery—" In the beginning was the Word, and the Word was with God, and the Word was God,"—and so it is clear from revelation, as revelation is the "root of truth," the rest of the doctrine follows, through necessary ideas. These ideas are necessarily connected with the infinity, oneness, and simplicity of God, attributes of which we have understanding even by the light of reason.

What is true of the generation of the Word is equally true of the procession of the third Divine Person—that it is a mystery, which is *above reason*, but which is not *contrary to reason*.

It is perfectly true that one is not equal to three, and there would be contradiction in the statement that it is so. The mathematical axiom—those things which are not distinct from a third thing, are not distinct from each other—is evident. It cannot, however, be therefore argued that, because, according to the Christian doctrine, the Divine Persons are not distinct from the Divine Essence, they are consequently not distinct one from another.

Mathematical axioms are evident, and the truth of them is necessary truth. Unless we had rational souls, we could not possibly believe; and if these first principles were not infallibly certain, we should not be able to know what is to be believed by us in Divine doctrine. Revelation itself supposes, and we also in our believing of revelation, suppose the evidently true, namely, that one is not three. Were it otherwise, revelation of the Trinity, which propounds one essence and three persons, would not render us certain that there are not three essences, and one person. Further, the revelation of the Trinity supposes the fact as evidently true, that when two are said not to be distinct from a third, it is under a formal idea in which they are not distinct from that third, and are not under that idea really two, and are also not that third, but are one, and without any real distinctness.

Apart from this evident principle, we should not understand that there is one Divinity, which is in no way distinct. When it is revealed that there is God the Father, and God the Son, and that there is nevertheless one God—and when it is revealed that God the Father, and God the Son, are identically the same God—there are two who, under the formal idea of *Deity*, are said to be one, or not distinct from a third, namely from Deity.

From that evident principle, therefore, we understand that there is revealed one Deity, which is not distinct from these two Persons, although these two are revealed as being at the same time distinct one from the other, *under another formal idea;* namely, under that of their being substantially related one to the other, by relations which are opposed to each other. These relations are opposed to each other, as is the personal relation of a father to the personal relation of a son—or as is the relation of the producer to that which is produced by him—or as is the relation of a begetter to him who is begotten. "I and the Father," said Jesus, "are one." "There are three who give testimony in Heaven, the Father, the Word, and the Holy Ghost, and these three are one."

One, under that idea in which it is one, is evidently not three; and so there is one Divine essence. The one God is not three essences, and not three Gods. The three Persons are not one Person.

Mathematical formulas are not, moreover, to the point in this matter. Termini, in mathematics, cannot under one idea be the same with a third, and under another idea be not the same as each other. This is because abstract quantities have the idea of one only, and not of one and another. In the physical and metaphysical order of finite substances, there is distinctness under the idea of *hypostases*—one and another; and there is a oneness under the idea of a *nature*, although this oneness is only a specific oneness. Peter, formally as he is this one, is other than Paul. Formally, as concerns his *nature*, he has a greater oneness with Paul than the oneness which he has with an animal in the genus of the *animal;* and he has greater oneness with an animal than the oneness which he has with a stone in the genus of *substances*. Peter's oneness with Paul is a *specific* oneness, or oneness of *species*. Both belong to that species, the *human* species, which constitutes both of them *men*. The Divine oneness is more than this. It is not a *specific* oneness. The three Divine Persons do not belong to one Divine *species*. They are numerically one, and so there is one God.

www.ingramcontent.com/pod-product-compliance
Lightning Source LLC
Chambersburg PA
CBHW031955300426
44117CB00008B/770